Everything you need to grow a MESSIANIC YESHIVA

Phillip E. Goble

Library of Congress Cataloging in Publication Data

Goble, Phillip E., 1943 -
Everything you need to grow a messianic yeshiva

Bibliography: p.
1. Converts from Judaism. 2. Christianity and other religions - Judaism. 3. Judaism - Relations - Christianity. I. Title.
BV2620.G6 248.2'46 81-1032
ISBN 0-87808-181-X AACR2

Published by William Carey Library
P. O. Box 128-C
Pasadena, California 91104
Telephone (213) 798-0819

In accord with some of the most recent thinking of the academic press, the William Carey Library is pleased to present this scholarly book which has been prepared from an author-edited and author-prepared camera ready copy.

PRINTED IN THE UNITED STATES OF AMERICA

Contents

Foreword

By Sid Roth

Ten years ago when I became a Jewish believer in Yeshua, there was no such option as a Messianic congregation. When I started attending a Presbyterian church I remember my discomfort as the minister singled me out by saying, "You're Jewish aren't you?" I just wanted to be like everyone else. Why did he have to single me out? At that time there were few Messianic Jews, and the minister was excited at the novelty of a Jewish believer at his church. It's hard to believe now, but initially as a new believer, I tried to hide the fact that I was Jewish.

At a picnic of the Messianic Jewish Alliance several of the leaders felt the need to start a Messianic synagogue. I was negative initially. But as an experiment I announced we would try one Shabbus service.

I remember stopping by my Dad's house to ask his advice. It had been years since I had been to a Friday night service. My father almost kicked me out of the house. He couldn't understand why all of a sudden I would be interested in Jewish things after accepting Jesus.

The next best place to turn to was a Jewish book store, where I purchased a prayer book. Somehow we got through that evening. We had twenty brave souls attend that first service seven years ago and we haven't missed a service since.

Since I was president of the Messianic Jewish Alliance Washington, D.C. chapter, that made me the logical leader of the synagogue. I was two years old in the Lord and knew very little Scripture.

It was only God's mercy that kept our congregation together over those early years. What about members? Could gentiles become members? Should we call our spiritual leader, rabbi? How much Hebrew should be in the service? Do we meet on Friday and Sunday or Friday and Saturday? Should we wear yarmulkahs? What about funerals? Should we use a Christian cemetery or a Jewish cemetery? Would a Jewish cemetery allow us to even participate?

The questions were endless but God resolved them one at a time. Now there are Messianic synagogues throughout the world. So many in fact, we have seen the formation of the Union of Messianic Congregations. Today our congregation, Beth Messiah, located in Rockville, Maryland has its own building, day school, and full time spiritual leader.

I wish I had this book before we started pioneering ... You are very fortunate. God really loves you!

Sid Roth
Founder and Host of the Messianic Vision

Preface

In 1974 I began to see that many churches were not willing to change the routine of their style of ministry in order to reach the Jewish neighborhoods where God had placed them. I saw that new congregations needed to be planted, messianic synagogues, in those areas. I have never advocated putting Jews under the law, but if a Jewish community like Williamsburg, Brooklyn, is on its way to eternal death (under the law) and a church in that area insists on worshipping in the style of White Anglo-Saxon Protestants, something must be done. A new congregation -- one that will identify in hymnology, liturgy, architecture, and worshipping style -- must become as if it *were* under the law to win those who *are* under the law (I Cor. 9:20). An ivory tower theologian or a novice may not see the difference between putting people under the law and becoming *like* people who already *are* under the law. Such critics attacked my first book, *Everything You Need to Grow A Messianic Synagogue*. At the time I wondered, will they throw the baby out with the bath water? Will they outlaw cultural identification along with judaizing and legalism? If they do, they will hardly notice in their comfortable W.A.S.P. churches that they have given the Judas kiss to so many, and hell will not stop burning.

In my book, I wanted to allow for enough cultural elasticity to identify radically with orthodox Jews in Brooklyn or reformed Jews in Los Angeles, so that different kinds of messianic synagogues could be planted in different areas. Some people misunderstood me. I spent so many pages writing on water baptism, some got the impression I was teaching one must be baptized to be saved. Actually I was trying to prove only that baptism is a Jewish ritual, not a traitor's or a Gentile's ceremony foisted on the Jews.

In 1975, when I spoke at a special Fuller Seminary convocation, I felt impressed that God would give me several messianic synagogues in Florida. God wanted to prove that what he was saying through me was possible, that several congregations *could* be planted simultaneously in the same area. And that these congregations could help sustain a Jewish people movement, providing such things as a potential Jewish marriage market, so that the Jewish people would have the freedom to keep their identity as Jews. This is important, because if the Jewish people totally assimilate and become non-Jews, so that there *are* no Jews, then how can Yeshua still return as King of the Jews? Dr. Donald McGavran, my teacher, said we should work to see five hundred of these congregations in the United States, and an equal number overseas. He told me to get some of the key leaders to help me put together this book, so that many training centers can emerge.

By 1976, Jewish men from all over the country were calling me in Florida, telling me they felt led to get into the ministry because of their faith in Yeshua, explaining they had somehow heard about me, asking me if I needed help in Florida. We began a little Yeshiva class in conjunction with an agape feast which occurred later the same day, when new believers took the mikvah. In the Yeshiva class, the Jewish ministers brushed up their Hebrew and learned how to turn Jewish home Bible classes into messianic congregations. I was reliving Paul's experience in Acts 19:9. When the first messianic synagogue formed, I was free to turn that congregation over to a Jewish minister, so that I could go with another Jewish minister to start another one. In less than three years, three congregations were formed and growing. What my critics said couldn't be done, God did, using even a person like me, of Gentile background, to show that anyone could do it, with his help. By simply ordering my time in a disciplined way, one night of visitation ministry, one night of bus ministry, one day of Yeshiva classes, God did the rest.

This book shows that there is a way revealed in the New Testament to be loyal to the law without legalism, to become like Rabbinic Judaism without syncretism, to become indigenous without Scriptural compromise. The purpose of the book is to provide a tool to help accelerate the in-gathering of God's ancient people in these last days. It is my prayer that God will use it to wake up the Church to the Great Commission and to the fact that the Good News is to Israel first and last! God bless you!

Phillip E. Goble
New York City
October 11, 1980

PART I

The Biblical Basis for a Messianic Yeshiva

1

The Biblical Basis for a Messianic Yeshiva

The Mistakes of the Past

The centuries between New Testament times and the Reformation were indeed dismal ones for Jewish Christianity. After the Hadrianic war, Jerusalem became a pagan city from which Jewish Christians were barred, just as they were practically excluded from both the Catholic Church and the synagogue. From 135 A.D. until the conquest of Palestine by the Mohammedans in the 7th century, we hear very little of Jewish Christians, other than a few passing remarks on certain Ebionites or Nazarenes from such sources as Jerome or Origen or a certain Jewish bishop of Constantia named Epiphanius. The story of Jewish Christianity from the 7th century to the Reformation is one of confused church strategy that ranged all the way from the enticement of studied polemics in compulsory audience to the intimidation of forced baptism by threat of death. Thus we move through the crusades and the inquisitions roughly to the time of the Reformation. The historian Hugh Schonfield offers a summary of this period:

> Many a mission, which might have proved successful if the Jewish converts had been left alone to present their case in their own way, was turned into a massacre by ecclesiastical interference or popular malice, to the great sorrow of those who were unwittingly responsible. In the instances of definite fanaticism which have to be recorded, the harsh polemics and burnings of the Talmud, one must

> remember that blasphemy was a much more grievous sin in those days, that the torment of the damned in hell was a reality that made any present suffering worthwhile if it could secure immunity, and that cruelty in word and act was less tempered by social custom.(1)

It is a matter of record that many Jewish people became disciples of Jesus during this pre-Reformation period. However, whom to credit with their evangelism is another matter. For example, we have no way of knowing how instrumental the Dominican preachers were, since many of their efforts backfired. The overzealous Dominicans were instrumental in petitioning inquisitorial interference with the Jews in Ferdinand and Isabella's Spain. Also they were responsible for engaging Pfefferkorn who in turn initiated Emperor Maximilian's book confiscation order which brought on untold burnings of the Talmud and other Jewish writings. Like the Dominican evangelists, the medieval church was a mixed blessing to the Jews.

THE POST-REFORMATION PERIOD

Then, with the Reformation there came to the Jewish people two forward-thinking defenders, John Reuchlin and Martin Luther. Reuchlin, a non-Jewish Hebrew scholar, exhorted against the confiscation of Jewish writings, and for that plea he was rewarded with a charge of heresy and branded as an instrument of the devil. Later, in 1523, Martin Luther wrote a treatise entitled *That Jesus Was Born a Jew*:

> Those fools the papists, bishops, sophists, monks, have formerly so dealt with the Jews, that every good Christian would rather have been a Jew. And if I had been a Jew, and seen such stupidity and such blockheads reign in the Christian Church, I would rather be a pig than a Christian. They have treated the Jews as if they were dogs, not men, and as if they were fit for nothing but to be reviled. They are blood relations of our Lord; therefore if we respect flesh and blood, the Jews belong to Christ more than we. I beg, therefore, my dear Papists, if you become tired of abusing me as a heretic,

> that you begin to revile me as a Jew. Therefore, it is my advice that we should treat them kindly; but now we drive them by force, treating them deceitfully or ignominiously, saying they must have Christian blood to wash away the Jewish stain, and I know not what nonsense. Also we prohibit them from working amongst us, from living and having social intercourse with us, forcing them, if they would remain with us to be usurers.(2)

However, finding that the Jews made little response to his overtures, Luther turned on them with the most vicious and scathing anti-semitism. Here is a quote from another book entitled *Of the Jews and their Lies*:

> Burn their synagogues and schools; what will not burn, bury with earth, that neither stone nor rubbish remain. In like manner break into and destroy their houses. Take away all their prayer-books and talmuds, in which are nothing but godlessness, lies, cursing and swearing. Forbid their rabbis to teach on pain of life and limb.(3)

Therefore, for more than two centuries after the Reformation, scarcely a Protestant voice was heard in behalf of the salvation of the Jews. A major exception was Phillip Jacob Spener, who was the first to work out a detailed missionary plan for the Christian approach to the Jews. Another bright light was Johann Henrich Callenberg, founder of the Callenberg Institute and sometimes called the father of missions to the Jews.

However, of the surprisingly high number of Jewish Christians in this period we have testimony in DaCosta's *Israel and the Gentiles*:

> Those who have gone over to the Protestant Churches from the synagogue have been more numerous during these few last years in Germany than they ever were elsewhere or before. Amongst a multitude of Israelites who have doubtless been led by very different views to receive baptism, a remarkable number have distinguished

> themselves by the sincerity of their profession....The number of Jews baptized in Germany during the last twenty years is estimated at five thousand.(4)

The increased number of Jewish believers in 18th century Germany, the modern pioneer country for Jewish missions, was the result of a new era in Christian-Jewish relations. In the early Reformation church there arose a new consciousness for the evangelization of the Jews. A symptom of the new age was to regard the methods employed by the medieval church as not at all in keeping with the spirit of Christ. Therefore, there was a gradual relaxation on synagogue building restrictions, circumcision prohibitions, and mandatory attendance at sermons in Christian churches. Here Spener went further. He was an advocate of complete freedom for the Jews in the exercise of their own religion, an entirely novel idea even for pietistic Germany.

In the Netherlands as early as the Synods of Delft and Leiden, 1677 and 1678, there was action taken on behalf of the Jews. Not only were ministers to use Hebrew in winning Jewish people through preaching Moses and the prophets, but also the professors of seminaries were to emphasize the study of Hebrew by requiring examinations of their students.

Two extremely important Hebrew Christians who emerged from a later "Jewish awakening" in the Netherlands were Abraham Capadose and Isaac DaCosta. Capadose founded the association of "Friends of Israel in the Hague" in 1846. In 1861 Capadose and DaCosta founded the "Netherland Society for Israel." These societies were important in promoting prayer services for the salvation of the Jews in Holland's cities and towns and also in promoting interest in Jewish evangelism.

THE JEWISH MISSION CENTER APPROACH

In London in 1808 another society was founded, the "London Society for Promoting Christianity among the Jews." This became the oldest and most extensive Jewish mission organization in the world as well as the mother of many other societies. With it we see the development of the so-called "Jewish mission center" which was developed in its most grandiose style in London in 1813 on a five acre plot of ground called Palestine Place.

When completed, Palestine Place comprised a church building, a chaplain's residence, a boys' school and a girls' school, a "cooperative Jewish converts" institution, a missionary college and several residences. This facility lasted for a period of 70 years during which there were some 1,765 baptisms. Palestine Place was staffed with specially trained missionaries and departmental workers and sought to meet every exigency which might arise in bringing the Jewish people to Christ. We are surprised, therefore, to find that the property was disposed of in 1895. A letter from Abraham Capadose provides an insight that may help in a post-mortem appraisal of Palestine Place:

> For I speak from my own experience: the Jew has a natural pre-possession against a missionary--against a man who advertises his desire to make him change his religion; but he respects a pastor of the Church. Now...it is not in the heart of an Israelite, that his pride should repel the idea of going to find or to hear a missionary whom he always suspects of wishing to deceive him, whilst the very man, if he could, without being noticed, ...would eagerly hear a sermon ...without that prejudice because the preaching...would not have for its express design the conversion of Israel. Oh, if the church of Scotland, of England, of Holland would unite in this, to engage mutually to announce once a week that there would be a sermon, not for the Jews, but for the church or its members, on the prophecies concerning Messiah, from this or that part of the Old Testament, I am heartily convinced that we would see quietly coming into the assembly a number of Jews, who, if invited by any missionary would have refused or gone with prejudice.(5)

Here we see one of the first criticisms of the so-called "Jewish mission center approach" in favor of what has come to be called the "parish approach." However, in spite of much criticism of mission centers unrelated to parishes, non-ecclesiastically constituted mission societies have set the pattern even for today. Four of the best known and largest which have operated on a national or international scale are the American Messianic Fellowship, the American Board of Missions to the Jews, The Friends of Israel Society, and the American Association for Jewish Evangelism. Lest this be taken as criticism, the absence of churches in Jewish ghetto areas in large cities explains what has often made the mission station approach appear to be the only feasible alternative. Rev. J. S. Conning, Department of Jewish Evangelism, Presby. U.S., has summarized Jewish missionary methods in the immigrant ghettos of American cities:

> A mission hall in the crowded Jewish neighborhood, meetings in Yiddish for adults, street preaching, visitation in homes, the circulation of Yiddish literature, and the distribution of relief to the needy. To these methods have been added within recent years the use of the community center with its wider appeal to women and young people as well as the summer camp with its daily vacation Bible school programs, post evangelism, and some work through the local churches.(6)

Until the disappearance of the first, second and third settlement communities in the Jewish ghettos of American cities, the apparent need for traditional Jewish mission stations did not lessen.

A critique of the mission station, however, is that typically it lacks the body of Jewish believers whose faith is the proper atmosphere to encourage faith in other Jews. Instead of being genuine body expressions of Christian grace and charity, many mission stations, because they are struggling to show a following in order to survive, simulate Christian graces by certain token charity approaches to the Jewish community. These of course are often unneeded and appear to be a come-on, as does all the hoop-la of the "community centers" which always try to pretend that they aren't what they are -- namely, a missionary station dressed up as a Jewish community center.

THE MESSIANIC SYNAGOGUE APPROACH

It is naive to say that any one organization or method offers the best approach. However, a long-neglected and yet highly promising approach is that of the Messianic synagogue, because it is scripturally tested and sanctioned. Unlike the typical mission station, the Messianic synagogue does have a body of believing Jewish disciples. That their faith is a fertile environment for Jewish people to come to believe is shown in the large-scale additions in the early Messianic synagogue community of Acts (Acts 2:41-47; 5:11, 14; 9:31).

The first important modern Jewish Messianic synagogue was founded in 1882 by Joseph Rabinowitz. Rabinowitz was born at Resina in 1837 and grew up in Chasidic circles. At 13, he was betrothed but did not marry until six years later. His future brother-in-law Jehiel Hershensohn (Lichtenstein) introduced him to the New Testament by lending him a Hebrew copy and remarking that perhaps Jesus of Nazareth was the true Messiah. Rabinowitz took the Hebrew New Testament to Jerusalem with him, and, sitting on the Mount of Olives viewing the Mosque of Omar where formerly the Temple stood, his mind went back over the tragic history of his people. Why was Israel suffering? The answer came to him: "The key to the Holy Land is in the hands of our brother Jesus." Filled with the glory of a great mission, Rabinowitz returned to his homeland and was baptized in 1885 in Berlin. Rather than joining the Lutheran or the Russian Church, however, he built a hall which became a Jewish Messianic synagogue. His sermons became available in Hebrew, Russian and Yiddish and numbered in the thousands of copies reaching the masses of the Jews in eastern Europe.

Thus we see in the Jewish Messianic synagogue not an imposing of the Christian faith on Jews from without, but a reclamation of Christianity from within. The Messianic synagogue which both Lichtenstein and Rabinowitz were instrumental in reviving perhaps for the first time since the apostolic age was a forerunner of similar modern synagogues rapidly mushrooming today throughout the Jewish community.

For centuries Messianic Judaism was not possible as a coherent, lasting tradition. This was so not only because of the de-nationalizing tendency of the Christian faith, which tended to stop any lasting people movement from the Jewish community, but also because of the social ostracism of both the church and the synagogue. Then, too, the policy of the medieval church had really been one of anti-semitic gentilizing which claimed that the Jewish community must collectively and individually make a complete break with its whole way of life in order to accept Jesus as Messiah and Lord. However, there is a new understanding in missionary thinking today. The philosophy of modern missions is that people do not have to commit ethnic suicide by throwing over their culture or assimilating into another culture in order to become believers in Jesus. The gentilizing of past Jewish missionary efforts is recognized today for what it is.

Also, from the Jewish side, modernism has given the Messianic Jew more toleration in the eyes of the Synagogue. In fact, Christianity is not ruled out as a fatal error in itself, and if it has been conceded that it is all right for gentiles to come to know the God of Israel through Christ, the next logical step is that it is also right for Jews to come to this knowledge through him. Although many Jewish religious authorities are not willing to go this far, there are many Jewish people today who are tolerant of Messianic Jews and more open than ever before to the claims of Jesus.

Modern missionary thinking concedes that there is no one "Christian culture" but that all cultures must be Messianized (brought under the Messiah's Lordship) by culturally relevant Messianic congregations. We have black churches to minister to the black community, we have Spanish churches to minister to the Spanish community. In the same way we must have Jewish Messianic Synagogues to minister to the Jewish community and these should surface as such wherever there are bodies of Jewish believers in Jesus. They should be staffed with Messianic Jews, or ethnically sensitive gentile personnel, and they should have a non-cultic, non-discriminatory but culturally sensitive and focused outreach to their own Jewish communities.

Albert Huisjen has some extremely insightful recommendations for the Christian church at large:

> The church has lost sight of the fact that concern for the salvation of the Jews rightfully belongs to the primary considerations of the church. It does

> not belong at the perimeter of her missionary programming, where it is now generally found, but at its very center. Our salvation is not only of the Jews but, also for the sake of the Jews. Salvation is come to the Gentiles to provoke the Jews to jealousy. To the Jew first is a Biblical concept that was first projected in prophecy by Moses, first practiced by Jesus, and first promulgated by Paul. So we repeat what we have said before, namely: To the Jew first has a unique continuance so long as the Jews remain in unbelief and the church has temporal existence. If her mission to the Jews is to come into its own it must be given its rightful place in the mission programming of the church. How this might be brought about should be of real concern in Christian circles...For a church rightfully to answer to her calling respecting the Jews, concern for their salvation should be placed at the center of her interests and missionary programming. Then in accordance with her organizational structure an exhortation should go out from her denominational assembly that this be observed alike by all her congregations, her ministers, her office-bearers, and members. In turn the ministers should pass this pronouncement on to their respective congregations and exhort them with the goal in mind of conditioning them to take in the Jew whenever contact with him is made, whether within parish bounds, as a fellow resident, or in the common ways of life.(7)

In modern times, the best example of just such a top-down denominational zeal for the Jews as Huisjen advocates was the Scotch Presbyterian Church in 1838. That church began by overtures to several presbyteries and then by following up with an enactment of the General Assembly. A commission studied Jewish missions and a mandate was given to the congregations by official pronouncement that there should be an education of the entire church in things Jewish by means, among other things, of an official letter course. Needless to say, the response was a great harvest of Jewish souls. Huisjens advocates that something of this nature is needed in all denominations.

A great modern breakthrough occurred November 8, 1974, when a major Protestant denomination's National Home Mission department agreed that Jewish people could form "fully operative" messianic synagogues within the Assembly of God denomination. This historic decision meant that perhaps for one of the first times since the New Testament period, a Christian denomination was organizationally making room for the kinds of synagogues that can sustain the Jews *both* spiritually and culturally from generation to generation.

Such a long-awaited rapprochement between church and synagogue in the one Body of our Lord is the hope of Christians everywhere and is also the all-pervading goal of this study. It is hoped that all evangelical denominations will soon find messianic synagogues among their congregations world-wide, and that there will be interdenominational and non-denominational or independent messianic synagogues, as well.

This is not to say that the messianic synagogue method of ministry is the only way to win Jewish people to their Messiah. Any local Bible-believing congregation will soon find Jewish people in attendance, because a great end-time ingathering is presently beginning, and Jewish people are being won anywhere and everywhere. However, just as in the past maybe only four or five Jewish people might be won in a given geographical area, now four or five *congregations* of Jewish people can quickly be planted in the same location! This is a sign of the lateness of the times (Luke 21:24-31; Matthew 23:39).

The purpose of my first book, *Everything You Need to Grow a Messianic Synagogue*, has been misunderstood in some circles. I wasn't writing a book to tell Jewish ministers the one and only way they should run their ministry. I wasn't writing a book to tell Jewish people how Jewish they may or may not be, according to the New Testament. Some may not want to join a messianic synagogue. Some may join a messianic synagogue that has no Saturday morning Torah service. Some may join one that does. My book was just a primer to begin to move in the direction of an indigenous Jewish congregation and should be helpful to Jewish people in the initial stages, while they're feeling their way along, trying to see what the style of the Jewish community is where they're ministering.

My book does not tell Jewish people they *must* do anything (except face the eternal consequences of rejecting the Good News). There is no legalism in my book, just the strategic pragmatism of Paul's admonition in I Cor. 9:19-23. Does this mean my book puts Jewish people back under the law? Absolutely not. A Jewish believer in Messiah is in essence a new creation. He is in the world but not of the world. He may observe the law but he is not bound under it (I Cor. 9:20-21). His heart and life, allegiance and authority, mind and spirit, is hidden in heaven with the risen Messiah. He has died to all but the New Age, and he has been born into a new spiritual existence. He has received the spirit of the New Age. He is free, free to become all things to all men (that he might eliminate misunderstanding and culture shock) in order to, by all means, save some (I Cor. 9:22).

Since he is in essence a heavenly citizen, an enlightened new creation (even already in this dying, evil age), a believer is now free (according to the constraints of holiness and love) to become like any unenlightened people. The believer is not lawless (II Peter 3:17), he is under the law of the Messiah (I Cor. 9:21). His life is not controlled by mere rules, but by a Holy person, the indwelling Word of God, the Messiah, whose Spiritual and Scriptural control leads him in a holy life (Jeremiah 31:31-34). See Colossians 2:20-23.

When an actor becomes *like* someone else in order to persuade an audience, it is not a sham. When a believer in the Messiah becomes like a Jew to win a Jew to the Messiah, it is not a hoax. If it is an act done in sincere love, it is an act of truth. An actor knows when he is "doing the truth" on stage. He does not literally *become* the part (that would be insanity or reincarnation); he becomes *like* the part. When a messianic Jew becomes like an orthodox Jew (under the law), the messianic Jew is not under the law but *like* one under the law. *Paul was not under the Law* (I Cor. 9:20-21, NIV). Therefore, no one can interpret Matthew 5:17-20 and 23:2-3 as meaning that Jesus bound the messianic Jews in Jerusalem under the law. To show one's loyalty to traditions while keeping the ethical demands of the law is not the same as legalistic, pharisaic bondage. Neither Jesus nor Paul advocated the latter.

To be literally under the law means to be outside the Messiah (unsaved) and depending on legalistic self righteous religion for salvation. To be *like* someone under the law is to lead a similar life style, but for different reasons. If I legalistically avoid eating pork, or driving on Saturday because I feel I am thereby a superior ethical and religious specimen, I am under the law. If I avoid pork and Sabbath driving to be able to have a more credible witness for the Jewish Messiah to my unsaved orthodox Jewish neighbors, I am under Messiah's Gospel and not Moses' law. An actor sees the truth and integrity of this kind of "acting" because he sees the sincere motive and not the artifice. An orthodox Jew who becomes a believer may still keep the law but he should do so not because he is under the law but because the Messiah's love constrains him to do so in order to win his orthodox family and friends.

When Jewish ministers and congregants don't understand the difference between becoming *like* an orthodox Jew and *becoming* an orthodox Jew, they make a serious mistake and lose the *reality* of the freedom from the law that we have as new creations in the Messiah. This is true in the same way an actor loses his head if he doesn't see the difference between becoming *like* Napoleon on stage and *becoming* Napoleon on stage.

If we go to the Muslims, do we bind ourselves under the Koran? Do we fasten ourselves into that book as though we were unenlightened Muslims? Of course not! We may identify with Koran-believing Muslims, and use the Koran to proclaim the Messiah when it says the same thing as the Word of God, but we shine God's light on the Koran, we do not put ourselves under the bondage of its darkness. The same is true, to a lesser extent, of the Talmud and other rabbinic literature. We become *like* talmudic Jews, but a messianic Jew does not *become* a talmudic Jew. A Messianic Jew is a new creation. As new creations we put on Christ and become all things to all men as God's holy actors. This is important because my book has been misinterpreted by a few Jewish ministers. Instead of preaching *like* rabbis, they began preaching *as* rabbis. In other words, instead of preaching the substance of the New Covenant in a rabbinic style with "kosher" terminology, they began preaching the substance of what rabbis preach (e.g., only on anti-semitism and pro-Israelism). When that is *all* that is preached and the Good News is pushed "underground" in the public services, the sheep don't hear the Shepherd

Messiah's voice and are not fed. They soon drift away. Proof is offered that the *substance* of the Gospel can be preached in a rabbinic style by my play, *The Rabbi from Tarsus*, where Paul preaches the height and depth of the Good News in a thoroughly rabbinic style, so that even a chasidic rabbi hearing it might be spiritually stirred positively or negatively, but not culture-shocked.

Messianic indigenous synagogues that are thoroughly Biblical, that do not compromise the Good News or its manner of acceptance (repentance-baptism) that are open to all and led by men who endeavor not to "culture shock" anyone, Gentile or Jew, reformed or orthodox, are desperately needed today in the Jewish communities of the world. These congregations can be multiplied as quickly as Messianic yeshivas can be organized to equip and train their leadership. As Jewish leaders are trained, they will learn through the yeshivas how to plant a new congregation, how to preach in a Jewish style with New Covenant substance, how to counsel and minister to the needs of Jewish people, and how to become a rabbi surrogate able to perform Jewish weddings, funerals and bar mitzvahs (8). It is hoped that this book will be useful in multiplying these yeshivas wherever there are Jewish population centers in the world.

2

A Jewish Contextual Theology for a Messianic Yeshiva

One of the first things that a messianic Jewish student or teacher in a yeshiva must do is to arrive at a thoroughly Jewish contextual theology that does not compromise the Word of God. Judging from Acts 24:10-21, there can be little doubt that one of Luke's objects in writing Acts is to show that the religion which has since been given the post-biblical label "Christianity" is in fact the true Jewish "way," the true Jewish religion -- true Judaism, and is therefore rightfully the *religio licita*. Luke emphasizes that even the apostle to the Gentiles knows his religion is most relevant to Jews. Paul, is depicted by Luke as a rabbi who always goes to his own people first, and does not normally turn to the Gentiles until he has first been rejected by the Jews. Paul is pointedly shown to be a practicing Jew who takes Nazarite vows (Acts 18:18), and is eager to celebrate the Jewish feasts in Jerusalem (Acts 18:21; 20:6, 16), even willing to purify himself in the Temple (Acts 21:17-27). Furthermore, Acts 23:6-10 indicates that the Judaism of Paul has more in common with the Judaism of the Pharisees than even the Pharisees and Sadducees have with one another. Acts 2:46 asserts that from the very beginning this true Judaism was loyal to the Temple, where, significantly, the Gentile mission was given (Acts 22:17-21). Luke notes that it is only Paul's enemies that refer to his religion as a Jewish "sect," while Paul himself argues in Acts 24:14 that he worships the God of their fathers and believes the law and the prophets. Thus Luke demonstrates that Paul's Biblical Judaism is without taint.

Then Paul himself zeroes in on a basic tenent of Judaism, the doctrine of the hope of the resurrection of the dead upon which Paul bases his claim to Jewish orthodoxy. Those Jews who believe the Jewish doctrine of the resurrection of the dead and will listen to Paul's testimony regarding the resurrected Lord Yeshua will accept his authoritative teaching as true Judaism. Those who refuse to believe the doctrine of the resurrection historically fulfilled in Yeshua will deny Paul's teaching. But Luke makes it clear that if Jews reject the apostolic interpretation of Judaism, they reject true Judaism (Luke 10:22). Luke records Peter saying as much in Acts 3:22-24 where Peter quotes from Deu. 18:15-16 that Moses declared that anyone who would not listen to the Prophet that God would raise up would be extirpated from Israel. This warning is sounded by Peter immediately after his argument that God has raised Jesus from the dead. Arguing somewhat similarly, Paul defends his life in Acts 24:14-15 by defending the orthodoxy of his religion based on the generally accepted doctrine of the resurrection of the dead. Just as Peter claimed that David spoke as a prophet predicting the resurrection of the Messiah (Acts 2:30-32), so Paul says to King Agrippa (Acts 26:2-8), in arguing that the Messiah is the first to rise from the dead, "Do you believe the prophets?"

Because Luke is the only evangelist who both begins and ends his gospel in the Temple, it is clear that Luke is asserting that in a real sense "Christianity" is but a further extension of the Jews' national religion. For Luke's history tells the story of how the spiritual remnant from the Jews finds added to itself a spiritual remnant from the nations to form a nation not of this world, true spiritual Israel. That Luke is arguing that Christianity is true Judaism is shown by Luke's describing the Apostle to the Gentiles as a temple-loyal rabbi who "asserts nothing beyond what was foretold by the prophets and by Moses, that the Messiah must suffer and that he, the first to rise from the dead would announce the dawn to Israel and *to the Gentiles* (Acts 26:23)." Here Paul, as a Bible-believing rabbi, is asserting the truth of Isa. 42:6; 49:6; 53. Luke draws out the irony in Acts 26:6-8 that it is for the hope of the resurrection, the hope for which Jewish people are worshipping God with intense devotion day and night, for this very hope that Paul is impeached (and impeached by Jews, of all people!). Thus Luke drives home the point that this religion is Judaism in the truest sense of the word, and the people who should be the first to recognize it are somehow blind to the fact.

For Luke the true "remnant" Jews are not those who are uncircumcised in heart (Acts 7:5, 13), because they reject the apostolic teaching. Rather, the true "remnant" Jews are those who accept the apostolic teaching and are mikvehed (baptized), meet constantly to hear the apostolic teaching, and to share in the common life, to break bread, and to pray (Acts 2:42). Especially significant is the "breaking of bread" when one remembers that for Luke the Lord's Supper emerges from a Passover seder and has the same central covenantal significance (Luke 22:7-8, 20). Also, it should be carefully noted that for Luke water baptism is the initiation rite of faith whereby the nations must be discipled and whereby all men, Jews and Gentiles alike, must receive through faith the all important gift of the Holy Spirit without which there is no membership in the true people of God (Acts 2:38, 39; Luke 3:7-9; 24:47). According to Luke (Acts 2:1), on Sunday morning, Shavuos (Pentecost), A.D. 30, the proclamation went forth that if Jews were to remain committed to the true faith of Judaism, they must personally commit themselves to the Messiah of Judaism. Since the key ritual for making proselytes to Judaism had been a mikveh bath of water baptism, the risen Lord Yeshua commanded his followers to go into all the world, making proselytes to Messianic Judaism by means of a mikveh bath in the name of the God of Israel.(1)

Today there is a great deal of confusion in the Jewish community as to who is a true Jew, since there is no unanimity discernible among Jews along even racial, religious, political, or national lines. Most Jews want to believe that there is some sense in which the Jewish people are a race, yet there are Japanese Jews. Many Jews would like to define themselves along religious lines, and yet there are Jewish atheists. Of course, many want to believe that the Jewish people are united as a nation, and yet an American Jew knows he's not an Israeli. Therefore, most Jewish people do not really know who the real Jews are.

However, the New Testament does know who the Jews are. Paul asserts quite clearly that the true Jew is the one whose praise (a play on words since "Judah" or Jew means "praise") is of God (Romans 2:29), who has submitted in faith to the rite of spiritual circumcision (Col. 2:11-13), thus becoming a spiritual child of Abraham by faith (Gal. 3:7), and therefore a true Jew (Phil. 3:3). Such are "sons of the covenant," the New Covenant where the Torah is written on the heart (Jer. 31:31-34). For, as both the Torah and the Tenach show, God intended to "mark off" as his own not merely people who were circumcised physically but "in their hearts" (Deu. 10:16). So strong is this teaching that God threatens to destroy any Jew who is not spiritually circumcised (Jer. 4:4). Such a one will be shut out of Jerusalem (Isa. 52:1), as well as the Lord's sanctuary (Ezek. 44:7, 9) and salvation (Deu. 30:6). For not all God's physical people are his spiritual children (Rom. 9:6). In Gen. 17, circumcision (the bris) is the covenant sign of God's choosing out and marking men for his own. But in the New Testament the gift of the Holy Spirit, without which a man does not belong to the Messiah (Rom. 8:9), is offered in connection with faith and water baptism (Acts 2:38), which is identified (when it is an act of faith) with Messiah's way of circumcision (Col. 2:11-12). See Rev. 3:9 on who is not a Jew.

Many people do not know that Judaism used to be a missionary religion, and that the official leaders of Judaism were both zealous and apparently somewhat successful at making converts at the time of Yeshua.(2) Therefore the mission of Yeshua did not arise in a vacuum. It received the legacy of the zealous Jewish proselytizing movement, to which it added the world-shaking power of the Holy Spirit in order to make more proselytes to Messianic Judaism than anyone ever dreamed possible. According to ancient tradition,(3) the first proselytes to the Jewish faith were gentiles, Abraham and Sarah, and through their descendants, God intended to proselytize the nations (Gen. 12:3). Thus it was that Judaism was carried to all peoples, Jews and Gentiles alike by the followers of Yeshua. For Yeshua baptized Judaism with the Holy Spirit and brought God's people the Good News of the Kingdom which Judaism had for so long been waiting to take to the world (Matt. 28:19). Therefore the Good News of Messianic Judaism is that the hope of Israel has been fulfilled, the Messiah has come, the resurrection has already begun through him -- Yeshua Ha Mashiach, who has already begun to pour out the Holy Spirit on his followers; consequently, the people from every nation may receive the Holy Spirit and be assured of their own personal coming resurrection by obeying the Messiah of Israel as their Lord and King.

Just how Jewish the faith of Christianity is is made obvious by the startling fact that, judging from the Pauline epistles, people who had been heathen just a short time before were expected to be able to understand the complex rabbinic style argumentation of Paul (e.g. Gal. 4:21f). These people can no longer be considered heathen. Theologically they must be able to think like Jews. Therefore, it is no mere spiritualization to say that the converts to Christianity were in some sense Jews.(4) Theologically, there can be no better label for them. For how could one fully understand the Gospel without entering into a full understanding of the soul of Israel? If one rejects this conclusion, one is left with the absurd idea that only the false teachers (judaizers) could make true proselytes (Jews) out of the Gentiles.

That Luke is aware of the gentile Christian's privileged status as a Jew or Jewish proselyte is obvious in the fact that for him the Lord's Supper emerges from a seder. Whereas uncircumcised men could not sit at table with Jews (Acts 11:1-3), circumcised men who were uncircumcised at heart (Acts 7:51) excluded themselves from the privilege of sitting at the Lord's New Covenant "seder" (Acts 13:46). Those of the natural Jews who rejected the privilege of entering into a new covenant with the God of Israel condemned themselves as unworthy of eternal life and forfeited their privileged status to the Gentiles, the wild olive branches of the Chosen People of God.

Turning from Luke to the broader theological perspective of Christianity as true Judaism, it is hardly necessary to belabor the point that the Judaism taught in the New Testament preserves the essentials of the faith of Israel that other brands of Judaism have largely lost. For example, Messianic Judaism teaches Biblical monotheism, that the Lord our God is *echad* (Deu. 6:4). The Torah does not say, "Shema Israel ah-donai elo-hey-noo ah-donai *yachid*." Maimonides makes the unbiblical assertion in the second article of his "Thirteen principles of the faith" (5) that God is *yachid* (a simple unity), but no such assertion is ever made in the Bible, where God is always referred to as *echad* (complex unity).(6) The Jewish Scriptures teach that God has a complexity in his unity such that man must be created male-and-female-multiplying in order to adequately reflect the image of God (Gen. 1:27-28). God did not picture himself by creating a solitary man. The threefold picture of two human beings conceiving a third was necessary to reflect the complex unity of the one God of Israel. In Gen. 2:24, God says that when a man marries a woman the two become *echad*, one. This is not *yachid*, an absolute unity, which would make the two people simply, absolutely one human being! Rather a marriage is *echad* because it is a complex unity of two joined into a unity. On the other hand in Judges 11:34, Jephthah's only daughter is simply, absolutely one human being, so the Bible refers to her as *yachid*. If God's unity were that simple it would not be possible for King David to say, "The Lord said to my Lord" in Ps. 110. Moreover, if true Judaism is to be judged by Biblical standards, what is often called "pure monotheism" (7) is in reality impure and unbiblical and even "unjewish."

According to the Scriptures, God has always had a complexity in his unity, because God has always had his Holy Spirit and his powerful creative divine Word. The one God of Israel sent his divine Word among us as a man in order to make a blood covering for our sins so that we might receive the eternal life of God's Holy Spirit. This was God's gift of love to us, so that he could with mercy and justice forgive us and bring us into a new order of life. However, God's gracious provision through his divine Word Yeshua has forced the whole world into a crisis of decision. When we look into the Jewish face of Yeshua we are confronted by the divine Word of God himself. Whoever does not obey the God of Israel by heeding his divine word in Person is cut off from Judaism and from salvation (John 8:39-45).

Besides Biblical monotheism, the other essentials of the faith of Israel are not lost in Messianic Judaism although they have been largely lost or neglected in other kinds of Judaism. For example Messianic Judaism maintains in the death of Yeshua the Torah's demand for blood sacrifice: "It is the blood that maketh an atonement for the soul" (Lev. 17:11). Moreover, the Temple of Yeshua's body -- torn down by men -- has been raised by God. Messianic Judaism also preserves the true significance of such Jewish institutions as the high priesthood, the sage, and the prophet and such Jewish doctrines as those concerning the Messianic King, the Holy Spirit, and salvation. Through the resurrection from the dead of the great high priest (Heb. 7:24), sage (Matt. 12:42), prophet (John 7:40), and Messianic King (John 7:41) Yeshua and through the coming of the Holy Spirit on Shavuos A.D. 30, all these essentials of Judaism are imperishably maintained.

THE CHURCH IS A MESSIANIC SYNAGOGUE

Modern scholars such as Bousset, Oesterley, Baumstark and Werner have shown that the early church functioned liturgically very much like a synagogue. In fact, the church is referred to as a synagogue by both James (Jas. 2:2) and also frequently by such church fathers as Ignatius and Theophilus of Antioch. In Luke 4:16f the synagogue is the birthplace of the proclamation of the gospel, for it is here that Jesus first begins to preach. As we have seen, Luke is not giving the history of a new religion which he juxtaposes over against the old religion. Rather he is telling the story of the true religion and how Judaism opened beyond the Temple and Jerusalem to the ends of the earth so that Gentiles could be received into the true faith of Judaism and be saved. In fact, one could say that the story of Luke-Acts is the story of how the synagogue opened its doors to the world. For Acts tells the story of the world-wide Messianic Synagogue of Yeshua, at first composed exclusively of physical Jews and then, as the Holy Spirit overflowed Jerusalem and spilled out onto the world, comprising spiritual Jews from every race on earth.

That the Pauline churches are Messianic synagogues is clear from Luke's narrative. In fact, the unreceptive synagogues (which prove to be non-messianic synagogues as far as Yeshua is concerned) force Paul to find new meeting places for his authoritative teaching, and therefore it is the fault of an influential minority of Jews that the true way within Judaism becomes separate from the already established synagogues in the diaspora. Although these newly established Pauline Messianic synagogues are populated mostly by Gentiles, the fact that they are headed up by a rabbi and that they were, despite their heavy Gentile constituency, nevertheless clearly competitive with non-messianic synagogues explains the persecution (Acts 17:5; I Thes. 1:6) which they endured at the hands of representatives from other synagogues. All of this goes to show that even the Pauline churches, despite their cultural accommodation to Gentiles, were identifiable, even to hostile Jews, as synagogues. How much more like a synagogue must have been the primitive Jerusalem Church! For these Jewish believers in Yeshua are described in Acts as not only loyal to the temple but also to the law (Acts 21:20).

It's important to keep in mind that if the majority of Jews in a particular synagogue accepted the apostolic teaching, they did not thereby cease being a synagogue, any more than the Jews of Beroea in Acts 17:11 would have ceased to be synagogue members had they in fact determined that "these things were so." The earliest Christian communities continued the "traditional mode of worship to which they had been accustomed in the synagogue."(8) The "prayers" of Acts 2:42 would not exclude the *shema* and the *amidah* which all law-zealous Jews prayed daily. Therefore, it's important to remember that the first Jerusalem believers were not worshipping in churches. They were worshipping in fully operative synagogues and Jewish house fellowships, which should be fairly clear from the fact that there were among them not only many priests (Acts 6:7) but also many believers who were zealous for the law (Acts 21:20). Because she has so completely lost the Jewish flavor of her early worship life, the Church today does not recognize herself as a Messianic synagogue; therefore, she does not see the obvious priority and relevance that the Gospel should have to the Jews. For if the Church really understood herself to be a Messianic synagogue, then, of all peoples, she would be directing her Gospel to the Jew first.

THE UNITY OF MESSIANIC JUDAISM

When Paul was expelled from a synagogue in the diaspora he invariably planted another synagogue in the same town, a Messianic synagogue which acknowledged Yeshua as the Messiah and Lord. These synagogues did not make *cultural* conversion to Judaism a qualification for salvation, but these gentile-dominated Messianic synagogues, even though they did not live the life-style the law made possible, kept their theological unity with the law-zealous Jewish Messianic synagogue community in Jerusalem. They maintained a relationship of brotherhood with the saints at Jerusalem in order to witness to their unity in the one faith of Israel. The New Testament depicts Messianic Judaism as sustaining its unity despite its cultural diversity through the fact that the apostles were cooperating cultural specialists (Gal. 2:9). That is, Paul and Barnabas and James and Peter remained in contact and affirmed their theological accord despite the varied cultural expression that theological truth found among their apostolic constituencies.(9) The New Covenant Passover meal of the Lord's Supper comprised the center of the common worship life of both the gentile-accommodating Messianic synagogues of Paul and the Jewish-accommodating

Messianic synagogues of James and Peter. The "collection" is one piece of evidence we have for the contact that the Jewish believers in Jerusalem maintained with the Gentile believers of Paul's mission in the diaspora. Furthermore, in Gal. 2:2 we see Paul submitting his gospel to the Jewish apostles "that he might not run in vain," and we see Paul keeping amicable relations with James, even to the point of acquiescing to his request (Acts 21:23f) that Paul should go to the Temple and make a sacrifice to maintain his (and their) credibility with the local Jewish community.

The basic unity among the apostles has been undermined by those who attempt to see a theological disagreement about the law between Paul on the one hand, and James and Peter on the other. This basic difference begins in the minds of many scholars with Stephen whom Schmithals, Haenchen, Brandon and others attempt to make into an antinomian. (10) Schmithals asserts that it is "incredible in view of the variety of Messianic expectations in orthodox Judaism, that the Messianic hope of the believers in Jesus -- which was moreover politically harmless -- could have been the cause of bloody persecution." (11) Therefore, for Schmithals, if Stephen wasn't stoned to death because he advocated a Christianity free from the law then the violent reaction he stimulated is wholly inexplicable. Haenchen also believes this and says as much in his commentary on Acts. (12) However, the difficulty is that nowhere in Acts does Stephen attack the law. Furthermore, the question of the validity of an expression of Judaism which disregarded the ceremonial law would appear to be a later issue that could be theologically developed only on a Gentile mission field. To overcome this difficulty some scholars have postulated quite gratuitously a Hellenistic Christian mission preceding Stephen and developing outside Jerusalem which influenced Stephen and gave him his antinomian philosophy.

However, there is plenty in Stephen's speech to make the Sanhedrin murderously angry without postulating any such extraneous irritation. What was so enraging about Stephen was not his undermining of the law. Nowhere does the New Testament record any Jew advocating that his fellow countrymen repudiate the Holy Torah. This would have meant ethnic and ethical suicide for the Jewish people and cultural treachery of the highest order. Stephen was undermining not the law but the entire contemporary religion of the Jews, for Stephen asserted that since Jesus is the Messiah of Judaism and these Jews with their religion rejected the Messiah of Judaism, then their religion was not true Judaism and in fact they were resisting the Holy Spirit and were heathen at Heart (Acts 7:51-53). Such a stabbingly blunt confrontation could do nothing else but force the Jewish people in the Sanhedrin to either accept what he was saying as true or to violently reject it as blasphemy and heresy for which he deserved death. Peter had preached something of the same thing when he warned in Acts 3:23 that all Jews who rejected the Prophet that Moses talked about would be cut off from Israel. However, "Hebrew" Jewish believers appear to have been considerably less abrasive than the "Hellenist" Jewish believers in their presentation of the Gospel and the fact that the former were Aramaic-speaking Jews rather than Greek-speaking Jews may have worked somewhat to their favor as well. With Stephen then, the jarring fact begins to be asserted in Jerusalem that where there is no true apostolic teaching there is no true Judaism. Or, to put it another way, a Judaism which is unreceptive to the Holy Spirit and the Messiah is not Judaism at all, for where there is commitment to the law and the temple but no commitment to the Messiah, there is no commitment to true Judaism, for the Messiah is the covenant of Judaism (Isa. 42:6). Stephen is not being "anti-Judaic,"(13) but is voicing the warning of Ro. 2:28, 29 and Ro. 9:6 in Acts 7:51 when Stephen calls the Sanhedrin "heathen still at heart" (NEB), because they are resisting the Holy Spirit by rejecting the Messiah Yeshua (Acts 7:52) in favor of the temple and the law, which they have subverted (Acts 7:49, 52). See Rev. 3:9.

Therefore, if it can be shown that Stephen was not an antinomian, and if it can be shown that the religion of James, which involved Torah-zealous Jews (Acts 21:20), was as validly "Christian" as the religion of Paul, then it can be shown that early Christianity was not an antinomian reaction to Judaism. Unfortunately James, the brother of the Lord, has been given very unsympathetic treatments by several modern scholars. He is seen to be the one who "ousted Peter from his original primacy," the one who plotted to lead Paul into a trap in Acts 21 to get him out of the way, and the one who was manipulating the judaizers from Jerusalem but who was so clever and so powerful that Paul was supposedly afraid to take him to task by name.(14) However, it is interesting that every commentator who wants to present James unsympathetically has to undermine the credibility of Luke. Luke makes it clear (Acts 15:24) that James would repudiate any interpretation of the men "from James" (Gal. 2:12) which would imply that he himself sent the judaizers. Moreover, Gal. 2:1-4 shows that at a very early period the Jerusalem apostolic leadership did not argue with Paul's Gospel to the Gentiles, even though that Gospel disregarded the law as a means to salvation. They understood that the Gentiles waited for the Messiah's torah or teaching (Isa. 42:4), the Good News, which would supersede Moses' law (Deu. 18:19). However, "false brethren" among them disagreed and some of these law-zealous men may have agitated Paul because they feared persecution against the Jewish mission in Jerusalem at the hands of their own people (Gal. 5:11). Since a "Jew" at that time was by definition loyal to the Torah, it may well be that Paul does not criticize James in any of the Pauline epistles, because Paul realized that James would and could not publicly condemn anyone who was loyal to the law, for if he did so he would compromise his whole position in Jerusalem as a loyal Jew and a spiritual leader among the Jewish people. It is a testimony to the wisdom and the courage of James that he, the head of the law-zealous Messianic Jewish community in Jerusalem, despite all the pressure that must have been on him to the contrary, advocated that there be no "irksome restrictions" placed on Gentiles (Acts 15:19), which meant that they would not have to submit to circumcision nor depend on keeping the Law as the condition for their salvation (Gal. 5:3). If Luke's report (Acts 15:19-24) is correct, then, Paul must have been impressed that James and he were preaching the very same gospel.

If we may assume that the epistle of James was written by James, then we see that he had anything but a heterodox Christology. The Jesus Christ of James is both Lord and reigns in glory to come again (Jas. 5:8) as Judge (Jas. 5:9). There can be no doubt that James preaches the same gospel as Paul, for in Jas. 1:21 he speaks of the implanted word that is able to save your soul, a reference to the implanted law of the New Covenant (Jer. 31:33). James' allusion to the law of Lev. 19:18 as the "kingly law" (Jas. 2:8) must include a reference to the King of Israel, which for James is Jesus (Jas. 1:1). A law-loyal Jew of the synagogue, whose teaching is grounded in the authority of Jesus, his Lord and Messiah, James saw that the Christ event had made all the more pernicious exclusivistic snobbery (Jas. 2:1-9) and that the wall between Jews and Gentiles had been broken down. Therefore, James did not impose circumcision on the Gentile Titus (Gal. 2:3), but instead resolved to impose "no irksome restrictions" on Gentiles (Acts 15:19). James must have prayed for and received much wisdom (Jas. 1:5) to be a faultless and devout conformist to Judaism, daily frequenting the Temple courts for the observances of Judaism, and yet at the same time to understand that these were Messianic privileges, not burdens to be thrust upon Gentile proselytes as the precondition for their salvation. Not only was James an extremely wise man, he was above reproach, both according to his personal religion and even ceremonial criteria. Yet the Gospel James preaches in his epistle does not make its appeal on ceremonial criteria, but on the ethical demand of his religion. Here James follows Jesus, whose appeal was always ethical and for whom the perfect law of liberty, the kingly law of love both for God and for one's fellow man, was the goal of Judaism. Therefore, in James we see modelled the power of Jesus to make a man a good Jew, from anyone's estimate, one whose love for God is manifest by his devotion to *both* the law and the Spirit of the law, which is the Good News of God's Grace in the Messiah.

Moreover, like Paul, James knows that saving faith is not empty lip service but is active in love.(15) Both men gain a hearing from unbelievers by displaying the fruit of the spirit,(16) though James and Paul used different cultural strategies, Paul putting himself outside the law though not outside the law of the Messiah to win Gentiles, James putting himself as if he were under the law to win law-abiding Jews (I Cor. 9:19-23), though in fact he is under the kingly law of love (Jas. 2:8). Paul would not dispute James that we are justified by works and not by faith alone(17) unless it can be shown that James means by "works" not "faith active in love" (Gal. 5:6), but the works of the *law*. For the latter to be true, Acts 15:19 would have to be judged a Lucan fiction since here James is represented as acceding to Gentile liberation from the law.

However, it is crucially important that this liberation from the law not be termed antinomianism, for neither Paul nor James is an antinomian. Unfortunately, Paul's views concerning the law were susceptible to misunderstanding and abuse.(18) And just as Paul's view of the law has been misunderstood, so has James. Neither Paul nor James offers the law in itself as a means to salvation (Jas. 2:10; Gal. 3:10). Both men speak of the "torah of freedom" (Jas. 1:25; 2:12; I Cor. 9:21) in a way that implies Messiah (Jas. 2:1; Ro. 8:2), and James, no less than Paul, emphasizes the need for faith (Jas. 1:3, 6; 5:15), for love toward God (Jas. 1:12), and being born again (Jas. 1:21).

The epistle of James constitutes a re-evaluation of Judaism, but not in terms of its ceremonial dimension, for both James, Jesus, and Paul kept the ceremonial law and proved thereby that the Christian life is not antithetical with a life lived in loyalty to the Torah. However, since the Judaism of James is controlled by the authority of Jesus and by the Holy Spirit, he brings to his Judaism a new depth and power of ethics and love which reveal a fulfillment of all that Judaism intended to bring. The great ethical heart of James reminds one of an Amos or a Micah and especially of Jesus. But the epistle of James reveals more than courageous preaching against evil in high places. We see also in James the possibility for a new brotherhood within Judaism, one that is held together not merely by a common allegiance to various cultural traditions and legal demands, but one that is held together by the love of the Messiah. James kept the law as he worked to create this brotherhood among his people, even as he cooperated with Paul's mission to create brotherhood between Jews and Gentiles.

The deep Jewish piety of James earned him respect from every sector of the Jewish community of first century Palestine. Apparently only the wealthy Sadducean Temple party, whose calloused neglect of the poor brought them under the severe censure of James, were against him. Nevertheless, James became known as "James the Just," and was given a status of pre-eminent respect not only among Jewish believers in Yeshua but also among Jewish believers, so that the new movement with Judaism was left in peace to build itself up by increasing in numbers. Therefore, while Paul provoked the Jews to jealousy by winning some Jews and many God-fearing Gentiles away from the unbelieving synagogues, the Messianic synagogue community of James provoked Jews to jealousy by winning large numbers of priests (Acts 6:7) and Pharisees (Acts 21:20) *into* the synagogues that were permeated by the authoritative teaching of Yeshua *even though they were fully operative in loyalty to the law.*

Yeshua was the center of the worship life of this community because the mikveh and the Lord's "Seder" were the primary Jewish rituals that incorporated unbelievers into James' Messianic synagogue community. Yet at the same time, those who entered the Messianic community via the mikveh and the "Seder" also remained credible members of the Jewish community by their loyal attendance at Temple and synagogue. Therefore, there was no cultural "irksome restriction" that would stop a Jewish people movement and would keep priests and pharisees from joining the "church," since the Jerusalem "church" was a Messianic synagogue community.

Furthermore, since this equally valid form of Christianity was loyal to the law, we cannot then say that Paul was an antinomian. For in the New Testament, Paul is seen hurrying back to Jerusalem to have fellowship with these law-zealous saints, to even demonstrate his loyalty to the law with them (Acts 20:16), since the Jewish festivals were prescribed by the Torah (Lev. 23:4-8). Furthermore, Paul could hardly have begun persecuting the Church because of a misapprehension that the Jerusalem Church was antinomian, since there is no evidence that the religion of the early Jewish believers was disloyal to the law. Rather, Paul's initial persecution finds adequate motivation is his desire to suppress the assertion that a cursed dead man is the Messiah, the Holy One of Judaism, the goal and continuing center of the religion of his people. That this "Jesus" Judaism was gaining a large following sparked the zeal and fervor of Paul's attack, for he knew that such a growing movement of heretics could not be allowed to spread to other cities. Later, when Paul became the Apostle to the Gentiles, his quarrel was not with torah-loyal Jews. His controversy was with certain soteriologically heretical Jewish believers who were apparently undermining the gospel and putting a stumbling block in the path of Gentiles by asserting that salvation was not in believing in Jesus alone, but in getting circumcised and keeping the entire law. Whether these men believed this because they feared persecution by their own people in Jerusalem or because they genuinely believed that man, by keeping the law, can please God and thus save himself does not matter. What does matter is that Paul has no quarrel with Peter and James, and that he is not preaching a different gospel.

Paul himself was loyal to the law and remained a practicing Jew(19) who did not gentilize Jewish people, but rather even performed rabbinic ministry for them (Acts 16:3). Yet, he refused to be a separatist, both in regard to table fellowship between Jewish and Gentile believers in the same church (Gal. 2:14), and also in regard to his world-wide church's relations with the law-zealous Jerusalem Messianic synagoque community (Ro. 15:31).

In Gal. 2:3 we see that a similar desire on the part of James also meant that in the church at Jerusalem there was no exclusivistic separation between Gentile believers and Jewish believers. Undoubtedly Titus, when he stayed in Jerusalem with Paul, was allowed to have communion with the Jewish believers even though he was not circumcised. We see also in Acts 15 that James is so concerned that Jews and Gentiles be able to continue to have table fellowship with one another in the Body of Yeshua that he lays down just a few minimal rules that will make table fellowship between Gentiles and kosher Jews possible. Paul's equal concern is shown in Gal. 2:11-14 where Paul asserts that the unity in the Messiah must not be compromised by Jews withdrawing from table fellowship with Gentiles.

Paul's great reverence for the law meant that even though he loved the law he did not depend on his own legal rectitude for salvation. He was eager to show by both actions and speech that he was a zealous and orthodox Jew.(20) However, under the tension of the heretical soteriology of the judaizers, Paul had to hammer out a theology for Judaism wherein the yoke of the torah was not confusingly and unscripturally imposed on Paul's heathen proselytes to Judaism. James agreed with Paul's theology in principle (Acts 15:10-20, 24), since it was understood that when the Messiah came, the world would receive his law, his torah or teaching (Isaiah 42:4). No one -- Jew or Gentile alike -- could find salvation if the yoke of the Messiah's law was not taken (Deu. 18:19; I Cor. 9:20-21; Matt. 11:29).

Moreover, because the Pauline synagogues were stripped down to quickly accommodate people of Gentile culture and because the few Jewish believers in such an environment may have relaxed their Jewish scruples, Paul would be open to attack by Jews as encouraging antinomianism (Acts 21:21), despite the fact that there is no hint in any of his epistles written to his Gentile mission churches that he ever taught *Jewish* people to repudiate their sacred traditions. Anyone who quotes Gal. 4:8-10, Col. 2:16-17, or Romans 14:5-6 to prove that the Jewish festivals are forbidden to Jewish believers in Yeshua is reading the Bible entirely out of context. Paul is not addressing these epistles to Jewish believers who are celebrating these days in the name of the Yeshua; therefore, his words cannot be taken as criticism of believers who *are* celebrating these days in the name of Yeshua.

Against Brandon,(21) James does not question Paul's Jewish orthodoxy in Acts 21:20-22. Rather, James warns Paul that thousands of law-zealous yet born-again Jewish believers in Yeshua have been led to question Paul's Jewish loyalty, that he has been teaching Jews in the diaspora to betray their religion. It can well be imagined that there was tremendous pressure on James to repudiate Paul, and that he certainly might have thought that not to repudiate Paul would completely destroy his credibility with the local Jewish community. However, there is no hint in Luke or in the epistles that James ever repudiated Paul. Rather, according to Luke, James was zealous to see Paul re-establish confidence in the "Way" among both the law-zealous Messianic Jewish believers and unbelievers in Jerusalem.

Many modern scholars distort James' position. Brandon thinks he detects in James a suspicion of Paul because for Brandon the logic of Paul's theology made the "peculiar religious status claimed by Judaism of absolutely no effect."(22) However, in Romans 11:25-26 Paul asserts the truth of a "mystery," that the hardening of Israel has always been *partial*, until the full number of Gentiles would come in, and then the whole of Israel would be saved. So the "peculiar religious status" of the Jew *is* relevant to Paul's view of the plan of salvation. Furthermore, James was concerned that true Judaism, the Judaism of Jesus conveyed to the world through the apostolic teaching, should be seen in the right kind of light by the Jewish community, that this Judaism should be seen to allow Jews to remain loyal to the Torah even as it allowed Gentiles to become engrafted into Judaism without becoming culturally Jewish. Both men understood that the Great Commission (Matt. 28:19) was to *disciple* the nations, not transculturate them. For Paul and his Gentile mission to be repudiated because Paul was considered to be a heretical Jew would have been just as destructive to the Judaism of James *which included the Gentile mission* as it would be to Paul.

Paul understood just as clearly as James that a man must live like a Torah-loyal Jew in order to win Torah-loyal Jews (I Cor. 9:20). However, the same man might have to identify with the lifestyle of a Gentile in order to win a Gentile. Therefore, Paul's life was directed not only by the Torah (he was a Jew and at that time to be a Jew meant to be loyal to Torah), but also by the Spirit in the interests of the gospel. Had Paul been the antinomian Jew he is often made out to be,(23) he would never have circumcised Timothy nor taken a Nazarite vow. Paul would say that Christians are free from the letter of the law (Gal. 3:10-13), but Christians are not free to shirk their responsibility to put themselves "as if" under that law to win those Jews (I Cor. 9:20) who are, in the case of James' constituency, zealous for the law. This putting oneself "as if" under the law to win those who are under the law is something that Christians have refused to do for the past 2,000 years, and this is why Messianic synagogue communities have almost entirely disappeared with James.

JUDAISM CULTURALLY ACCOMMODATING GENTILES

As we have seen, Paul's religion is not a "Christianity free from law."(24) It is Judaism accommodating Gentile culture. In fact, Pauline Judaism has plenty of room for the law. Paul is even willing to sacrifice his life if necessary in order to keep in fellowship with law-zealous Messianic Jews to whom he returns at the end of the book of Acts (Acts 21:13; Ro. 15:30, 31). For Paul, James and the apostles are a kind of spiritual substitute for an apostate Sanhedrin which does not accept the authority of the apostolic teaching that Jesus is Lord and Messiah. Paul never forgets that his gospel is not only his but also that of the Jewish apostolate in Jerusalem. Therefore, in spite of all of the assertions of his independent apostolic authority, he nevertheless freely submits to James and to the apostles at Jerusalem "that his gospel might not be preached in vain" (Gal. 2:2).

What we see in Acts 15 is the legitimization of two cultural streams within the one body of Yeshua, for there James lays down the Holiness Code of the Old Testament as the groundrules making possible table fellowship between Jews and Gentiles.(25) The picture of Judaism we have here is of two non-exclusivistic, mutually-fellowshipping, yet culturally *different* streams within the one body of Yeshua. The guidelines laid down in Acts 15:19-20 can be summarized in what Paul said, "It is good neither to eat flesh, nor to drink wine, nor to do anything that makes your brother stumble" (Ro. 14:21). In a Gentile situation, Jews should not offend Gentiles by withdrawing from them (Gal. 2:11-12), and in a Jewish situation, Gentiles should be willing to eat only what will not offend Jews. In this way every man does what is pleasing to his brother and not to himself to promote the unity in the Messiah (Ro. 14:13-15).

However, because the ceremonial law is culturally foreign to Gentiles, it is often naively assumed to be burdensome to all and antithetical to the freedom of a Christianity which can be valid only if it is antinomian. To Gentiles a more or less Torah-loyal form of Christianity (call it Messianic Judaism) is either unimaginable or inferior. However, the Jewish-accommodating Judaism of James is just as "Christian" as the Gentile-accommodating Judaism of Paul. Neither relied upon the law for justification or communion. Simply there were Messianic bodies within Judaism who, because their congregants were Jews, lived a lifestyle loyal to the Torah, whereas also within the one Body of our Lord there were synagogues that, because their congregants were Gentiles, did not observe the ceremonial law. Since Acts presents the church essentially as a unity with its center in what could only be described as a fully operative Messianic synagogue community (Acts 21:20), then there is every reason that Gentile Christians should understand that their religion is Judaism, Judaism which has accommodated itself to Gentiles and must not be constrained from accommodating itself fully to Jews. The ironic situation of modern times is that, although initially Torah-loyal Jews allowed Gentiles to enter Judaism without being loyal to the Torah, now there are those who would attempt to redefine the faith so that it has no room for Torah-loyal Jews, only "antinomian Jews and Gentiles." So zealous is one Gentile scholar to assert the irreconciliation of "Torah Judaism" with "Antinomian Christianity" that he depicts Hellenistic Christianity as antinomian from the beginning, even though this requires postulating a Hellenistic Christianity which preceded Stephen and originated outside Jerusalem.(26) In this way Gentile Christians forget that it is not they who sustain the root, but it is the root that sustains them (Ro. 11:18).

To Paul, the Jew was the true and original object of God's concern, and Gentiles were grafted on to become spiritual Jews and true -- though non-transculturated -- proselytes to the Messianic faith of Israel. This is why spiritual Jews must never make themselves superior to the natural branches (Ro. 11:18), for God has not rejected the Jewish people he foreknew (Ro. 11:2). The plan of salvation that Paul sketches in Romans 9-11 is that Gentiles temporarily supplant the non-remnant of Israel (Ro. 9:24-29) like Jacob did Esau (Ro. 9:10-13). But the Jewish remnant is not supplanted (Ro. 11:1-5), and when the full number of Gentiles has come in and the partial hardening of Israel is over, the Jewish remnant will expand so that it can be said in fact that all Israel will be saved (Ro. 11: 25-32). Therefore, for Paul the success of the Gentile mission is never seen as an end in itself but as a means to provoke the Jews to jealousy that they too might be saved (Ro. 11:11). In fact, for Paul as for other Biblical writers(27) the hope of the spiritual revival and salvation of the Jews is fraught with the very eschatological excitement of the Messiah's final coming, and this must be kept in mind lest Acts 13:46 and 28:29 be interpreted to mean that Paul believed God was finished with the Jews.

Rather, for Paul the true faith of Judaism is proliferated throughout the world as congregations are called out of the old synagogues to form new synagogues thriving on the apostolic teaching and the charisma of the Holy Spirit. However, the men who direct the planting of these new synagogues are not insensitive to cultural diversity and therefore recognize the need and in fact the necessity of cultural specialization in their missionary work along ethnogeographic lines. James assumed the Jewish mission in Jerusalem while Peter and John went to the Jews in the diaspora.(28) Likewise, although he was the Apostle to the Gentiles, Paul always went to the synagogue first. He realized that even though he was the Apostle to the Gentiles, he was still planting synagogues. Yet, because he was a specialist in Gentile missions, the synagogues he planted were specifically designed to accommodate Gentiles. For example, these synagogues would probably not celebrate all the Jewish festivals, and they would certainly not circumcise Gentile babies, avoiding the practices the Jewish-accommodating synagogues of James and Peter would allow. Since Jews and Gentiles don't live similar lifestyles and since the one religion of both James and Paul permeated all of life, the synagogues that were planted by James, Peter and Paul had to accommodate these cultural differences. This was so, even though James and Paul were concerned that the synagogues remain in fellowship with one another and that neither place any "irksome restrictions" on the other.

Within the Body of Yeshua, then, there is only one gospel, but it has different cultural expressions. Since the apostolic office implied cultural specialization (Gal. 2:7-10), a Jamesian pastor must surely have functioned more like a rabbi than, for example, a Pauline pastor. Therefore, in Acts 21:20 we see the possibility of a "Christian" ministry by Jews among their own people which allows for all the scripturally compatible observances of the Jewish religion, including the practice of circumcision, as well as the bar mitzvah,(29) and the observance of all the Jewish holidays.

The Messianic synagogues planted by Paul were stripped down to put no greater burden on the Gentiles than that they celebrate their Messianic faith through the Jewish rituals of the mikveh and the Lord's "Seder," and that they adopt the Jewish scriptures as the ethical guideline for their life. The apostolic office took culture seriously, recognizing that theology can never ignore culture though culture must always bow to theology.

Therefore, the picture of the religion of James and Paul given us by the New Testament is not a Jewish religion "designed to serve the essentiality of Judaism while admitting a qualified possibility of Gentile participation in the new faith."(30) Rather, the religion of the New Testament is one in which the law of love allows *both* a radical accommodation to Jewish culture and a radical accommodation to Gentile culture, where the Torah may be *both* adhered to by gospel-believing Jews and where the Torah is not imposed on gospel-believing Gentiles. However, because the Pauline churches were designed to accommodate Gentiles and carefully avoided imposing Jewish distinctives on them, these same churches were destined to have extremely limited cultural appeal to the Jewish community. For these Gentile synagogues were stripped of the vital culture-sustaining traditions (the bar mitzvah, the shabbat and festival services, etc.) that, generation after generation, a normal Jewish synagogue offers the Jewish community for her cultural sustenance as a people.

For Gentiles, the law means one thing: a heretical and futile effort to win salvation. However, for Jewish people the law has a different purpose than is often supposed. Jews are not in the business of spending all their time trying to figure out a nice heretical way to get salvation. Jews are in the business of sustaining themselves culturally as a people, and the law helps them to do that. When the Jewish mother does the things that the law says she should do, she is helping to sustain her ethnic consciousness as a Jew. Does anyone think that the Jews could have sustained themselves ethnically as a people all these millennia without the law? Could the Jews have remained Jews if, instead of bar mitzvahing and Sabbathing and koshering all this time, they spent their days intermarrying, eating pork chops and playing hillbilly guitars?

Strumming hillbilly guitars (or even singing Lutheran hymns in church) would not have kept the Jewish people Jewish. Besides the Jewish home, the religious institution for promoting the cultural identity of the Jewish people has for thousands of years been the synagogue. Unlike the modern Gentile church, the synagogue does not force Jewish people to find their cultural identity outside her sacred walls. For this reason, the synagogue, together with the Jewish home, is the great reservoir for the religious and cultural survival of the Jewish people. This was also true of that messianic synagogue community which was the early church, for we read in Acts 21:20 that the first believers in Yeshua were "zealous for the law." They worshipped in the synagogue as Jews and their faith in Yeshua did not lead them to reject the law and the Jewish lifestyle that the law insured them: rather, their faith in Yeshua made them even more zealous to be loyal Jews who raised their children to be Jews. Thus the early church accommodated great people movements from the Jewish community (Acts 2:41; 5:14; 6:7; 21:20); there was no lack of cultural commitment to scare unsaved Jews away. Indeed, her zeal for the law encouraged unsaved Jews to have zeal for the Lord Jesus.

Anyone attending a synagogue today is likely to see the bar mitzvah candidates sitting up front on the platform with the rabbi. This eloquent picture intends to say to the Jewish congregation that if Jewish people will come to the synagogue every week, the synagogue will keep them Jewish and their children will be culturally incorporated into the Jewish community when they reach the age of their religious majority. The bar mitzvah ceremony is very old and functionally it has had its equivalent from the very earliest times. When Jesus was blessed by the sages upon the occasion of his twelfth birthday, we can assume that the ceremony was the functional equivalent of a bar mitzvah at that time, because it was the custom during the period of the Second Temple for the sages to bless a Jewish child who had reached his first fast day at age twelve or thirteen.(31) This would surely mean that it was very much a part of the life of the first "church" in Jerusalem to have the children of the law-zealous messianic Jewish believers in Jesus go into the temple and have this bar mitzvah-equivalent ceremony. Therefore, faith in Jesus was not for the Jew in the first century a road to cultural assimilation because the first church had room in her life for Jewish culture and even for the bar mitzvah!

Of course, when a Gentile reads this he has a tendency to think that these Jews who had their children bar mitzvahed even as they taught them that Jesus was the Messiah must have been leading schizophrenic lives where they did some things entirely as Jews and other things entirely as Christians, with the former being entirely dispensible. One can readily see why Gentiles would feel this way. Gentiles do not want to see their own children bar mitzvahed because they do not want to culturally incorporate their children into the Jewish community. However, Jewish people are not Gentiles, and since God has a vested interest in keeping Jewish people Jewish until his Son, the King of the Jews, returns, it must have been very important to God that there be a messianic synagogue community in Jerusalem for Jewish people to become incorporated into once they discovered that Yeshua is the Messiah.

The Gentile-accommodating Pauline churches could not sustain Jewish people culturally because the churches of Paul were stripped of the very culture-sustaining traditions that are vital to the survival of the Jewish people, but a stumbling block to the salvation of the Gentiles, Paul's mission field. Therefore, how tragic it is that the centuries have not seen men after the tradition of James, the apostle to the Jews, pioneering messianic synagogue communities among the Jewish people. Somehow the Jewish cultural specialization died with James and with him died the messianic synagogue movement which has only recently found new life all over the world. One can only lament that both rabbis and Christian ministers have not read Acts 21:20-21 more carefully: "You see how many thousands there are among the Jews of those who have believed: they are all zealous for the law, and they have been told about you that you teach all the Jews who are among the Gentiles to forsake Moses telling them not to circumcise their children nor observe their customs. What is your position then?" In Acts 28:17, Paul gives his position to a Jewish audience in Rome: "Brethren, *though I had done nothing against the people or the customs* of our fathers, yet I was delivered prisoner from Jerusalem into the hands of the Romans." And elsewhere Paul affirms "to the Jew I became like the Jew to win Jews; to those under the law I became like one under the law -- though not being myself under the law -- that I might win those under the law" (I Corinthians 9:20). If only rabbis and Christian ministers had read those verses with discernment, there may have been many, many more Jewish children that would have been bar mitzvahed in the body of our Lord and might have come to know the Supreme Living Rabbi as their Messiah. Both the rabbis and the Christian ministers will stand God's judgment for this, because the Scripture says "Let not many of you become teachers, my brethren, for you know that we who teach shall be judged with greater strictness" (James 3:1). Unscriptural teaching both within the Christian community and the rabbinic community have militated against large-scale people movements from the Jewish community into the body of the Lord.

Even Paul, the head of the Gentile mission, knew how to circumcise the Jewish boy Timothy in order to put Timothy "as if" he were under the law that he might win those who are under the law. Note that the operation of circumcision that Paul performed is part of his "Christian" ministry since Paul does it in order that Timothy might win the Jews in that area *to Christ!* (Acts 16:3). Tragically, there will be no large-scale people movement from the Jewish community until there are thousands of messianic synagogues led by messianic teachers who know not only how to preach the Gospel and how to baptize, but how to supervise the circumcision of Jewish babies as well as how to perform the ceremony of cultural incorporation found in the bar and bat mitzvah.

A Friday evening service is critically important not only because many Jewish people take Exodus 20:8-11 seriously and want to keep the Sabbath, but also because the Hebrew prayers of the synagogue liturgy provide an appropriate setting for the bar and bat mitzvah services as well as the other vital culture-sustaining traditions of the synagogue. Thus, when the church finds herself in a Jewish neighborhood she must take cultural specialization as seriously as the apostles did (Galatians 2:9), and become a fully operative messianic synagogue with Friday night services. Only in this way will she give opportunity for large-scale Jewish people movements into the Body of Yeshua as whole Jewish families and webs of relatives and friends join messianic synagogues where they can celebrate their faith in Jesus *as Jews* and sustain their cultural identity from generation to generation even as they are sustained in their spiritual life as believers.

There are those who would concede that messianic synagogues are not guilty of "judaizing" when they allow Jewish believers to celebrate their faith in Yeshua through Jewish customs and traditions and raise their children as Jews. Granted, messianic synagogue planters are not judaizers, since judaizing is requiring someone to keep the ceremonial law *in order to be saved*. Using the ceremonial law to sustain one's culture is not the same as using the ceremonial law to win salvation, and there are many critics who would have to concede this. Nevertheless, these same people might quote verses like Galatians 3:28 ("There is neither Jew nor Greek ... male nor female") or Galatians 6:15 ("For neither circumcision counts for anything, nor uncircumcision, but a new creation") and use these to try to dismiss the entire case for a messianic synagogue or for Jewish people being committed to their own culture. But to use a text which shows that being born again is the only thing that really matters to argue against the apostolic cultural specialization (Galatians 2:9) is hazardous in the extreme. Why did God have men set aside to be apostles to the Jews and other men set aside to be apostles to the Gentiles if there is no difference between the Jew or Gentile? Obviously, there is a difference just as there is a difference between men and women.

Moreover, Acts 21:19-21 warns against anyone teaching Jewish people not to circumcise their children or to celebrate their customs or to keep the law of Moses. And nowhere in the Pauline epistles can it be found that Paul taught Jewish people to repudiate their Jewish heritage. On the contrary, the book of Acts presents Paul as a temple-loyal rabbi who performs circumcision and vows in the temple and keeps the Jewish holidays with his Jewish brethren in the Lord in Jerusalem. The Paul of the New Testament is a Gentile-accommodating rabbi, not a Torah-free libertine!

It would be a misinterpretation of the book of Hebrews to see its author's intent as a call for cultic reform. There are those who would so interpret Hebrews 8:13: "In speaking of a new covenant he treats the first as obsolete. And what is becoming obsolete and growing old is ready to vanish away." It would be reading into the book more than is there to draw from the author's typological comparisons a call for Jewish Christians to divorce themselves from the observances of the old covenant ceremonial law. The author's message is theologically-ethically oriented, aimed at persuading his readers to keep their New Covenant faith and messianic zeal and the author has no discernable interest in purifying or reforming the observances of Judaism or in taking his readers to task for their involvement in taboo Jewish rituals. The question of a strategy of using old covenant observances to lead Jewish people to a new covenant faith, a missionary method plainly recommended in I Corinthians 9:19-20 ("to those under the law I became like one under the law, though not being myself under the law, that I might win those under the law") is not addressed by the author of Hebrews and therefore his words cannot be taken as criticism of such a strategy.

The church's rejection of Jewish culture has compounded and confused many Jewish minds. When the ordinary Jewish person attends a Gentile-style church and hears the pastor speak of how the Jews killed Christ, he reads into the situation a rejection not only of himself, his people, and his heritage, but of his culture as well. He hears, in effect, something like this: "We Christians don't like you Jews; and we don't like your Jewish customs or your Jewish ways of doing things." It's as though someone is saying to him, "Not only did you kill Christ, but your whole religion is wrong in every way, as is your culture and heritage."

It is easy to see how this type of confusion would put a Jewish person into a defensive, basically anti-Christian posture.

We see this phenomenon of confusion in the Book of Acts where certain Jewish people in Jerusalem were extremely puzzled by the strange Gentile style that the Pauline churches were beginning to take on. These Jews began to confuse the guilt applied to Israel in the proclamation of the Gospel and the Gentile cultural style of the Pauline churches which appeared as a combined threat to their peoplehood. This is why in Acts 21:21 and 28:17 we see Paul on the defensive himself as he denies Jewish accusations that the church is trying to destroy the ethnicity of the Jewish people by outlawing circumcision.

The Jews rightly perceived (and Paul did not deny) that their whole culture as a people would be threatened by the teaching and practice of a church which would not allow Jewish people to circumcise their children. Paul did not outlaw circumcision. He did not preach it (Gal. 5:11), but he did allow it for Jews (Acts 28:17).

On the other hand, Paul did not allow Gentiles to be circumcised as a conversion ritual, even for the purpose of missionary identification, any more than Paul himself would remove the mark of his own circumcision for the same purpose. Perhaps the Hellenized Jewish atheletes of his time could do this to identify with their Greek competitors in the games, but the race Paul was running was of a different sort. For Paul the human medium could never obscure or compromise the divine message, which for him was that the true Jew is never the result of mere human activity, whether in birth or in physical circumcision; the true Jew is always the result of a spiritual rebirth and heart circumcision in which God creates an eschatological new man.

Otherwise, however, Paul's martyrdom was really his life's sacrifice to prove that no Jewish custom (even a temple vow) was per se at issue in the Gospel. For Paul, the decision to follow the Messiah was always a spiritual issue, never a mere matter of externals (Romans 2:28, 29; 14:5, 6; Philippians 3:3).

Rabbi Paul gave the church a strategy in the New Testament. First, in his message in Galatians 3:13 Paul made it clear that Christ is essentially a curse *for* everyone, not a curse *against* anyone (unless rejected).

Paul would surely make that message clear today. He would emphasize that Christ is a curse *for* the Jewish people and *for* Judaism, not a curse against the Jewish people or against Judaism. Judging by Paul's radical willingness to go into the temple to make a vow and be present at a sacrifice -- despite the anachronistic implications that such a sacrifice must have had as far as Paul's theology of the cross is concerned -- we can see that Paul was willing to make a radical identification with his people if he could by any means save some (I Corinthians 9:22).

How would Paul identify with his people if he were trying to reach them in our world today? Would he not shock the Gentile church we see so timidly involved with Jewish culture today? From Paul's ministry to Timothy we *know* he would be willing to help his Jewish associates enculturate in any way necessary for them to identify radically with Jewish people to win them to Christ. Of course, what and when and how they would do these things would depend, for one thing, on what type of Jews they were dealing with, whether they would be Chasidic, Orthodox, Reformed, or agnostic Jews. In any case, Paul would not become like an Orthodox Jew to win a reformed Jew, or require a reformed Jew to become Orthodox. No, Paul would identify with the person where he was to lead him to the

Messiah (I Cor. 7:17-20). Paul would not put Jews under the law who were not under the law in order to free them from the law's curse. Nor would he plant an Orthodox-style synagogue in a Reformed neighborhood. He would use a pastor's wisdom. Paul took a very *small* representative delegation of his Gentile converts with him into Jerusalem and took no Gentile with him into the temple. We can imagine that in the twentieth century he would take few, if any, Gentiles with him into a Brooklyn Chasidic ghetto in order to become like the Chasidic Jews to win the Chasidic Jews in Brooklyn.

It's a tragic shame that the church has been guilty of not really following Paul's admonition in Philippians 4:9 (Revised): "What you have learned and received and heard and seen in me, *do*; and the God of peace will be with you."

Paul made it clear in Acts 28:17 he had nothing against the Jewish customs and that the issue in dealing with his Jewish people was a question of faith in the Jewish Messiah and not faith in cultural taboos.

In Romans 14 he shows that culture is a matter of individual freedom and conscience, and the rule of love would dictate that each man should allow his brother this freedom and not destroy a work of God by abusing another man's cultural freedom (Romans 14:20).

In fact, Romans 14 goes even further to suggest that a Christian should give up his own freedom out of love rather than create a stumbling block for others. So there's a sense in which it is a sin *not* to become like a Jew to win a Jew -- if by exercise of his Gentile cultural freedom one puts a stumbling block in the path of a man of another culture and thereby keeps him from experiencing the love of God.

Paul climaxed his ministry as the leader of the Gentile mission of the church by a love offering for Israel. In effect he was saying then that the church must not detach herself from Israel, nor could she give a mere lip service type of loyalty pledge.

Paul declared a message of critical importance when he carried a love offering to Israel at the risk (and finally at the loss) of his own life. Paul declared by his death that the ultimate fate of Israel and the ultimate fate of all believers in Yeshua are intertwined.

It is a shame that the church has erred so far in this respect. Many churches have not seen the need for their missionary budget to reflect the priority of Jewish evangelism, despite Ro. 15:27.

Therefore, the church must correct her own guilt. In the same way that the Jewish community shares a collective guilt with *all men* for the death of Christ, so the Christian community has a collective guilt for confusing and obscuring the clear gospel of the New Testament in proclaiming it to the Jewish people and to the nation of Israel.

Every scriptural Jewish ceremony may be acknowledged and pleasing in God's sight if done in the name of the one in whom all scripturally compatible Jewish ceremonies are fulfilled. The Scripture teaches that these are matters on which everyone should reach conviction in his own mind (Ro. 14:5). Jewish believers in Yeshua can also remain kosher, if they desire (Acts 21:20; Ro. 14:3). The scriptural principles here are "whatever you are doing, whether you speak or act, do everything in the name of the Lord Yeshua, giving thanks to God the Father through him" (Col. 3:17), and "to the Jew I became like a Jew to win Jews" (I Cor. 9:20).

Of course only the Bible is authoritative for the faith and practice of a Messianic synagogue, and the Talmud can never be placed on a par with the Holy Jewish Scriptures, Genesis through Revelation. However, where the Talmud agrees with the Bible, the Talmud may serve as an occasionally or frequently useful illustrative teaching for Biblical truth, though its assertions must always stand the test of God's Word, which is true of any non-Biblical book.

Choosing the wrong cultural specialist as their mentor, Jewish evangelists have typically tried to mimic the apostle to the Gentiles (Paul) and have largely ignored his highly successful (Acts 21:20) cultural counterpart, the apostle to the Jews (James). James was concerned that no "irksome restriction" (Acts 15:19) be imposed on Gentiles. He would have also been concerned to have no "irksome restriction" placed on him and the Jerusalem Messianic synagogue of which he was the spiritual leader. Can you imagine James' reaction if some Gentiles had told his Jewish congregations they could no longer practice circumcision or keep kosher or celebrate their new faith through the traditions of their people (Acts 21:20-21)? Unfortunately, the dismal history of Jewish missions has been the largely futile effort to impose the irksome restrictions of Gentile culture on Jews. Instead of planting and pastoring New Testament-patterned Messianic synagogues with cultural integrity in Jewish neighborhoods like James did in Jerusalem, Jewish evangelists typically function as unwitting twentieth century "gentilizers," trying to persuade Jews to transculturate -- a culture betrayal the Jewish community understandably resists as ethnic suicide. The church in a Jewish neighborhood must not forget where she is (I Cor. 9:20-21), nor should she confuse spiritual and cultural conversion. When the church finds herself in a Jewish neighborhood she should be used by God to form a fully operative Messianic synagogue. Otherwise, she may betray the example given to her by James and Peter and thus lose sight of the cultural specialization involved in the apostolic office and in the planting of churches.

In the twentieth century we see that the table has turned completely from what it was in the first century. The Jewishness of Christianity was once so pronounced that it was possible to have a debate as to whether Gentiles as Gentiles could have membership in the synagogue of Yeshua. Now the gentileness of the church is so pervasive that it is a debatable point as to whether the Jews as Jews can become members of the Gentile church of Jesus. The first believers in Jesus who were Jewish kept their credentials with the Jewish community and we see as a result that they had great evangelistic effectiveness. (32) Even Paul's ministry, though he was specializing in Gentile-mission synagogue growth rather than Jewish-mission synagogue growth, carried the authority in learning of a rabbi and therefore his gospel was keenly heard by Jews everywhere he went because of the fact that he preached like a rabbi. We need ministers in the church today to have more Jewish training and understanding so that they will not be gentilizers but rather will be able to sustain the Jew culturally as well as spiritually from one generation to another wherever they find him. Only then will they be able to make an impact on the Jewish community and to compete with the rabbinic ministry for the winning of the Jewish community to the Lord Jesus.

Indeed, a Gentile pastor who knows nothing about the bar mitzvah ceremony shares some of the incompetence in Jewish ministry of a rabbi who knows nothing about the

New Testament. This ignorance was not always present in the Body of our Lord. Because of the apostolic cultural specialization, the apostles gave the church flexibility in her cultural expression, and consequently the New Testament faith in the first century was just as viable an option for an orthodox Jew as it was for a Roman centurion. Because the Jewish apostolic specialization nearly died with James there has been no real cultural option available to the orthodox Jew ever since. Since James undoubtedly functioned as a rabbi (how could he be the spiritual leader of men who were zealous for the law if he didn't?), what is needed is a new army of spiritual leaders like James who will come on the scene and give the rabbis of the Jewish community stiff competition so that fully operative, culture-sustaining Messianic synagogues begin to compete with non-messianic synagogues for the religious allegiance of the Jewish community. In Jerusalem the local church could culturally compete with the local synagogue because the local church was a Messianic synagogue. This must become true today, and where the church finds herself in a mixed community where the proportion of Jewish people is not large enough to warrant her becoming a fully operative Messianic synagogue she must at least be so aware of her Jewishness and the Jewish origin and significance of the sacraments and of her indebtedness to Israel that she can make herself once again the most relevant of places for the Jew, so that the Jew will feel at home in the church and will understand that of all people the Gospel is most relevant to him and is to him first.

For the Jewish evangelist, James will continue to be the apostle to the Jews *par excellence*. The only differentia between Jamesian Judaism and first century Judaism was the authority of Jesus as Lord in the center of the worship life of Judaism. There was no cultural differentia between Jamesian Judaism and first century Judaism. James did not endeavor to purify or reform Judaism. He simply allowed a new center of authority to direct his Judaism and that was the acknowledgment of Jesus as Lord. James proved by his life that the law of love can be fulfilled within the pale of ceremonial law just as surely as it can without. Both Paul and James had a theological quarrel with the judaizers. But whereas Paul could repudiate legalism openly because his believers lived outside the ceremonial law anyhow, James had to show a "more excellent way" *within* the context of the ceremonial law under which he lived out his Messianic witness to Yeshua.

Even though the term "rabbinic Judaism" is actually a post-Biblical term describing a post-Biblical religion, nevertheless what the New Testament does in effect is to slam the door shut on rabbinic Judaism and open it wide to a Jamesian Judaism which in many cultural manifestations would be similar to rabbinic Judaism, but in terms of its authoritative center would have the Messiah. Because for the Jew the synagogue is a vehicle of his cultural identity and longevity as a people it is the task ahead to messianize the synagogue and to even messianize rabbinic Judaism to the extent that any scripturally compatible Jewish custom may be baptized into the service of preaching the Gospel and leading men to the One in whom every Jewish custom is fulfilled. Since even Paul the apostle to the Gentiles could keep the requirements of the law, if thereby he was enabled to clear an obstacle out of the path of the Gospel, it is all the more important for Jewish evangelists to become like the Jews and put themselves "as if" under the law to win orthodox Jews who are under the law. All these men need do is to keep the issue clear. The crucial issue between Messianic Judaism and any other sort of Judaism centers on the hope of the resurrection from the dead. The only question is whether there is such a hope and whether that hope has been realized in the historical resurrection of Yeshua Ha Mashiach. Is Yeshua the king of Israel or not? Is he alive today to rule the hearts of men, even as in the age to come, he will rule the world or not? There is no other issue.

Just as in the year A.D. 49 at the Jerusalem council, a Messianic synagogue formally made room for Gentile churches, so today the Gentile church must make room for Messianic synagogues. Messianic synagogues such as have been outlined in this chapter will give the world-wide body of Yeshua an enriching, fresh look at her origins. For the leaders of these Messianic synagogues will not be able to content themselves with blindly imitating reformed, orthodox, and conservative congregations or rabbis down the street, but will have to continually re-examine the Scriptures to steer Messianic Judaism on its own distinctive course within the world-wide body of Messiah's people. A good place to begin is with the Passover, which is the subject of the next chapter.

3

Toward a Jewish Contextual Theology: The Old Covenant Meal of Judaism

The ritual observance of *pesah* has changed somewhat over the centuries. The rites of the "*pesah* of Egypt" have sometimes been abandoned in the "*pesah* of (later) generations," as even the Mishnah admits.(1) But it is not the purpose of this study to discuss the various forms which the feast has taken in Biblical and post-Biblical Judaism (which is the subject of the Mishnaic treatise entitled *Pesahim*). Nor is this study interested in speculating on the origins of the Passover, whether its beginning is to be traced to a fertility sacrifice,(2) or to a Semitic nomad's springtime feast,(3) or on such questions as whether the *Pesah* and the *Massot* festival was originally two separate festivals. Rather, the interest of this investigation is to draw together the motifs in the Old Testament references to *pesah*, especially as these shed light upon the covenantal nature of the religion of pre-Christian Judaism.

If we restrict ourselves to the Old Testament, we see that we have two kinds of Passover texts: liturgical texts and historical texts.(4) In the category of liturgical texts, we have the ritual of the Passover in the story of the Exodus from Egypt (Exod. 12), the religious calendars in Exod. 23:15; 34:18, 25; Deut. 16:1-8; Lev. 23:5-8, the rituals in Num. 28:16-25 and Ezek. 45:21-42, and the story in Num. 9:1-14. In the historical texts, we have descriptions or mentions of particular Passovers: the first Passover, at the Exodus (Exod. 12); the first Passover in Canaan (Josh. 5:10-12); the Passover of Josiah

(II Kgs. 23:21-23; II Chr. 35:1-18); finally, there is the Passover described in II Chr. 30.

The Hebrew word for the Passover which appears in these passages is *pesah*. This verb means to "pass over" or "to leave out" or "jump over" in the sense of "to spare the life." The God of Israel spared the lives of those in the blood-sprinkled Israelite houses, while he did not pass over the Egyptians.

THE MEANING OF THE BLOOD

The immediate question to be answered is, what was it precisely about the blood smeared on the Israelite thresholds that prompted this divine "passing over"? Was there an expiatory cause -- that is, is the theology of blood atonement at the center of the matter? Or was an apotropaic cause involved -- that is, was the blood functioning as a repellant of evil? Gray asserts the latter,(5) completely ruling out any cathartic value in the blood-smearing ritual. Other scholars, though they would disagree with Gray and assert that the death of the paschal lamb at the time of the Exodus was redemptive, at the same time would agree with Gray that this expiatory value was later entirely absent.(6) These scholars would lead us to assume that the paschal victim either never had, or, at the very least, entirely lost its function as a sacrificial offering for the expiation or removal of sins.(7)

Yet no one, not even Gray, denies that the passover victim was a sacrifice,(8) and that the paschal meal was a sacrificial meal.(9) Therefore, the critical question is, what kind of sacrifice was the *pesah?* We are greatly helped in our attempt to categorize it by Exod. 34:25 where the *pesah* sacrifice is labeled a *zebah*. This was a communion sacrifice, what Vaux defines as, "the tribute offered to God to maintain or to re-establish good relations between him and his worshipper."(10) Although the *pesah* sacrifice cannot be strictly categorized as a sin offering because it is eaten by the worshipper, nevertheless, because it is a sacrificial meal, expiation is very much in view. Vos is right in showing the error involved in thinking that expiation was offered only in the sin offerings: "Wherever there is slaying and manipulation of blood there is expiation and both of these were present in the Passover."(11) In Jewish thought there can be no notion of communion with God without an implicit notion of antecedent expiation, for the God of the Jews is a holy, sin-hating God and therefore the communion he has with sinful men is always an act of reconciliation requiring expiation. In a word, then, the *pesah* offering was a sacrifice of redemption.(12)

Whether the *pesah* offering was ever a firstlings sacrifice is debatable,(13) but that the redemption of the first born of Israel is an important Passover theme has attestation by a divine oracle dated on the very day of the Exodus.(14) The motif of the redemption of the first born has covenantal significance and serves to point the Mosaic covenant back to the Abrahamic covenant, as we shall see.

But one does not even have to read very far in a Passover *Haggadah* to see the rich covenantal significance that this Jewish festival has invested in it. A glance at the Hallel Psalms,(15) or at the *haftorah* portion read during Passover week (see Josh. 3:5-7) reveals the preeminence of the covenant in the liturgy of Passover.

The covenantal relationship between the God of Israel and the Jewish people is assumed at every turn during Passover. For example, the sacramental scrupolosity regarding cleanliness in the preparation of the Passover meal presupposes a special relationship between Israel and her holy God. *Pesah* was in fact a solemn sacrament.(16) Everyone who participated in the meal was required to observe strict rules of ritual cleanness. It was a long-established practice that those who had ceremonially defiled themselves should take a sacramental bath.(17) In the same category would be such symbolically potent acts as gathering up and throwing out the old leaven -- the annual cleaning out of old impurities at harvest time is a sacrament of repentance -- and it has been persuasively argued that the reason the *pesah* victim was eaten in one place and its remains burned was to avoid ritual pollution.(18) This strong ethical-sacramental strain is built into the *pesah* meal because throughout the Old Testament the covenant idea is "one which demands from the people a strenuous morality."(19) That excommunication is threatened in connection with *pesah* (Exod. 12:19) underscores the covenantal character of the meal quite clearly.

It has been said that there is no univocal concept of "covenant" in Scripture.(20) Both human and divine covenants, it is true, take various forms in the Bible. However, through all the Bible's divinely imposed covenants, one covenant promise in particular is unfolding:

> By myself I have sworn, says the Lord; because you have done this and have not withheld your son, your only son, I will indeed bless you and I will multiply your descendants as the stars of heaven, as the sand which is on the seashore, and your descendants shall possess the gate of the enemies, and by your descendants shall all the nations of the earth bless themselves, because you have obeyed my voice (Gen. 22:16-18).

It is possible to view all the covenants of Scripture as means of supplementing, implementing, or fulfilling this basic Abrahamic covenant.

Throughout the Bible, blood, the precious receptacle of life and also a symbol of death, is used by God to make an awesome and sacred seal upon his covenants with men. The importance of blood in covenant-making is underlined in the experience of Abraham by both circumcision and animal sacrifice.(21) Without the memory of Abraham, the "remembrance" of the Exodus in the Passover festival would be quite incomprehensible. As Trumbull has aptly stated, the Passover feast was "the feast observed by the Jews in commemoration of that blood-covenanting occasion in Egypt when God evidenced anew his fidelity to his promise to the seed of Abraham, his blood-covenanted friend."(22)

The covenantal character of the Passover is evidenced by Exod. 12:48 where the Abrahamic covenant sign of circumcision is the requirement for participation in the ritual meal. This requirement shows that the Mosaic Covenant, in view in the Passover festival, is grounded in the Abrahamic Covenant. In the latter, God required both Abraham's blood in his circumcision as well as substitute blood in animal sacrifice for the redemption of Abraham's first born, Isaac. Thus the Passover festival uses both circumcision and the theme of redemption to keep not only the Mosaic Covenant but also the Abrahamic Covenant in remembrance at *pesah*. Further covenantal emphasis is given to *pesah* by the fact that at a very early period it was customary and in fact obligatory "for every individual male adult to offer a sacrifice on visiting the shrine as at every *hag*."(23) Furthermore, the primitive *pesah* was a New Year festival and involved an assembling of all males of the age of twenty and over who had undergone the initiation rite of circumcision.(24)

This note of emphasis on the Abrahamic Covenant underscores again the covenantal significance of the Passover.

To determine the precise covenantal meaning of the Exodus *pesah* sacrifice, it is necessary to decide the exact meaning of the blood on the threshold. Gray sees the blood used to keep some power out of the house.(25) Trumbull says that the blood is used to welcome some power into the house.(26) The latter's evidence is more convincing.(27) He states, "Jehovah did not merely spare his people when he visited judgment on the Egyptians. He covenanted anew with them by passing over or crossing over the blood-stained threshold into their homes."(28) Trumbull argues that God did not invent a new ritual or ceremony at every stage of revelation but he took a ritual with which the people were already familiar and he used it to make his message heard. The ancient threshold covenant with which the Semites were familiar was made when the head of the household offered a blood sacrifice at his door in order to signal the welcoming love that he had for a visitor. In fact, the welcoming love was measured by the preciousness of the sacrifice.(29) It makes perfect sense that, since it was a covenant-making God who passed over the Israelites and since the *pesah* blood met the terms of his covenant, then the blood on the thresholds constituted a welcome to such a God. This welcome would be a deterrant to the judgment of this God but not to his saving presence. The rich Semitic symbolism of Trumbull's threshold covenant fits well with the New Year's festival motif of Passover, when the Jewish people stood at the threshold of a new harvest and a new year.

Trumbull says that God did not pass over the houses of the Israelites but only the blood of the victim on the threshold as he entered the houses.(30) The fact of the story is that he crosses everyone's threshold in Egypt. For those who have the blood sacrifice, he crosses their threshold to save. For those who do not have the blood sacrifice, he crosses their threshold to judge. And the blood sacrifice itself distinguishes the Lord's people from his enemies; that is, it is the mark to distinguish those who are in a covenant relationship with him and those who are not. The blood mark on the threshold functions for the household as the blood mark of circumcision functions for the individual: both mark people as the covenant property of God.

THE MARRIAGE MOTIF

Without Trumbull's researched conclusions on the threshold covenant it is very difficult to explain the origins of the idea that Yahweh married Israel and carried her out of Egypt over the threshold of the Exodus (see Jer. 31:32), or to explain the ancient customs of the *mezuzah* with its covenantal scripture nailed to the threshold,(31) or the primitive threshold blood welcome to the bridegroom.(32) In describing the Exodus, Trumbull states:

> Obviously the figure here employed is of a sovereign accompanied by his executioner, a familiar figure in the ancient East. When he comes to a house marked by tokens of the covenanting welcome the sovereign will covenant-cross that threshold, and enter the house as a guest, or as a member of the family; but where no such preparation has been made for him, his executioner will enter on his mission of judgment.(33)

The figure of God being made welcome as a bridegroom and family member at the national threshold is very significant. Because the bridegroom rescues his bride, the figure is very close to the *go'el*, the next-of-kin redeemer who comes to ransom his relatives that they might be freed. When God is pictured as a *go'el*-like bridegroom we see how the theology of atonement and the theology of covenant come together in a vivid scriptural image.

In Israel the solemn declaration of a covenant was formally confirmed by a meal(34) and there are numerous examples of this in the Old Testament.(35) In fact, the word *berit* has been found possibly related to the root *brh* which indicates food and eating. Kohler believes that the original idea of covenant came from a covenant meal and that the characteristic phrase "cut the covenant" came from cutting up food for the meal.(36) In Exod. 24:3, after the people make their solem covenantal pledge to obey the Lord's law, we are told that Moses took the blood and sprinkled it on the people, saying to them, "Here is the blood of the covenant which God has made (literally 'cut') with you, on these terms." Then in verse 9 we are told that Moses, Aaron and the Elders went up and beheld the God of Israel, and "they looked at God and ate and drank" (Exod. 24:11). Here we see that the covenant does not go into effect until it is cut. This, of course, necessitates the death of the sacrificial victim. The victim itself, then, becomes a communal meal called a *zebah selamim,* which is a "sacrifice which produces a union between God and the people."(37) So in Exod. 24 the same kind of sacrifice as we see identified with the *pesah* victim in Exod. 34:25 is eaten in a sacrificial meal climaxed by a theophany. With the sprinkling of the blood, the covenant was made operative so that communion was possible. The communal meal that followed was of great importance because from this point forward Israel would share a unique relationship with her God, and both covenant and communion could be annually reaffirmed and re-experienced in the covenant meal of the Passover.

Therefore, the bitter herbs, the wine, the *massot* and the *pesah* victim were all covenant pledges. As such they were offered by the sovereign to his subjects to reaffirm the covenant relationship. Jer. 31:32 throws a great deal of light on the nature of this covenant renewal. In this passage God refers to himself as the husband of Israel who brought her out of Egypt and gave her a covenant. Also, elsewhere in Scripture we see Israel referred to as either a virgin or a whore, depending on the covenant loyalty she keeps to her sovereign. The Passover, then, if not in the cult, at least in the motifs drawn from Old Testament references, is a kind of yearly wedding anniversary dinner in which the God of Israel and his bride commune together as they remember the glorious day on which they were married. On this day, the people of Israel feasted on the very one whose blood sacrifice sealed their national and individual relationship with the God of Israel.

This marital imagery stands out all the more clearly in light of Trumbull's research on the threshold covenant.(38) Trumbull states:

> (The remembered Egyptian Passover) sacrifice was on the threshold of the homes of the Hebrews on the threshold of a new year, and on the threshold of a new nationality. Then Israel began anew in all things. Moreover, it was recognized as the rite of marriage between Jehovah and Israel; as the very threshold covenant had its origin in the rite of primitive marriage.(39)

Trumbull(40) has shown that the stamp of a red hand of a bridegroom was the certification of covenant union on the doorway of the family. However, in the Egyptian Passover, it was the virgin of Israel, the bride who certified the marriage covenant by the bloody hand stamp on the doorway and the stamp was made with the very feminine symbol of hyssop which symbolized the holy purity of the stamping.

Mowinckel has shown the importance of covenantal renewal in the feast of tabernacles.(41) Yet it is important to note that all of the three annual feasts had covenant renewal as their primary theme and of these the concept of covenant shines out most clearly in the Passover.

THE PEACE MOTIF

From the very outset of scripture, communion with God is seen as the end of man, and all covenant-making is the means to that end. But of all the sacrifices in the Old Testament the one sacrifice most clearly covenantal in significance and communal in design is the *pesah* victim. The *pesah* sacrifice was specifically designed to create communion. Notice that it could be sacrificed by the head of the household, but the whole victim had to be shared by the *same* household. Furthermore, the members of each household could not leave the house all night, but had to stay together to eat the lamb in its entirely at night. Thus one can see that everything was ordered to require the people to have a common meal from which to share common benefit. Moreover, the victim was designed to turn their minds backward to a great covenant-making, communion-creating, national sacrifice. Segal is right in saying that the *pesah* was "a communion ceremony in a class by itself in Israelite ritual."(42)

The *Pesah* victim was a peace offering, but a peculiar kind of peace offering, one that could not be enjoyed individually, but only corporately, one victim per household. It was a corporate peace offering. As we have said, there was an element of the expiatory sacrifice in the *pesah* offering, because wherever there is manipulation of blood there is the thought of expiation. But paramount in this *pesah* offering was the idea that God was mediating through this sacrifice not only reconciliation and peace but covenant union with his people so that they might experience the presence of God even as Moses and the Elders did in Exod. 24. Therefore, the strong commemorative aspect of Passover was for the purpose of re-experiencing covenant renewal and personal communion with God.

Proof of this is that the rabbis stressed the importance of the first person singular in the text of Exod. 13:8, "what God has done for *me* when *I* came out of Egypt."(43) Because the people of God had been manumitted into freedom, they were to personally re-experience the peace and joy of the freedom which God had personally given to their nation through his saving presence and mighty action at the Exodus.

Therefore, the *pesah* meal is an annual celebration of a peace treaty signed in blood on the thresholds of the homes of Hebrew slaves. Each person sitting at the Seder peace table is to remember both the former unrest of slavery and that great national experience of God's covenant peace experienced at the Exodus. In order that the experience may be reappropriated by each succeeding generation, the Mishnah says "in every generation a man must so regard himself as if he came forth himself out of Egypt, for it is written, 'and thou shall tell thy son in that day saying it is because of that which the Lord did for me when I came forth out of Egypt'"(Exod. 13:8).(44)

THE ESCHATOLOGICAL MOTIF

This covenant renewal ceremony is a ritual-recalling of the total experience of the covenant that God made. As the elements are explained the story unfolds in a wonderful visible parable where each edible detail adds a sensual note of re-experience. The pledges of the "cut" covenant provide the communion meal, the consumption of which seals the covenantal relationship and confirms the covenant promises. As the meal directs the attention of its participants backward to the action of God, it also remembers the promises that God made in the past, and these promises point the eyes of the participants toward the future.

Therefore, the eschatological emphases that the Passover had at the time of Jesus were very much in keeping with the message that the Passover had always proclaimed: namely, that the same faithful covenant-keeping God who rescued his people from Egypt will continue to rescue them, and ultimately send the Messiah to bring them their final deliverance. Even the post-Biblical ritual of the seat for Elijah and his cup have definite Messianic symbolism which in theology at least is a very old and long-standing feature of the covenant-deliverance motif of the Passover celebration.

As we have seen, the prerequisite for communion with the God of Israel is always covenant relationship, and this would include an expiatory sacrifice since a holy God can not commune with sinners without expiation. Therefore expiation, covenant, and communion are all values which are present in the *pesah* victim's offering. But that the *pesah* victim was also a meal shows that it was a peace offering as well, and this again underlies its importance in creating communion.

The motif of the first born, both in terms of the Egyptians and the Israelites can be seen in chapter 12 and 13 in the Exodus account. God struck the first-born of Egypt and saved the houses marked with the blood of the Passover victim, sparing the first born of Israel as well as the whole nation. A sacrifice which sealed the covenant and which spared Israel her first born looks back to the Abrahamic covenant and to the sacrifice that Abraham made in place of his son whom God spared. For, as a result of the Exodus, part of the covenant promise made to Abraham came true at Sinai: there God formally constituted Abraham a great nation and, through this nation, prepared to bless all the nations of the world. Therefore, both the Abrahamic and the Mosaic sacrifices look forward to the nation's Lamb of God that would be slain to free men from sin and death in order to lead all the nations on a New Exodus toward a New Promised Land as spiritual Jews and members of the common-wealth of Israel.

4

Toward a Jewish Contextual Theology: The New Covenant Meal of Judaism

Many scholars agree that the Last Supper occurred in an atmosphere permeated with the Passover, possibly even as an actual Passover Seder.(1) However, as far as strict historical detail is concerned, there are those who find the Johannine narrative more persuasive than the synoptic account. But even John makes it clear that for him the Last Supper is at least a proleptic *pesah,* for he emphasizes that Jesus was executed at the exact time the Passover lambs were being slaughtered in the temple (see John 19:36-37). Moreover, it seems clear from our Lord's words of institution that Jesus wanted the Last Supper to be thought of as a Passover, for he identifies the elements in the same way the *pater familias* identifies the various food in the Passover *Haggadah.*

THE NATURE OF THE MEAL

Even if the meal that Jesus had with his disciples was not, according to strict calendar date, a formal Passover Seder, nevertheless it seems clear that Jesus considered himself to be the Lamb of God. He saw his death in clear paschal terms, and he saw that his meal, this memorial meal of him, would be completely understandable only if linked to the salvation history of the Jewish people beginning at the Exodus, which the Passover proclaimed. Therefore, in the Gospels, Jesus uses the Passover Seder not as the strict, formal vehicle for the Last Supper, because he completely ignores any mention of the Passover lamb which would have been on the table. Rather, he uses the Passover Seder as the theological vehicle to explain the significance of his death.

When he states "this is my body" and "this is my blood of the New Covenant," in those few words he is able to say libraries of meaning, because those few words he can direct toward the institution of the Passover and all of its meaning in salvation history. This seems to be very clearly part of God's plan. Obviously, when the Messiah came, he could, as only one man during a short lifetime, say a very few words. How could he on this his last night with his disciples explain in just a few words the meaning of his death and the significance that it had for the whole of salvation history? He couldn't, without the institution of the Passover and all of its intended theological significance which he could invest with an even richer meaning by stepping into the center of the Passover and saying, "I am the Lamb of God. The whole meaning of Passover revolves around me. This enormous institution has been prepared in order that you might understand what I will tell you this night about the meaning of my death." An illustration that comes to mind is of a sixteen decker cake with all kinds of decoration on the icing, and yet the whole structure is somehow ill-defined until the groom and the bride are placed on the top. Then, what the whole thing means becomes clear with just the addition of those two elements. Suddenly, what was not entirely identifiable and meaningful becomes clearly a wedding cake. Something similar happened when Jesus and his disciples moved into the upper room. Jesus picked up the *matzoh* and the wine at a meal which, if not an actual Seder, was at least permeated with anticipation of the Seder. Jesus explained just two elements, the matzoh and wine, as himself, the Passover lamb. But with those brief revelations, the whole of salvation history becomes clear and the true meaning of the Passover bursts forth.

It is truly amazing, therefore, that so many modern scholars have totally overlooked the paschal character of the Last Supper. It has been seen as a mere prophetic or symbolic act, as an ordinary table fellowship meal, as an essene-type communal meal, as a mystery-cult meal, as a sabbath *kiddish,* as a *chaburah,* even as a mere eschatological meal.

Of all of these, the *chaburah* hypothesis is most appealing because Jesus apparently expected his disciples to be taking meals together frequently, and these meals would be the occasions whereby they could remember him. However, the *chaburah* hypothesis worked out in such elegant detail by Dix seems somewhat too formal for these Galilean Jews. At any rate, whatever *chaburah* atmosphere the evening of the Last Supper may have had must have been overshadowed by the paschal tone which Jesus set when he identified the elements of the meal. Of the two, the *chaburah* meal is unquestionably a less imposing theological vehicle than the Seder, which Jesus could well use to carry more of the freight of his message to his disciples.

Furthermore, the question of the dating of the meal is not all-important. As long as the meal was close enough to Passover to be imbued with paschal overtones, then the theology of Passover is relevant to the Lord's Supper wherever Jesus chose to make it relevant, as we will see when we look at the words of institution.

Unfortunately, many scholars, when they decide that the Johannine account is more covincing historically, dismiss the paschal meaning of the Last Supper entirely, because they say it could not be an actual Seder since it does not fall on the proper evening. Others dismiss the paschal content to the Last Supper because they say there is no lamb. However, if Jesus *was* the Lamb of God and if in this case the Lamb of God himself was conducting the Seder, then we would have to say that this particular Passover did not lack a lamb. Also, if it were the Lord's will to die with the lambs at the same hour they were being slaughtered, then it would be necessary for him to conduct his Seder at least one day in advance. Consequently, it would be the Lord's prerogative for a Seder of this special order to occur one day early, and still be no less a Seder, regardless of its unconventionality.

As we have seen, what is exegetically decisive for identifying the paschal character of the meal is the fact that Jesus explains the elements just as the narrator of the Passover *Haggadah* explains the elements of that covenant meal. Against Martin,(3) who says that by his words of institution Jesus transcends the Passover, he does not transcend it in the sense that he exceeds its true meaning. Rather, he plumbs the depth of it, using the Passover to infinitely reverberate his message. Thus every motif in the Passover can be enlisted to proclaim the significance of Jesus' death in all its covenantal, communal, and eschatological depth of meaning.

We should not be surprised that Jesus' mind was dominated by the Passover during the night of his arrest, for the New Testament itself is dominated by paschal imagery. As in the Old Testament so in the New Testament, the Passover is mentioned more frequently than any other festival.(4) Also when we look at I Corinthians we see that paschal ideas dominate Paul's view of the Eucharist.(5) Like the Jewish Passover, Paul's Eucharist emphasizes the new community and does this even to the minimization though not the complete neglect of the expiatory value in the Lord's death, just as in Judaism the expiatory value of the lamb was often neglected. Thus Paul sees the death of Jesus as the sacrifice making operative the New Covenant and bringing into existence a new community which is spiritual Israel. Paul thinks of the death of Jesus primarily in covenantal terms.(6) Therefore, to the extent that one dismisses the paschal overtones of the Lord's Supper, one also loses its Pauline and Scriptural significance.

By referring to himself as the Lamb of God, by explaining the elements of bread and wine as his body and his blood, Jesus was saying that he was going to die the death of a sacrificial victim, and that if one looks at the Passover lamb and the meaning of its death, then one will see the meaning of his death. We know that the Passover lamb had the value of an expiatory sacrifice because all sacrifice involved expiation. However, its primary use was as a communal peace offering which brought men together as a family to commune with the head of their family, the Lord himself. Thus the *pesah* offering gave Israel the knowledge that she had indeed been "passed over," reconciled and renewed in her covenanted relationship with the God of Israel in order that she might experience the inexhaustible peace of God.

The words of institution given to us in Matt. 26:28 assuredly refer to the "many" of Isa. 53. The Servant's "sickness" was regarded as having "a redemptive significance, since the agony of his soul was likened to the sin offering *(asham)* of a sacrificial victim (Isa. 53:7,10). If the "Servant of Yahweh" bore the sins of his people, and worked out their salvation in the travail of his own soul, vicarious suffering is given an expiatory value."(7) In Isa. 53:5 we see that the wounds of the Servant are for transgression and iniquities. Moreover, there is something of a peace offering involved because "the chastisement of our peace was upon him and by his stripes we are healed." The paschal victim was also a peace offering. The purpose of its sacrifice was to offer divinely instituted reconciliation and communion through a meal wherein the sacrificial victim was divided up among the worshippers.

Following Jeremias, it is likely that Jesus had in mind Exod. 24:8 when he spoke of the covenant blood being poured out, though it is possible that Zech. 9:11 is also in view.(8) With Jesus' command to "take and eat," he implies that all men need to be "passed over" or spared the wrath of God's punishment, and that it is only through his death that men can find reconciliation with a holy sin-hating God. When Jesus says, "This is my blood," he is saying that his blood on the threshold will be a welcome for God to come in and commune with his people and to take them as his covenant bride on an Exodus out of the bondage of their former ways. By offering his death through the breaking of the bread and the outpouring of the wine, Jesus is proffering the only covenant pledges through which men can come into true covenantal relationship with the God of Israel. When he asks his disciples to remember his death in the Last Supper, he is asking them to remember a great historical event where an Exodus was occuring and was prophetically celebrated, even before it occurred.

In the Lord's Seder, bread broken and wine outpoured symbolize death. But the death symbolized is one that brings communion between God and men. All of God's people experience oneness with God and each other as they feed on the one loaf even as all the Israelites in each house fed on the one lamb. The wine symbolizes the joy that the community experiences united in peace, the peace that can only come through the expiation of a sin-atoning death. Just as bread and wine were symbols of the divine peace that the high priest Melchizedek mediated to Abraham (Gen. 14:18), so the Great High Priest Jesus offers himself through the bread and wine as God's peace offering to men. His broken body and outpoured blood are the only acceptable peace terms to bring reconciliation between a just, holy God and sinful men, for without the infinite injury which the Father inflicted on the Son, God in all justice would have had to declare an eternal war in hell upon all rebellious men. God's peace offering, the blood of the Lamb of God, is his only acceptable restitution for the sins of guilty, God-alienated men, and the Lord's Seder is the only real peace table in this world. The task of Messianic Judaism (or Christianity) is to persuade men everywhere to submit to a mikveh of repentance so that they may gather around the Prince of Peace and be assured at his Seder table that they have been "passed over" and given the eternal peace of God. This means that all men must be persuaded to accept the Messiah of Israel, who is the Lamb of God, as their king and Lord.

At the Lord's table, the fellowship of Spiritual Israel is gathered as the people of the New Covenant (Jer. 31:31-34). Here Spiritual Israel is brought to remembrance of the great Exodus that occurred when she was taken out of Egypt's judgment through the sacrifice of the Lamb of God and given a special relationship to God. Cullmann can explain the joy of the primitive Christian cultic meals only by rooting the remembrance of the Lord's Supper in meal-related resurrection appearances from Easter to Pentecost rather than in the Last Supper, which for Cullmann holds no joy. However, he overlooks that the communion joy comes not only in reexperiencing the risen life of the Messiah through his presence, but also in re-appropriating the benefits of his atoning death, which is the whole significance of the Last Supper. It is *both* the atoning death and risen life of Jesus remembered in the Lord's Supper that bring the Eucharist its joy, for it is through the blood of the cross that God has made peace (Col. 1:20), and with the death of the Son of God, the "great obstacle to communion with God has been removed."(9)

However, what is most thrilling about the Lord's Supper is the nature of the communion that is available. The communion of the Lord's Supper is with a God who is a covenant-keeping God. In the Lord's Supper, it is this covenant-keeping God who himself comes and himself offers his own death as the seal of the covenant which he personally extends to all men who will take and eat.

Because of Jesus' death, a covenant has been made bringing into existence a new people of God. The word for covenant in the New Testament is *diatheke*. It means either "covenant" or "will." But when it means "will" it always has the same basic meaning as "covenant," because there can be no benefits until the death of the benefactor, whereupon his will goes into effect as an operative covenant. So where there is no death there is no inheritance for the heir. This means that had Jesus not died there would have been no New Covenant.(10)

In the gospel of John, Jesus proleptically offers himself as a covenant meal and is rejected. The people do not understand what he means when he asks them to feed on him.

When he feeds the hungry as a sign that the true paschal lamb has come (John 1:29, 36) "who is to die that he may become for them the bread of eternal life,"(11) the people don't understand the gift that Jesus is trying to give them because they don't understand that he must die a sacrificial death as a paschal lamb in order to bring them to God (John 6:41f). They don't understand that their personal, covenant-making God has come himself to unite with and renew spiritually the inner being of men. He comes as the bread of life that can provide nourishment enough for eternal life since he offers men the eternal, Holy Sprit of God. Trumbull states: "Having in his own blood the life of God and the life of man, Jesus Christ could make men sharers of the divine nature by making them sharers of his own nature; and this was the truth of truths which he declared to those he instructed."(12) Jesus comes to men able to give them his Holy Spirit, his mind, his joy, his love, his example, his commandment, and his body, for he promises to give them a body like his in the age to come. With such a one to come and commune with men, with such a King to bring men God's covenant, it is no wonder that the Lord's Seder is the covenant meal and the focal point of Messianic Judaism.(13)

John and Paul each speak of the importance of relying on Jesus as one's true covenant meal and feeding on him as the true bread of life. In John 6:31-49 we see that Jesus is likened to manna or bread from heaven. In both I Cor. 10 and John 6 the people make the same mistake: they fail to recognize and rely upon Jesus as their true bread, since in both cases they rely on something else instead. In John 6:53-58 Jesus commands that men must depend on him, nourish themselves in him, rely completely on him, or they will not receive the eternal life of the Father which he himself is. There is no eternal bread for spiritual Gentiles who have not yet become born-again spiritual Jews.

THE REQUIREMENT OF REPENTANCE

Exodus 12:43-49 excludes Gentiles from participation in the Passover Seder. Likewise, the Lord's Seder, the Passover meal of the Jewish New Covenant, excludes spiritual Gentiles. To sit at the Lord's Seder table, one must be a spiritual Jew, circumcised of the will and the spirit, having undergone through faith the rite of spiritual circumcision which is the mikveh.(14)

Repentance is the ordeal demanded of all men before they can approach the Lord's Supper. To be admitted to the Lord's Supper in the first place, one must be in a covenantal relationship to the God of Israel. But the sign of the New Covenant is no longer circumcision, which was the sign of the Old Covenant. Now the token of a man's status as in a right relationship with the God of Israel is his mikveh or baptism, which is a sign of his repentant turning toward God. As I Cor. 10 shows, a man who is still living in idolatry may partake of spiritual food and drink, but he is going to die in the wilderness nonetheless because he has not yet repented of his idolatry. Everyone in the world is guilty of the body and blood of the Lord until he repents. If a man's lifestyle shows that he has not at all repented, then he is again guilty of not discerning the imperative of repentance in view of the Lord's death. He does not understand the nature of the covenant meal that God is offering to men in the body and blood of Jesus. Therefore Paul urges believers to make a new beginning, to turn in repentance with a new hope toward God, setting aside their old ways (I Cor. 5:7-8). He therefore asks that all believers approach the Lord's Supper in an attitude of repentance.

In the Old Covenant Moses sprinkled blood on the people, the blood of the covenant, and this blood brought into effect a covenant curse. People identified with the victim whose fate would be theirs if they betrayed the covenant loyalty.(15) Similarly Jesus' fate on the cross will be ours if we reject him. The proclamation of the New Covenant is that the Son of God has gone to hell for men. If unrepentant men reject him men will go to hell for themselves.

I Corinthians 10:16 states that the benefit received from the Lord's Seder is communion in the blood of Christ and communion in the Body of Christ. By sharing in the blood of Christ we share in the benefits that come from his atoning death.(16) Sharing in the Body of Christ means to share with other believers in a corporate life of fellowship in and through his resurrection power. The covenant community consists of everyone who has entered into a solemn oath-bound relationship of loyalty to the Messiah and to one another by their repentant participation in the sacramental reality of the work of the Messiah for the salvation of the world through an oath-bound water rite and an oath-bound meal.

In the mikveh, Yeshua summed up and signified in a symbolic action what he would do to save the world: he would bring in the New Covenant of the Kingdom of God by his death, burial and resurrection; and he would lead all who would follow him to a similar experience of death and new life: death to the old life of sin and rebirth to a new life of eternal sonship through the gift of the Holy Sprit. Therefore the mikveh is burial and resurrection in water as a sacrament of repentant oath-bound union with the Messiah. Similarly, participation in the one loaf and the one cup as an oath-bound meal (signifying Jesus' death as the grounds for God's communion with men) manifests covenant unity not only with the Lord but also with other believers.

The Mishnah says that "so long as a Gentile has not been immersed, he is still a Gentile."(17) Likewise, if a Jewish person, even if he has been physically circumcised, has not yet taken the mikveh, he is also ceremonially uncircumcised because he has not yet submitted to the faith ritual of spiritual circumcision, the seal of the New Covenant, which is the mikveh of Messianic Judaism. For in the same way that a non-Jew coming up out of the water of his baptism was considered at that moment to be a Jew, ceremonially, when a person comes up from the mikveh of Yeshua he becomes a spiritual Jew, one who is in a New Covenant relationship of faith to the God of Israel.

The rabbis said that a proselyte was like one who had touched a corpse. Touching a corpse was like contracting seven days of uncleanness (Num. 19:16). Therefore, a proselyte, like a ritually unclean Israelite, needed to take an immersion in water as he approached God, particularly if he were to share in the Passover (see Mishnah *Pesahim* 8.8). Likewise Rabbi Saul warned that those who eat and drink the Passover covenant meal of the Lord's Supper unworthily eat and drink judgment on themselves (I Cor. 11:27-30). Verse 28 says that a man must examine himself; that is, he must approach the elements in an attitude of moral self-scrutiny. In verse 29 the meaning of the word "body" must refer to the body of the Lord. Not only does this fit the context of how the word is used throughout the chapter, but it makes sense in terms of what Paul had just said in verse 28. To discern the body of the Lord is to see that it is his body which is broken for our sins and therefore if we partake of his body we must not continue to partake of our sins but must approach the Lord's Supper in an attitude of moral self-examination and reverence, knowledgeable of the awesome fact that the Son of God had to be killed to make restitution for what we have done.

Here we see the ethical dynamic of the Lord's Supper. Just as an Israelite had to take a ritual bath for uncleanness in order to partake of the Passover, those who would renew their covenant with the Lord in this New Covenant Passover meal must approach the Lord in the same repentant attitude. They must recall the attitude they had when they first covenanted themselves to the Lord through the mikveh, which even in pre-Christian Judaism had a built-in value of repentance. Of course, anyone who partook of the Lord's Supper without having previously repented through the mikveh would be eating and drinking judgment on himself, for he would be approaching the covenant meal in an unworthy manner, not having previously covenanted himself as the Scriptures require (Matthew 28:19-20) to the Lord. Though this is not Paul's primary thought in the passage, it is implicit in everything that he is saying in the passage, for coming to the Lord's table in a truly repentant attitude also necessarily implies that one has taken a mikveh of repentance in the name of the God of Israel.

Jewish proselyte baptism has its roots in the levitical immersions of the Torah (Num. 19). These purification baths were for ritually unclean Israelites who had defiled themselves by touching a corpse or other taboo object. Both pagans and ritually unclean Israelites were excluded from the Passover, because both were ritually unclean: one, because he was not circumcised and baptized into a covenant relationship; the other because he had not taken a mikveh bath to remove his ceremonial uncleanness; and neither, of course, had the sacrifice commanded by the Torah (see Lev. 15:13-25). A sacrifice was required of both pagans becoming Jews and unclean Israelites, and was offered by both after they took their water immersions. Therefore, in order to gain entrance to the covenant meal of the Passover Seder the same three conditions were required of proselytes as natural-born, yet ceremonially unclean Jews. These three conditions were circumcision (required on the eighth day of the life of a natural born Jew), water immersion (see Lev. 15:13; Num. 8:7-8, Lev. 14:1-32), and sacrifice.

In the New Covenant Scriptures none of these three aspects of covenantal incorporation into the people of God is omitted. For where there is faith, water immersion into Messianic Judaism in the name of the God of Israel includes an eternal (spiritual) circumcision (Col. 2:11-13), an eternal (spiritual) purification bath (Tit. 3:5), and a perfect, eternal blood sacrifice for sin (Heb. 9:12). Only those spiritual Jews who have covenanted themselves to the Lord Jesus in the mikveh may sit at the table of spiritual Israel and partake of the Passover Covenant meal of the Lord's Supper. Therefore, the precondition for covenantal admittance to the Lord's Supper is repentance, always and every time in attitude, and once for all time in the mikveh of repentance.

COVENANT RENEWAL THROUGH REMEMBRANCE

Now we come to the *anamnesis* (remembrance) to see what it is exactly that we are to remember when we partake of the Lord's Supper. Jeremias claims(18) that in Palestinian Judaism, Jesus' call for remembrance is best understood as divine remembrance, that God would remember him. However, J. J. Tetuchowski has argued against Jeremias' theory by the use of the word "*zkr*" ("remember") in the Passover Haggadah.(19) Tetuchowski argues that it is the disciples who are to remember. This means Jesus' covenant subjects are to remember the work that he has done and also the work that he is about to do. Following Millard, "at all times the covenant-subjects are to be prepared against a visit from their Lord (GK. *parousia* as in Hellenistic Egypt) or a summons to his presence, and their readiness is shown in the regular recollection of their promises and of his in a solemn repetition linking past, present and future."(20)

Concerning the question of what the disciples are to remember, it should be noted that Biblical covenants are always concerned with the conduct of the covenant subjects. In the Old Testament this can be verified by looking no further than the Ten Commandments. In I Cor., the apostle Paul also feels the need to teach the covenantal significance of the Lord's Supper in terms of the personal responsibility of the Corinthians who are the Lord's covenant subjects. From the outset of the epistle the covenant unity of the Corinthians is shown to be in jeopardy (I Cor. 1:10). For there are found to be divisions among the Corinthians. Furthermore, we see that the ground of their unity has been misplaced, since some are rallying around Apollos, others around Peter and others around Paul. In I Cor. 1:13, Paul has to remind the Corinthians of the ground of their unity, that they were baptized in the name of not Paul but Christ, and that covenant loyalty must be grounded in the Messiah. Indeed one of the objectives of the epistle of I Cor. is to bring these "babes" (I Cor. 3:1) into a more mature grasp of their covenant responsibility (see I Cor. 3:1-4). The first four chapters of I Cor. are used by Paul to break down jealous rivalries and carnal notions of wisdom which the Corinthians had used to take sides against one another.

But in chapter 5 he begins to deal with another area of ethical conduct: that is, sexual morality. Paul demands excommunication for the incestuous offender, and here we see a covenant curse go into effect. It has a redemptive purpose "for the destruction of the flesh, that his spirit may be saved in the day of the Lord Jesus," but, nevertheless, until the man repents he is to be cut off from covenant identity and can not in his present state experience covenant renewal in the Lord's Supper. The people of the covenant are to cut themselves off from him.

In chapter 5 Paul makes a direct reference to the Passover and demands that the Corinthians scour their mind searching for the leaven of sin in order that they might "celebrate the festival" in an attitude of repentant sincerity and truth. Commentators have spiritualized the Paschal theme of I Cor. 5:6-8 so much that they completely divorce it from the context of I Cor. 11. Consequently, they miss the Paschal character of the Lords' Supper, which like the ancient feast of Israel, is also a covenant meal and one that is also sacramentally approached in an attitude of repentance. This notion of repentance is so crucial Paul demands that any one who is living in an unrepentant state is to be cut off from the brothers (see I Cor. 5:11). All fellowship is to be curtailed, not only the covenant eating of the Lord's Supper, but all eating in general.

In chapter 6, Paul again is concerned with his Lord's subjects and their covenant standing. They are undermining the covenant in two ways. First, by their disunity which has reached the point of lawsuit, and second by their going to another sovereign to settle their disputes rather than to the One in whom they are covenantally related. Paul says he would rather suffer wrong or be defrauded than do what the Corinthians are doing (see I Cor. 6:7), for their actions undermine the very sovereignty of the covenant maker and sustainer, the Lord himself. In I Cor. 6:9-11 Paul enumerates quite specifically the kind of immoral behavior worthy of the curse of excommunication from covenant privilege. The Corinthians are commanded to separate themselves from any vassals of another authority who would have them join them in sensual pursuits. Indeed throughout the epistle of I Cor. there are reprisals threatened against the covenant breakers.

In chapter 10 Paul reminds the Corinthians that although the Old Covenant subjects, the Hebrews, had their form of baptism and eucharist, they were idolators. Therefore God cut them off from covenant privilege. Paul explains to the Corinthians that this was a warning and that they must not take part in the outward form of covenant renewal by eating and drinking with the Lord and then engage in immorality, for this is putting the Lord to the test (see I Cor. 10:9). In I Cor. 10:20-21 Paul shows that a sacrificial meal implies communion with the one to whom the sacrifice is made. Therefore they are not to commune with demons by joining pagans in ceremonies of eating food consecrated to idols. "You cannot drink the cup of the Lord and the cup of demons. You cannot partake of the table of the Lord and the table of demons." In I Cor. 11:29 Paul warns that where there are covenant offenses against the Lord there will be covenant reprisals. This explains why many were sick or weak or even dead. The Corinthians were coming together in a manner that was unworthy of the covenant and its sacrifice. Consequently, instead of renewing the covenant by eating and drinking they were bringing on the covenant curse of judgment on themselves. In verse 32 we see that the judgment of the Lord is a chastening judgment that has the purpose of bringing them back into a state of salvation and not pushing them away into condemnation, since the Lord is not willing that any should perish (II Pet. 3:9). Nevertheless, this curse is in fact a real curse and Paul is making clear that the Lord's Supper is deadly serious business. In fact, it is very probable that the curse which falls at the end of the epistle comes from the liturgy (see I Cor. 16:22).

Millard is right in comparing the covenant reprisals against the Corinthians for their misbehavior to the Old Testament where the Lord takes his people to court for their faithlessness.(21) Exod. 12:22 is relevant here, for at the Old Covenant Passover the man who left the house showed by his leaving that he did not believe in the promised protective power of the blood and was therefore not relying on the covenant relationship it provided for his safety. The Corinthians had in effect "left the house" by fraternizing with demons and by entertaining attitudes wholly out of keeping with the Lord's nature and his covenant demands. Therefore, these Corinthians were likewise exposing themselves to death.

Against Jeremias, who could not see how the disciples could possibly forget the Lord,(22) it is not God who is in danger of forgetting his Messiah, but it is men who are in danger of forgetting Jesus. Not that they would forget Jesus, but that they would forget Jesus as the Lord who is also the Lamb and whose covenant depends on men remembering that the Lord died as the Lamb for their sins lest they sin again. Therefore the Corinthians must remember the great price their sin cost God in order that he could institute a covenant with them, and they must trust the Lord at his Supper with that same repentant attitude that they had when they were initiated into the Lord's community through the act of baptism.

In sharing the Lord's Supper the Corinthians attested, however hypocritically, to the covenant that the Lord's Supper proclaimed. Millard gives two purposes for remembering the death of the Lord. "Thanksgiving which involved renewal of loyalty to the gracious Suzerain, and recollection of the commitments undertaken in response."(23) To these there could be added a third purpose, and that is remembering the Lord's death in order to proclaim it. Here eating and drinking become preaching (I Cor.11:26), for in the Lord's Supper, the covenant is remembered in both its inauguration and its saving benefits, and the call to remembrance is responded to in a form that is itself proclamation. Eating and drinking, the response to preaching, is itself preaching in that it calls other men to eat and drink. Therefore, the covenantal response to the gospel (of eating and drinking) is a form of preaching that calls men to make the same covenantal response to the gospel. The Lord's Supper points men to the covenant-making rite of baptism and leads them to the Passover celebration of the Lord's Supper, for only those who have covenanted themselves to the Lord by obeying him in the mikveh may partake of his Passover covenant meal of the Lord's Supper and be accounted part of his community which the Lord's Supper concretely symbolizes.

Just as the Old Testament Passover sacrifice is designed to create communion since a common lamb was consumed by each household as each family communally remembered the benefits from the same sacrifice, so in the New Covenant, "because there is one bread we, many as we are, are one body for we all partake of the same loaf"(I Cor. 10:17).

Just as in the Jewish community the passover lamb which was shared by households also included strangers and neighbors and yet made them part of the same spiritual family, our Passover Supper brings strangers together as one family and has constituted us one people, even as the *pesah* sacrifice did in the Exodus from Egypt.

5

Toward a Jewish Contextual Theology: Celebrating the New Covenant of Judaism

The key liturgical theme of the Lord's Supper is, of course, remembrance. In constructing liturgy for a communion service, the primary question is, what exactly does the Lord's Supper remember? A good means of criticizing the liturgy of a Communion Service is to ask the question, "Does this Lord's Supper celebration remember *enough?"* For the Lord's last meal was framed in a season of remembrance, in a Passover setting, the memories of which permeated the Lord's Supper with Paschal and covenantal significance. Jesus took full advantage of this fact by asking his disciples to remember him in this same context, enlisting the very matzoh and wine of the Passover season for use as his instituted reminders. By thus declaring himself to be the eschatological Lamb of God, he pointed backward to the Exodus and forward to Calvary in a way that placed himself at the center of salvation history. Then he endeavored to frame the memory of himself in a way that would make it impossible to grasp and fully remember the significance of the Last Supper without also remembering its Paschal and covenantal overtones. Yet too often Christians celebrate communion with the barest of liturgical expressions, usually with very little hint that anything transpiring has to do with the Passover or any sort of covenant, old or new.

There's a price to pay for such superficial liturgies. Dropping the Old Testament depths of meaning from the Lord's Supper makes the death of Christ less a matter of prophetic history and more a matter of coincidence.

It also makes Christianity less a matter of covenant faith and more of a mystery cult. The Old Covenant still is a "schoolmaster" to bring us to Christ (Gal. 3:24-25). However, ever since the first century Judaizers, those heretical "schoolmasters" with a penchant for circumcision, began to plague the Church with their "Old Covenant" guise, the Church has forever after overreacted to anything too "Jewish." Consequently, it has only been recently that scholars have been willing to take a very open-minded and thoughtful look at the Lord's Supper as a genuine Jewish Passover Seder, if not in its actual time of institution, at least in its theological significance. However, what is yet to be done is to frame liturgy for the celebration of the Lord's Supper which will make plain the paschal and covenantal values of the Lord's Supper.

THE SEDER IN THE CHURCH

Let it be said, first of all, that it is a mistake to say that the Lord's Supper "transcends" the Passover if that is meant to make the Passover somehow irrelevant and obsolete. Furthermore, it is now apparent that Paul would be misread entirely if he were interpreted to teach that believers in Jesus can no longer celebrate the Passover. Paul himself continued to celebrate the Passover and we find him in the New Testament continually hurrying somewhere to do so. When Judaizers came and tried to impose certain festivals on the Gentile believers, these Judaizers were not doing this in Jesus' name or in order to glorify Jesus, but in order to glorify themselves. Therefore, it would be misreading Paul to say that Jewish festivals *per se* are totally out of place in the Church of Jesus Christ. For in fact the very first church of Jesus Christ celebrated *all* the festivals (Acts 21:20) and Paul celebrated these festivals with the church. When he was in Jerusalem, Paul's quarrel with the Judaizers was not with the festivals but with the heretical soteriology involved in their imposition of these festivals on Gentiles. Far from discarding the Passover, in I Corinthians Paul is very concerned that the paschal and covenantal character of the Lord's Supper be preserved, as we saw in Chapter IV.

Therefore, the church would do well to have a special Seder with extended communion on Passover each year,(1) not only as a witness to the Jewish community but also as a witness to itself. For the church must understand her historical links to Israel and to the Exodus, or she will not understand that she herself is covenanted to God as spiritual Israel and that she has also begun an Exodus pilgrimage. What a tremendous witness it would be to the Jews throughout the entire world if all churches celebrated the Passover each year! For Christians to remember that it was "our people" that were in Egypt would be a great testimony to Jewish unbelievers and would be a mighty weapon against anti-semitism in the Church. How much more meaningful would such a Seder/Communion service be when all the baptized spiritual Jews stood to take the same matzoh that had been in use throughout the evening and the same Seder wine to proclaim to all "the death of the Lord until he comes."

THE JEWISHNESS OF THE LORD'S SUPPER

But even an ordinary communion service cannot be shorn of its paschal character, if justice is to be done to the covenant-keeping God of Israel that the Lord's Supper is intended to uplift. For it is the same God keeping covenant in the *Lord's* Seder who kept covenant in the *Passover* Seder, and he chose to institute and perpetually teach the Mosaic Covenant and the New Covenant through the continuity of the same Jewish feast.

The Lord's Supper is a very Jewish meal. When you take away its Jewishness by playing down the paschal and covenantal significance of it, you also dehistoricize its content. You can't get rid of the Jewish and paschal character of the Lord's Supper any more than you can get rid of the Jewishness of Jesus. Allmen said it very well:

> This Jewishness of Christ seems to me as irrevocable as the election of Israel (cf. Romans 11:29), and equally scandalous, and to wish to reject it threatens to separate Christ from his incarnation and turn him into a vague spiritual principle. Because in a certain sense you cannot avoid becoming a Jew when you become a Christian, it seems to me that these elements of the Jewish Paschal meal (or of other Jewish religious meals), the bread and the wine, must be honored. It is in no sense a question of Judaizing after the manner of those who wish to impose circumcision on those pagans who became believers. Judaizing is a soteriological anachronism; it calls

> into question the decisive, radically renewing nature of Christ's advent. To remember that this advent must be respected in its uniqueness and particularity (of race, place, date) is not Judaizing, it is preaching the gospel.(2)

This ignorance of, and overreaction to, Judaizing is what has made the church aloof and calloused to the salvation of the Jewish people and has also made the church ignorant of herself as she closes her eyes to her own Jewishness. If a Christian cannot understand that he himself is a spiritual Jew, he will be less apt to love and to identify with the Jewish people and will be more prone toward anti-Semitism. If a Christian does not see the Church universal as a spiritual nation not of this world yet linked historically to the Israel of old, who herself was born at the Exodus and spiritually liberated (at least in remnant) at Calvary, then the Christian does not recognize in reality what the Church is. Jesus left us the Lord's Supper in order to teach the Church who she is, but he left us a Lord's Supper rooted in the Passover. Therefore, we have no theological or liturgical right to cut the Eucharist loose from the Seder in a way that makes the two appear unrelated or mutually independent.

It is a strange commentary on many American churches that they could wink at a Halloween party in their fellowship halls but never tolerate a Passover Seder. Gentile Christians have for too long suffered from a Marcion-like aloofness from the "mere shadows" of the Old Testament which really borders on anti-Semitic repugnance of the Jewishness of Christianity. And here Karl Barth is worth quoting in full:

> (The Church) has certainly not succeeded in making it (Israel) jealous, in making clear to it the nearness of the Kingdom of the son of David, in making Jesus of Nazareth dear and desirable and in writing to it. In this sense, the church as a whole has made no convicting impression on the Jew as a whole. It has debated with him, tolerated him, persecuted him, or abandoned him to persecution without protest. What is worse, it has made baptism an infant start into the best European society.

> It has seriously sought the conversion of individuals. But for the most part it has not done for the Jews the only real thing which it can do, attesting the manifested king of Israel and saviour of the world, the imminent kingdom in the form of the convincing witness to its own existence, and thus it still owes everything to those to whom it is indebted for everything. This failure, which is often unconscious, or perhaps concealed by all kinds of justifiable charges against the Jews, is one of the darkest chapters in the whole history of Christianity and one of the most serious of all wounds in the Body of Christ. (3)

Two of the by-products of new liturgy for the Lord's Supper developed along more Jewish and more paschal lines are that (1) the church will magnify her ministry to the Gentiles and (2) the church will liturgically "go to the Jew first." Paul, the apostle to the Gentiles, magnified his ministry to the Gentiles in order to make his fellow Jews jealous. Paul would come to a synagogue and preach the gospel and certain Jews in the synagogue would throw him out, and Paul would be forced to start a new synagogue next door, one that would sometimes be more Gentile in cultural character, but one that was clearly *competitive* with the local synagogue. This was so because, although Jesus the Messiah was in the center of its worship, yet its worship forms were still Jewish enough to be jealousy-provoking to the local Jews. Paul was magnifying his ministry to the Gentiles, and he was making his fellow Jews jealous. They could not simply ignore his church planting as something that had absolutely nothing to do with them. They saw that Paul was in fact a synagogue planter, except the synagogues he was planting had Jesus in the center instead of the Torah.

If the Lord's Supper is celebrated in a very Jewish manner with the paschal and the covenantal values clearly in evidence, then Gentiles -- whether they are Italian, French or whatever their ethnic or cultural background may be -- will be led to understand that they are also spiritual Jews and should have a special place in their heart for the Jewish people. For their part, whenever Jewish people would witness such a communion service, they would see by its paschal and covenantal overtones that the Church has not forgotten them and that the Church still views the evangelism of the Jews as a priority. As Jewish people see the relevance of the communion service, they will begin to see the relevance of the Gospel.

In fact, more than ever, when the Lord's Supper is Jewishly observed, it has evangelistic power, for when both baptism and the Lord's Supper are publicly and properly administered, with only baptized believers allowed to receive the Lord's Supper, the Lord's Supper Jewishly observed becomes a corporate sermon (I Cor. 11:26) calling men to make the faith response of water baptism in order that they too may be no more excluded as spiritual gentiles from the *Lord's* Seder, but may, as baptized proselytes to Messianic Judaism, gather with Spiritual Israel around the Messiah of Israel. As I Cor. 11:26 says, every time we eat this bread and drink this cup we are, by that very eating and drinking, preaching. We are preaching the saving significance of the Lord Yeshua's death, which is the chief task of Messianic Judaism until the Lord comes again.

When unbaptized people, especially unbaptized Jewish people, see that responding to the gospel is a very Jewish thing to do because baptism is a *Mikveh-bris* and the Lord's Supper is a Seder, then the tension is on them to confess Yeshua as Lord by getting into the water in order to be no more excluded from the Lord's Seder. Since making disciples is drawing lines and persuading men to cross them, the Lord's Supper, properly administered, persuades men to cross the baptism line into discipleship. In effect, then, when we partake of the Lord's Seder, part of what we are celebrating is our spiritual circumcision, our spiritual Exodus, and our actual water baptism that incorporated us into spiritual Israel, in the same way Israel remembers her Red Sea national birth in the Passover. For in eating and drinking, we are celebrating our new life as spiritual Jews. And as we corporately participate in the Lord's Seder, by that very participation, we are defining who we are: spiritual Israel. As a matter of fact, the Seder is itself visual proclamation in that it calls men to realize that they are either inside or outside the circle of spiritual Israel (and therefore salvation) and must make a decision either to remain outside spiritual Israel or (via baptism) to enter spiritual Israel and eat at the Messiah's table. When men see the Lord's Seder celebrated, they must understand that a line is being drawn which they either cross or do not cross, depending on whether or not they will or will not receive the word of the God of Israel. In the Lord's Seder, people are confronted with a choice: they can either remain "Egyptian," spiritual pagans and be left behind in the Egypt of this dying world, or they can respond to the Seder's proclamation and (via baptism) can sit with spiritual Israel and her Messiah and enter that pilgrimage and Exodus upon which we, as born-again spiritual Jews, have already embarked.

Therefore, preaching corresponds to immersion and the Lord's Seder in that in all three ways the Word of God draws a line confronting men with a decision to either cross that line or not cross it, get in the water or not get in the water, eat and drink or not eat and drink, become a spiritual Jew or remain a spiritual pagan. Preachers need to understand the Jewishness of their role, functioning as they do as Moses figures who call people out of Egypt into a new Exodus of salvation and offer them the opportunity to exit death and sin via a Red Sea of water immersion and a Seder table of salvation. Gentile preachers who are ignorant of the Jewishness of their task blur the definition of what the church is in relation to Israel, what the Jewish New Covenant Scriptures are in relation to the Jewish Old Covenant Scriptures, and they blur this not only for Jews who have traditionally been unresponsive to the proclamation of the Church and have not seen the relevance of it, but they also miss the significance for Gentiles. For a Christian can only know who he is himself when he understands who he is in relation to the Jews at whose table he is eating.

The call to discipleship that is implicit in Holy Communion can be brought to the fore by a simple and historically valid tradition: to have the believers stand as they partake of the elements. To the modern Christian this may seem like an innovation, but Dix has remarked: "It appears to have been the universal tradition in the pre-Nicene church that all should receive communion standing."(4) Whether we agree with Dix's interpretation of the Last Supper along strict *chaburah* lines is irrelevant to the important point that standing for Communion was a widespread practice in the early Church. Regardless of the actual historical reason for such standing, we can think of many reasons why this might be done in the Church today. If eating and drinking is preaching, we normally think of preaching as something that one does standing up. And if the whole Church is participating in a kind of acted confession when the Church celebrates the Eucharist, then we can see why the Church might stand. A second reason might be to make sure that the Lord's Supper is properly administered, meaning in the case of the theology set forth here that only those who had been baptized could partake. Furthermore, since the Lord's Supper is no more private or secret than water baptism, there is no good theological reason for dismissing catechumens prior to communion, in spite of any venerable traditions to the contrary. In fact, it makes better theological sense for the baptized to take communion standing in order that their eating and drinking might be preaching to the unbaptized as well as to themselves. With the simple action of asking those who have been baptized to stand up, a line, so to speak, is drawn and those who remain seated understand that they have not yet crossed that line and that now they must sit to listen to a sermon, a corporate sermon, which the baptized ones will now preach as they eat and drink the body and blood of the Passover Lamb of God.

Cochrane(5) seems to miss the significance of the confessional value in the Lord's Supper with its attendant discipling tension. He advocates that the Lord's Supper be eaten in a seated position in the Fellowhsip Hall, and seems to think the important concern is that the congregation be gathered at tables, since how can there be a "Supper" in pews? However, a staged re-enactment of a "Supper" is not the essence of the matter. Arndt comes much closer to the mark when he states that baptism and the Lord's Supper are "'objectivizations' of the Christian message. They objectify the gospel by means of objects and actions in association with the interpreting words." (6)

The idea of a sacrament as a visible word goes back to Augustine. This is the concept that the sacraments make the gospel visible to the eye even as preaching makes the gospel hearable to the ear. But what many evangelistic churches of today seem to overlook is that the sacraments provide an objectivization not only to the message but also to the *response* to the message. If you want to accept the gospel, what do you do? You get in the water. That is something quite concrete, and when you get into the water you *know* you have responded to the gospel. If you want to become part of the body of Christ, what do you do? You partake of his body with others who are also your fellow partakers by eating the bread and drinking the wine. That is something quite objective that you can do as a response. And your doing it puts objective discipling tension on others to do it.

Churches that have no concept of a response to the gospel other than the "altar call" are usually the churches that find the sacramental response of a believer as a kind of irrelevant afterthought to "coming up front." These churches usually have a rather low sacramental theology and their celebration of the sacraments have little theological depth of understanding or perception. However, when the baptized ones stand to take the matzoh and the wine of a very Jewish meal celebrated in a Jewish way, then it is clear to everyone observing that the people in this place either have or have not linked themselves up with the Israel of old, depending on whether or not they have turned in repentant obedience to the Jewish Messiah. Stibbs hints at this when he says:

> Participation in the Lord's Supper, therefore, should be for all who share in it a dramatic or acted proclamation of the gospel. In such oral announcement the scriptural record suggests that all who communicate should share. For, the apostle wrote, 'as often as you eat this bread and drink the cup, you proclaim the Lord's death till he come.' One may compare in possible illustration what happens when the royal toast is proposed. In response not only do all stand to drink, but also audibly they all proclaim 'The Queen.' Similarly, it may be, when at Corinth the Lord's Supper was eaten, not only was the story of Christ's passion retold, but also every communicant shared in confessing his faith by declaring audibly the significance of his action. Certainly it would make our own worship more fully corporate and confessional if, when the sacrament is administered, every recipient proclaimed the Christian significance of his participation; and said, for instance, as he received the bread: 'I take and eat this in remembrance that Christ died for me, and I feed on him in my heart by faith with thanksgiving.' And similarly later on at the reception of the cup.(7)

Stibbs' suggestion of a possible confession is helpful. However, if the fact that all who are standing have been baptized is clear by the liturgical preparation for their standing, then the very fact that they are eating and drinking is proclamation enough without any particular verbal confession needed from them. Their mere standing to the question, "Will all those who have been baptized please rise?" will be sufficient to make the discipling tension felt that there is no eternal bread for spiritual gentiles and that one must become a born-again spiritual Jew by obeying the Jewish Messiah as Lord. As the standing ones eat we see, following Allmen, "the supper makes manifest the baptismal, apostolic, and local character of the church."(8) That it is the baptized ones standing shows that the meal is the meal eaten by the covenanted ones. What makes the words of institution significant is that they plunge the whole body into a union of faith and a unified preaching of that faith by their unified response to it in eating and drinking. As the gospel takes concrete form in the sacraments, it evangelizes the whole man, his physical being no less than his spiritual being. Thus the body is seen as the concrete manifestation of Yeshua'a own people and those who partake are confirmed in their faith which in the Supper is shown to be a corporate faith, one that draws strangers together and makes them one family.

The Passover Haggadah prescribes that the *pater familias* present the paschal elements and say, "Let all those who are hungry enter and eat; all those who are in need come and celebrate (the passover)."(9) This open invitation is for all those who are willing to covenant themselves to the Lord. For the Passover is a celebration of the covenant by the covenanted ones. The same is true of the Lord's Supper. If this interconnection is not made clear through the preservation of the paschal and covenantal character of the Lord's Supper, then the clear connection between baptism and the Lord's Supper will be lost and one sacrament will not point to the other as it was theologically intended to do. Arndt provides a good summary: "Preaching is the good news of a new life for man which God offers as a gift to man. Baptism is an initiation into the new life and the Supper is its food. They all have for their content what God has done, is doing, and will do to bring his reconciling purpose for all men to its fulfillment."(10)

For the Lord's Supper liturgy to have more apparent covenantal and paschal character, it is necessary for the liturgy to teach that to partake of the Lord's Supper is to engage in a covenantal response to a covenant-making God. Therefore, the liturgy needs to explain something of the means by which God inaugurates a covenant by blood, how he did so in the Old Passover and how he did so in the New Passover through the Messiah's death. Secondly, the liturgy needs to teach that this New Covenant is commemorated, remembered, reaffirmed and renewed by the universal breaking of bread by the church throughout the world. Thirdly, in order that our salvation be linked to history, the liturgy needs to say something about the fact that Jesus was a Jew, that he made his covenant with all spiritual Jews through a Jewish meal and that all those who respond to him become table partners with the remnant of Israel throughout the ages. To departicularize the Jewish historicity of the Lord's Supper is to seriously curtail the edification of the church and is to tragically hinder the evangelization of the Jews.

It is certain that Jesus did not partake of the bread or of the wine on the night of his betrayal without first speaking the traditional blessing.

> It was a strict rule for a Jew that he should eat nothing before a blessing is pronounced. All benedictions begin with the words: 'Blessed art thou, O Lord our God, King of the Universe. The blessing of a meal including wine would continue: 'who hast caused bread to come forth out of the earth and who hast created the fruit of the vine.'(11)

An inclusion of these blessings in the Communion liturgy would enhance the true Jewish character of the Lord's Supper. This is also a point in the worship life of the church when we might expect to hear some Hebrew: "*Baruch ah-tah ah-donai elo-henu meh-lech ha'olam hamotzi lechem min ha-ah-retz,* blessed art thou, O Lord our God, king of the universe, who brings forth bread from the earth." This we might hear before the words of institution, "this is my body, which is for you; do this as a memorial of me," and the attendant breaking of matzoh. Next, we might hear Hebrew in the blessing that Jesus said before he partook of the wine: "*Baruch ah-tah ah-donai elo-henu meh-lech ha'olam boreh p'ree hagafen,*" blessed art thou, O Lord our God, king of the universe, who creates the fruit of the vine." These are the words said before the institution over the cup, "this is the new covenant sealed by my blood, whenever you drink it, do this as a memorial of me."

Christians may be gentile in culture and birth but as far as their spiritual life is concerned, they are spiritual

Jews and members of spiritual Israel. They also have an obligation to preach the gospel to every creature, to make the Lord's Supper a sermon as relevant to Jews as it is to gentiles. Therefore, Christians have an obligation to let the Lord's Supper shine through as a Jewish meal, at least as Jewish as it was for Jesus.

If the Lord's Supper were celebrated on the last Sunday of each month, it could be the climax of the evangelistic outreach of the church so that those who were to be baptized could be baptized all together on each month's final Sunday. If this were also Communion Sunday, then all the newly baptized could celebrate their first communion together with the other believers. This procedure would draw the sacraments closer together so that they could mutually reinforce one another in the process of making disciples. Then on that "Acts 2:42 Sunday," when we stand from our seats to partake of the Lord's Seder, those who have not yet submitted to the mikveh-bris of water baptism would witness our visible confession. When the server steps in front of each of us with the broken matzoh of the Lord's body and the wine of his outpoured life, we are confronted with the very One who alone can free us and give us a new life of peace. As the server says to us, "Every time you eat this bread and drink this cup you proclaim the death of the Lord until he comes," we realize that we are concretely receiving the saving Word of God who is the Lamb of God who takes away the sin of the world. We also realize that our very eating and drinking has become preaching as we witness to the wonderful fact that we have been "passed over" and our sins have been forgiven so that we can have a new life. As servers move around the room, the words "for every time you eat this bread and drink this cup" reverberate over and over again even as the gospel is echoing right now all over the world. This is a corporate sermon, preached by both the servers and the served, and does not end until the Reader is himself served. When the last server has come forward and has served the reader, what a moment of intense worship ensues! For now we have just received the most precious person in the world afresh and by the power of the Holy Sprit he indwells us all anew with his presence most acutely experienced at this very moment. At this point there needs to be real overt expression of the unity that this covenant-making God has made possible through the Messiah's death. Our hands may be up in the air but they also may be around one another as we affirm our love for one another by our touching. As the Lord's Seder service is concluded, everyone who partook should be in prayer for the unbaptized who sat observing the corporate sermon that Jesus has just preached through us. We should pray that each one here today will stop excluding himself from our Lord's Seder but will instead obey Yeshua and submit to the mikveh-bris so that, as a spiritual Jew, he will be no more excluded from this Passover table.

One of the reasons the liturgy in the church has lost the paschal and covenantal quality it should have is because the church has not kept its liturgy closely enough tied to the Bible. As Dix has said, "Evidently liturgical practice was not understood by the primitive church to be in any way subject to the control of the New Testament documents, even when these have begun to be regarded as inspired scripture (C.AD 140-180)."(12) Certainly a liturgy based on I Cor. would have more paschal flavor and more covenantal significance, since, as we saw in Chapter IV, I Cor. has these built-in theological values.

Dix(13) has delineated a seven-action shape of the Biblical eucharist as (1) the Lord took bread, (2) he gave thanks over it, (3) broke it, (4) distributed it, saying certain words. Later he did the same thing with the cup. He (5) took the cup, he (6) gave thanks over it, he (7) handed it over to his disciples, saying certain words. However, the shape of the Church's liturgy traditionally began to fall into a four-action shape: (1) an offertory where the bread and wine are "taken" and placed on the table together, (2) the prayer where the reader gives thanks to God over the bread and wine, (3) the fraction where the bread is broken, and (4) communion where the bread and wine are distributed, one at a time or together. So the seven-action shape which the Bible uses becomes a four-action shape in the actual practice of the liturgy. The criteria for determining which of the two shapes to follow is not historical authenticity alone, but the question of the discipling dynamics involved and how the worshippers may be helped to receive the most vivid impression or remembrance of the Lamb of God, the Lord Yeshua. There could be equally impressive liturgies written with either of the two shapes.

A possible outline for a liturgy(14) could be (1) the Lord's Supper is framed in terms of the Passover, explaining its rootage in the New Testament "haggadah" as the institution of the new covenant and as a ceremony of covenant renewal; (2) all those who have been baptized are asked to stand; (3) the baptized ones receive cleansing of sins repented and pronounce in unison an oath of covenant relationship between them and the Messiah before the covenant pledges are distributed; and (4) the servers are served by the reader and go out in turn to serve the congregation. After everyone is served, the reader is served and then there is a time for the expression of worship and the expression of love for one another and for the Lord. This particular liturgy does not formalize any prayer but leaves open the element of spontaneity for any prayers given at any point in the Communion service.

The important values of any Lord Supper service should be (1) the paschal character of the meal rooting it in history and in the Jewish faith; (2) the covenantal character of the meal, making it a renewal of blood relationship between God and man; (3) the fresh and present assurance of complete remission of sins including the remission of sins committed since last the sacrament was received,(15) and (4) a sense of the presence of the covenant-keeping God of Israel and of his Messiah who comes to bring the new covenant.

Yeshua comes to us, and we are united to him, not only in the mikveh, not only in the Lord's Seder, but even in death when he will receive us as he did Stephen. We know that Yeshua will receive us then because we have received him now and enjoy his Spirit already as an actual down payment on our guaranteed eternal inheritance (Eph. 1:14). The Passover Seder of the Old Covenant looked backward to God's blood sprinkled deliverance of his people from enslavement. This same festival also looked forward to the coming of the Messiah. The Passover Seder of the New Covenant also looks backward to a blood sprinkled deliverance affected by the blood of God. This New Covenant Seder, however, looks forward to the second coming of Messiah. As little families all over the world gather around the common lamb to commune through his blood sacrifice with the God of Israel, an international spiritual nation, a nation of spiritual Jews, a people not of this world, are proclaiming the significance of the Lord's death. It is hoped that this study will contribute to the re-writing of liturgy, liturgy that will help spiritual Jews see the paschal and covenantal significance of the Lord's Supper in terms of its Biblical and Hebraic roots. The Lord's Supper is the covenant meal of Messianic Judaism. As the people of this culturally all-inclusive Jewish religion come to the Lord's Supper, their common

Jewish meal should become for them an ecumenical rallying point as well as a point of contact with the Jewish community, for all may become Jews not through pedigree or merit (Lu. 3:8-9) but through the God of Israel's gift of faith (Ro. 2:28-29; Phil. 3:3).

6

Toward a Jewish Contextual Theology: Celebrating Shabbat in Light of the New Covenant

A Sabbath service is critically important not only because many Jewish people want to keep the Sabbath, but also because the Hebrew prayers of the Sabbath service provide an appropriate setting for the bar and bat mitzvah services as well as the other vital culture-sustaining traditions of the synagogue. Thus, when the church finds herself in a Jewish neighborhood she must take cultural specialization as seriously as the apostles did(Gal. 2:9), and become a fully operative Messianic synagogue which offers not only Sunday services but Sabbath services as well. Only in this way will she give opportunity for large-scale Jewish people movements into the Body of Yeshua as whole Jewish families join Messianic synagogues where they can celebrate their faith in Jesus as Jews and sustain their cultural identity from generation to generation even as they are sustained in their spiritual life as believers.

Because the Lord Yeshua first resurrected and appeared to his disciples on Sunday (John 20:1), and appeared to them again the following week on Sunday (John 20:26), finally pouring out the Holy Spirit on them (Acts. 2:1) on Sunday (Shavuos A.D. 30), Sunday became known as the Lord's Day. Thus it became an established Jewish tradition to meet on the Lord's Day for chavaroot.

It was not enough for Jewish people to witness to the fact that God rested on the seventh day after the creation. It was now necessary also to witness to the fact that God worked a new eternal creation on the eighth day, the first day of the new creation, when his Son resurrected to become the head of a new eternal humanity who are experiencing their new life of fellowship in him already, even in this dying world in advance of the age to come. Therefore, the first Jewish believers did not fail to acknowledge both the Sabbath and the Lord's Day (Rev. 1:10). This is why it is so important for Messianic Synagogues to offer services on both Sabbath and Yom Rishon (Sunday), not in order to "lord it over anyone's faith" (II Cor. 1:24) in respect to legalistically dictating how each one should esteem one day over another (Rom. 14:5); rather, in order to follow the principle of love in I Cor. 9:20 that Yeshua and the early church applied to the Jews when they preached the Good News on the Sabbath (Mk. 6:2; Acts. 18:4). Thus these synagogues point to the continuity of their Jewish faith, preserving both its past and its future as they witness to the fullness of their Biblical Judaism for the benefit of the salvation of their local Jewish community.

The liturgical outline which is offered in this study is neither an exact historical re-enactment of a first century Palestinian synagogue service such as Yeshua may have attended nor is it a mere imitation of a modern Sabbath service. Rather it is an attempt to faithfully preserve the components of the basic liturgy without tampering with their integrity, while at the same time making whatever slight addition might be necesssry to Messianize the service and let Yeshua have his central place in the worship. This was done by adding only five words to the *Shema* -- *Yeshua Ha Mashiach Hoo Adonai*, and by adding the Lord's Prayer to the *Mourner's Kaddish*.(1) These slight additions state, in effect, that once Jewish people realize that Yeshua is the Messiah and the Lord of their Judaism, he becomes the central focus of their Jewish life and his authority is felt at the center of every aspect of their religion. Yet as far as their religious forms are concerned, all Yeshua really added to their religion was a new confession and a new prayer. Yeshua did not come to destroy Judaism. He came to fulfill it and therefore all the hallowed, scripturally compatible traditions and customs of Judaism need not be discarded once Jewish people believe that Jesus is their Messiah. Yeshua can be the Lord of their Jewishness and make them appreciate their heritage more than they ever dreamed possible.

However, a word of caution is needed here. In the somewhat involved analysis of liturgy that follows, an impression may be given that the Sabbath service is a burdensome straitjacket that is bound to quench the Spirit and bore the worshippers. This is not true, as experience has shown. Used with spiritual discernment and edifying explanation rather than legalistic inflexibility, the Sabbath liturgy provides a loose framework within which an exciting variety can be achieved through the selection and order of the ancient prayers. The Holy Spirit is free to spontaneously intervene and alter the flow of the service at any point. However, without the liturgy to supply a Biblically based and yet culturally relevant framework in which the Holy Spirit can move, the service may lose its vitally attractive indigenous appeal to the Jewish community.

The two basis components of the Friday evening Sabbath service are the *Shema,* which is the central confession of Judaism, and the *Amidah* which is the main prayer of the evening. The *Shema* and the *Amidah* are the two indispensable portions of the liturgy around which everything else revolves. The basis structure of the service is this: A) Opening prayers and hymns; B) The *Shema* and its framework of benedictions; C) The Amidah; D) Scripture reading and sermon; E) Closing prayers and hymns. There is a certain amount of freedom and flexibility in how the various prayers and hymns are selected for the evening but all Friday Night Services include the *Shema* and the *Amidah.*

In the opening prayers and hymns there is a prayer said on entering the synagogue. "How goodly are thy tents, O Jacob..." comes from Num. 24:5 and from Pss. 5:8; 26:8; 69:14. This prayer expresses the great love that Jewish people have always had for their synagogue and is an indication of the festive and yet reverent mood encountered in witnessing a synagogue service preparing to begin. Psalm 122 is included in many prayerbooks as an opening meditation to ready the worshipper for the Sabbath service.

In conservative and orthodox synagogues the Sabbath candles are lit already when the service begins because no work is done after nightfall. However, in many synagogues a Jewish lady is called to the *bemah* (front platform) to say the Sabbath blessing over the candles. The lady who is given this honor is usually the mother or grandmother of a son or daughter preparing for participation in the bar or bat mitzvah service. She may not light the candles but she does say the blessing over them. The Sabbath lights in the synagogue are a very ancient custom and symbolize the eternal hope of the Jewish people, eternal life.(2) This custom is a precious Jewish tradition which has been largely lost in the modern gentilized Jewish home. Therefore, it is all the more important, especially in view of the symbolism of eternal life -- the hope of the Gospel, that this ceremony not be excluded from the Messianic Erev Shabbat Service. Along with the benediction on kindling the Sabbath lights, there is also a special benediction for the lighting of the candles during the Jewish holidays.

A selection of opening hymns and songs should include such long beloved favorites as *Shalom Alechem* and *Lecha Dodi*. *Shalom Alechem* is a beautiful song which Jewish people sometimes sing swaying back and forth with their arms around one another. Sung in this way by Jewish believers in Yeshua, this song, which is about the King of kings, becomes an eloquent witness that the King of kings and the Lord of lords is Yeshua Ha Mashiach.

The most important opening hymn of the service is *Lecha Dodi*. In this 16th century Cabalist hymn, the Sabbath is personified as a queen who is welcomed by the worshippers. The fourth stanza is especially important for Messianic believers in Yeshua for it says, "Shake thyself from the dust, arise, put on the garments of thy glory, o my people through the son of Jesse, the Bethlehemite, draw thou nigh unto my soul, redeem it."

The other psalms are also important to the opening of the service. The theme of a "new song" in Psalm 96 is an especially relevant selection for a Messianic Erev Shabbat Service. Psalms 92 and 93 are beautiful expressions of thanksgiving and praise to the just, sovereign God of Israel and are included to set the tone of worship for the Friday evening service. The Psalms have always played an important part in the liturgy of the church and it is appropriate that a Messianic Erev Shabbat Service should begin with Psalms.(3)

After the opening hymns and songs comes the second section of the service, which is the Shema and its framework of benedictions. The *Shema* (Deut. 6:4) is set in a framework of four benedictions in which two precede it and two follow it. The first two benedictions are the *Baruch ah-tah* and the *Ah-ha-vaht*. The *Baruch ah-tah* is a prayer which celebrates God as the giver of physical light and glorifies him for his role in creation. The *Ah-ha-vaht* blesses God as the giver of the spiritual light of Israel, the Torah. Both of these benedictions are preceded by the Canter's leading the congregation in prayer by singing the *Bar-choo*. The congregation either sings or recites sections of these benedictions in anticipation of the *Shema*. In the daily morning service of the Temple, the Ten Commandments were recited just before the *Shema*. Indeed, there could be no better place for a recitation of the Ten Commandments in the synagogue than after the *Ah-ha-vaht* which blesses God for giving his Torah to the people. Since Jewish believers in Jesus are often accused of abandoning the Torah, including a recitation of the Ten Commandments in the liturgy of Messianic Judaism is an important witness to the Jewish community.(4)

The *Shema* consists of three sections of the Torah (Deut. 6:4-8; 11:13-22; Num. 15:37-42). The sections from Deuteronomy and Numbers are either recited or sung in Hebrew and/or English by the congregation. In Judaism's declaration of the unity of God is the heart of the Friday Night Service. Therefore, this is the place to put the heart of Messianic Judaism's confessional faith, that there is one God and that Yeshua the Messiah is the Lord. This total confession of Messianic Judaism should be sung in the synagogue on Friday night so that Jewish unbelievers present will understand that the saving confession is not the *Shema* alone (Jas. 2:19) but that Yeshua is Lord (Ro. 10:9). Therefore when the *Shema* is sung it would be good to have the congregation sing "Ah-donai, Ah-donai, Yeshua Ha Mashiach Ah-donai, Ba-ruch ah-tah ah-donai elo-hay-noo, Yeshua Ha Mashiach Ah-donai" (Sung to the tune of "He is Lord"). With these few words Yeshua is placed at the center of the worship life of the synagogue and everything that transpires all evening long is understood to be done in his name.

The final two benedictions which conclude the *Shema* portion of the Friday evening service are called the *Guellah* and the *Hahsh-kee-vey-noo*. The word *guellah* means "redemption," and it comes from the next to the last word in the benediction, *ga-ahl*. Here the Jewish people assert their unfaltering faith in the God of Israel whose Torah is of eternal validity and who is trustworthy to save them even as he did at the Red Sea. There are quotations from the Bible in this benediction including Job 9:10, Ps. 66:9. Exod. 15:11, 18 and Jer. 31:11. The *guellah* benediction includes the paragraph entitled "God our Redeemer" as well as *Mee Chah-moh-cha*. This latter portion, *Mee Chah-moh-cha*, is sung in the synagogue and there are many beautiful musical settings for it.(5)

The Fourth Benediction which is the concluding benediction to bring the *Shema* portion of the service to a close is called *Hash-kee-vey-noo* from its first Hebrew word. The prayer is for protection during the night, and is an expression of man's dependence on God to protect him from all enemies, including the devil (Hebrew, *sah-tahn*).

At the conclusion of the Fourth Benediction the Scripture from the Torah (Exod. 31:16-17) is normally recited. Besides this Scripture pointing to the significance of the day, there are also Scriptures inserted for the Jewish festivals such as Lev. 23:44 for Passover, Pentecost, and Tabernacles in the liturgy. Also there is a selection from Ps. 81:4-5 for the Jewish New Year, and Lev. 16:30 for the Day of Atonement. In some prayer books there is a *Kaddish* inserted at this point, but in a messianic Jewish service the *Kaddish* need not be repeated but may only be recited once, when it falls later in the service. Therefore with the recitation of the Fourth Benediction and the appropriate Scripture regarding the significance of the day, we have concluded the *Shema* portion of the service, which included two benedictions, the *Shema*, and two concluding benedictions.

The congregation has stood to sing the *Shema*, and will stand again for the *Amidah*, which is the prayer *par excellence* of the Friday night service. The word *Amidah* means "standing," because the congregation stands and faces the ark and reads the prayer silently. These prayers come from the *Shemoneh Esreh* which are the Eighteen Benedictions, the oldest congregational prayers of the synagogue, almost all of them going back to the time of Yeshua and even before. Although there are now Nineteen Benedictions, since one was added after the fall of the Second Temple, only six of these are silently read in the Friday night service. These are the first three benedictions, which are praises, and the last three which are thanksgivings. A "Benediction of the Day" is inserted in the middle to substitute for the twelve (now thirteen) intermediate blessings which are called petitions.

These six benedictions are referred to by name in the Mishnah (Rosh Hashana IV. 5). The first one is called *aboth*, which means "fathers," and praises God as the God of history who brings Messianic redemption to his people. Benediction one begins after the quotation from Ps. 51:17, "O Lord, open thou my lips and my mouth shall declare thy praise." Benediction one begins with the words, "Blessed art thou O Lord our God" and goes to the words "thou art mighty to save." Supplementing the rest of the benedictions are occasional small interjections that are to be made on the festivals, but for ordinary Sabbath service these interjections are ignored so that the worshippers may read silently only the benedictions. The second benediction is called *geburoth* and means "mighty acts." It begins with the words "Thou O Lord art mighty forever," and concludes with the words, "O Lord who quickenest the dead." This benediction celebrates God as the one who sustains both the living and the dead, and who is able to bring about the Resurrection. The third benediction is very short: "Thou art holy and thy name is holy and holy beings praise thee daily. Blessed art thou O Lord, the holy God." This benediction is called the *Kedushath Ha-Shem* which means the "sanctification of the name." With these three benedictions the first three praises are offered.

Next comes the so-called "Benediction of the Day" which is the *Ah-tah Kee-dahsh-tah*. This includes both a quotation from Gen. 2:1-3 and a prayer for the Sabbath which begins "Our God and God of our fathers." The thirteen intermediate petitions which would normally occur in the week day *Amidah* are replaced in the Sabbath *Amidah* by a special prayer which varies depending on whether the Sabbath service is the Evening, Morning, Musaf, and Afternoon Service. This special replacement prayer for the thirteen intermediate petitions is deemed necessary because petitions dealing with want or sorrow such as are found in the thirteen intermediate petitions are considered inappropriate and disturbing to the sanctity of the Sabbath. Therefore the Sabbath *Amidah* in the synagogue always substitutes for these thirteen intermediate petitions the special prayer called the "Benediction of the Day." On Friday night, the Benediction for the Day includes Gen. 2:1-3 and a prayer called "Our God and God of our Fathers."

The last three "Thanksgiving" petitions of the Friday night Sabbath *Amidah* deal respectively with the Temple, with God himself, and with peace. The first of these, Benediction Seventeen, is called *Avodah,* which means "Service," because it thanks God that he will restore the Temple worship service in Jerusalem. This benediction starts "Accept, O Lord our God, thy people Israel and their prayer" and concludes "who restoreth thy divine presence unto Zion." Benediction eighteen is the second of the "Thanksgiving benedictions, and it is called *Hodah,* which means "thanksgiving." It begins with "We give thanks unto thee" and concludes with "unto whom it is becoming to give thanks." The last benediction in the *Amidah* is Benediction nineteen which is *Birkath Ha-kohinim,* meaning "the Blessing of the Priests." This benediction was normally preceded by the Priestly Blessing of Num. 6:24-26 in the Morning Sabbath Service. Benediction nineteen is a prayer for peace, which begins "Grant abundant peace unto Israel" and concludes "blessed art thou O Lord who blessest thy people Israel with peace."

Following the last benediction in the *Amidah* there is a silent meditation, "O my God, guard my tongue from evil and my lips from speaking guile" which concludes with "let the words of my mouth and the meditation of my heart be acceptable for thee, O Lord, my rock and my redeemer." This concluding meditation was written by a famous fourth century rabbi named Mar and contains reference to Pss. 60:7 and 19:15. It is an appropriate conclusion because, since the last benediction of the *Amidah* concerns peace, this meditation deals with the evil tongue, which is the most terrible enemy of peace.

Finally, there is one more silent meditation beginning "May it be thy will." Although this particular petition has found its way into the liturgy, this might be a good place for spontaneous silent prayer where each person makes his own petition.(6)

The *Amidah* is sometimes concluded by a recitation of Gen. 2:1-3, repeated three times in some prayer books: once in the middle of the *Amidah;* once concluding the *Amidah;* once at the beginning of the *Kiddush*. Also, a summary of the *Amidah* is sometimes recited at the close of the *Amidah* portion of the service. However, these repetitions could be omitted from the liturgy for the sake of time, which could be taken instead by reading from the Torah and the Haftorah (the Pentateuch and the Prophets). There is no good reason why this scriptural reading from Moses and the Prophets could not precede the sermon, normally not preached on Saturday in the time of Yeshua but on Friday night.(7)

The congregation rises to its feet when the Torah is taken out of the ark so that the Scripture may be read. The Torah reading may be a set reading so that in regular annual periods the entire Pentateuch can be read. The word Haftorah means "dismissal" or "conclusion," since it probably came at the end of the service originally.(8) However, since the sermon may want to make reference to both the reading from the Torah and the Prophets, it would be good to have the Haftorah read before the sermon. The practice of reading both the Law and the Prophets goes back to New Testament times (see Luke 4:16 and Acts 13:14-16). The Haftorah readings have been set in more recent times, but originally the Haftorah selections were probably up to the discretion of the reader and may be so today.

Following the sermon comes the *Mourner's Kaddish.* This beautiful prayer speaks not only of the glorification of God but of the Messianic hope, and was once spoken at the conclusion of rabbinic discourses as a kind of doxology to conclude a sermon. This is one of the most ancient prayers in Judaism and is important for its promise of the resurrection and assurance of immortality as well as the establishment of the Messianic Kingdom of God. This prayer must surely have been on the mind of Jesus when he composed the Lord's Prayer and therefore it is most appropriate that the Lord's Prayer follow the *Mourner's Kaddish* to remind mourners reciting the *Kaddish* that the Messiah has come to bring mourning to a close. Therefore, it would be appropriate for the spiritual leader to ask for all those who have lost loved ones to stand and recite the *Mourner's Kaddish.* Then, following the recitation of the *Mourner's Kaddish,* the spiritual leader could ask the entire congregation to stand and to recite the Lord's Prayer. This would be a tremendous testimony to Jewish people of the hope that they have in the Messiah of Judaism. No thought here would be given of the eternal destiny of those who died. It is not our duty to tell Jewish people whether or not their loved ones are in hell. This is something that in the final analysis only God knows. But it is our responsibility to tell Jewish people who the one is who alone can take away their mourning and dry all their tears, and this one is the Messiah of Judaism, Jesus. Therefore, in the *Mourner's Kaddish* and the Lord's Prayer the sermon is given a double congregational amen. For the common theme in both the *Kaddish* and the Lord's Prayer is the glorification of God and the sanctification of his name, which of course is also the goal of any good sermon.

The important concluding prayer of the service is the *Ahleynoo* which means "it is our duty." This prayer contains Scriptures from the Tenach including Dan. 2:37, Deu. 4:39, Exo. 15:18 and Zech. 14:9. In the Messianic Erev Shabbat service the *Ahleyoo* is a prayer in which

Jewish people acknowledge their election by God as the people who are selected to preach God as the King of the universe to all men. The second half of the prayer visualizes a world which is one kingdom with one God as its King. The congregation stands for the *Ahleyoo* and bows toward the ark as it confesses its faith in the one God.

The *Kiddush* is a weekly ceremony ushering in the Sabbath. It is a sanctifying of the day, hence its name. Originally it was a home ceremony in which a benediction was said not only over wine but also bread. However, when wayfarers would lodge and eat on the synagogue premises, the blessing over the wine was made in the synagogue in Babylon and in some medieval European countries so that the travelers could have the benefit of the *Kiddush* away from home. The *Kiddush* came at the end of the service and it is especially important that the *Kiddush* be at the end of a Messianic Erev Shabbat service because of the remembrance of the Lord Yeshua it contains for all Messianic Jews. This portion of the service could even be a possible place for communion in some Messianic synagogues and as such would occur last as the spiritual climax of the service.

The spiritual leader has the choice of at least two favorite hymns to conclude the service: *Ayn keh-loh-hay-noo* ("There Is None Like Our God") and *Adon Olom* ("Lord of the Universe"). *Ayn keh-loh-hay-noo* glorifies God as Lord, King and Saviour of the Jewish people, and it answers the question that Moses asks in Exo. 15:11, "Who is like our God?" The answer is, "There is none like our God." *Adon* Olom is a centuries old hymn which glorifies God as the Lord of the Universe and is the traditional closing hymn for the Friday Night Service.

The Priestly Blessing of Num. 6:24-26 is an appropriate benediction for Messianic Jews who have realized the priestly role to which they have been called. The spiritual leader can at this point raise his hand and dismiss the congregation with the blessing as the people prepare to be greeted by him and to join one another for the *Oneg Shabbat* ("Joy of the Sabbath") which is a social/religious refreshment time following the service.

The only portion of the Friday Night Service which has been omitted in the Messianic Erev Shabbat Service described here is the *Yigdal*, which is a poetic hymn that summarizes the "Thirteen Principles of the Faith" according to Maimonides. The unbiblical theology of this document makes it inappropriate for a Messianic Erev Shabbt Service because it gives Moses a pre-eminence belonging to the Messiah Yeshua and it makes certain assertions about the nature of the God of Israel that are unbiblical: namely, that in his unity he is simple *(yachid)* rather than complex *(echad)*, which the Bible nowhere asserts; and that he is incorporeal, an unfounded and unbiblical argument against the Incarnation which is out of place in a Messianic synagogue.

Rather than end the service on the gloomy note of an unbiblical *Yigdal* confession, the order has been changed so that following the sermon comes the *Mourner's Kaddish,* 2) Lord's Prayer, 3) *Ahleynoo,* 4) *Kiddush,* and 5) Concluding Songs and Benediction. As the service approaches its conclusion, the wine upraised in the *Kiddush* cup symbolizes the "Jubilee Judaism" of Yeshua. For he is the one who changes water into wine and who brings the joy of the Kingdom of God to us even now in this dying age. In him God revealed that he is *echad,* a complex unity, and in him God dwelt bodily. In him Judaism finds its fulfillment and its true joy and peace.

Credit should be given here for groundwork laid by other scholars, which should be helpful in constructing messianic Jewish liturgy for the festivals and other occasions. Dalman's chapter on the synagogue in *Jesus-Yeshua* is very helpful for getting a sense of what synagogue worship was like at the time of Jesus. Idelsohn's book, *Jewish Liturgy and Its Development,* gives an analysis of the liturgical components of the Sabbath and other services. The annotated work of *The Authorized Daily Prayer Book* edited by Joseph Hertz is most useful in understanding the religious significance of the various prayers in the Sabbath service. Eric Werner's book, *The Sacred Bridge,* is helpful in seeing the liturgical parallels between the synagogue and the early church, as is also Oesterley's book, *The Jewish Background of the Christian Liturgy.* All of these works plus the personal experience of attending many kinds of synagogues were helpful in this study. It is hoped that the development of Messianic Jewish liturgy can be used by the Body of Yeshua to reach out to the Jewish community and to show Jewish people that the church is really a Messianic synagogue herself and has the freedom to become as much like the Jewish community to win the Jewish community as she does to become like the Gentiles to win Gentiles. (I Cor. 9:20-23). With services such as these in operation the Rabbinic interpretation of Judaism will find stiff competition from the Apostolic interpretation of Judaism, and the Jewish community will find itself faced with a real theological alternative to Rabbinic Judaism which takes her culture seriously and offers her not only the opportunity to be Jewish but the opportunity to live in the peace which comes from belief in the Good News of Judaism.

There is freedom in the New Testament for Messianic Jews to meet not only on Sunday but also Saturday (Acts 21:20; I Cor. 9:19-20; Romans 14:5, 6).

The Saturday morning Sabbath service follows an outline similar to that of Friday night: A) Opening prayers and hymns; B) The Shema; C) The Amidah; D) Torah and Haftorah readings and sermon; E) Closing prayers and hymns. Leaving aside the somewhat repetitive task of analysing the liturgy, let us focus on the highly important Torah section (D). In many of the coming messianic synagogues this will be the portion of the religious service where the climax of the Jewish education of young adults will occur. The Bar and Bat Mitzvah services, which represent the fruit of Jewish Biblical, cultural and language training, may be conducted during the Torah-Haftorah readings.

When time comes in the service for the study of Scripture, readings may be in both Hebrew and in either English or the native language of the congregation. The Messianic bar mitzvah boy may recite one of the blessings for the reading of the Torah or Haftorah, or he may read part of the Torah or Haftorah portions -- either those set by the calendar or one of his own selection and dear to his own personal testimony. Furthermore, he may lead the service. For their part, the Messianic Jewish girls may read or chant a portion of Scripture on Friday evening or Sabbath morning.

Some of the important prayers during the Scripture readings are as follows:

> Bahr-choo et ah-doh-nye hahm-voh-rahch,
> Bless the Lord who is to be blessed.
> Bah-rooch ah-doh-nye hahm-voh-rahch l'ohlahm vah-ed. Blessed be the Lord who is blessed forever and ever. Bah-rooch ah-tah ah-doh-nye eloh-hey-noo melech ha-oh-lahm ah-sher

bah-chahr bah-noo mee-kahl ha-ah-meem v'nah-tahn lah-noo et toh-rah-toh bah-rooch ah-tah ah-doh-nye noh-tain hah-toh-rah.

Blessed art Thou, Lord our God, King of the universe, who hast chosen us from all peoples, and hast given us Thy Torah. Blessed art Thou, O Lord, Giver of the Torah.

Bah-rooch ah-tah ah-doh-nye eloh-hey-noo melech ha-oh-lahm ah-sher nah-tahn lah-noo toh-raht eh-meht v'chah-yay oh-lahm nah-tah b'toh-chey-noo bah-rooch ah-tah ah-doh-nye noh-tain ha-toh-rah.

Blessed art Thou, Lord our God, King of the Universe, who hast given us the Torah of truth, and hast planted everlasting life in our midst. Blessed art Thou, O Lord, Giver of the Torah.

May he who blessed our fathers, Abraham, Isaac and Jacob, bless (*person called to read)* who has been called to the reading of the Torah. May the Holy One bless him and his family, and send blessing and prosperity on all the work of his hands; and let us say, Amen.

Two concluding points are relevant here. First, the importance of the Bar Mitzvah service can not be overemphasized. Without it, the religion of Jesus appears to many Jews as a sure road to cultural assimilation (in three, if not two generations). Many Jews, even non-religious Jews who care little for the synagogue, think of the Bar Mitzvah for their children when they think about their religion with any positive sentiments. Of one thing these parents are sure: their children will have at least as much Temple identity and Jewish religious education as the training prior to Bar Mitzvah will offer them. The church is not at all a viable option to such people because to them a religion which does not offer the Bar Mitzvah could not be truly Jewish. In short, a real cultural barrier exists here and a real cultural adjustment must be made if these Jewish people are to ever know that Yeshua is their Messiah and become disciples of his Body.

Second, the Jewish parochial school is an important tool for preparing Jewish children to witness to their New Covenant religion in the Bar Mitzvah service. With the rise of immorality stemming from secularism in public schools, churches have already seen the need for parochial education; however, an even greater need exists in the case of the coming Messianic synagogue. Education retards cultural assimilation. The Jewish community's corporate fear of assimilation may prevent it from flowing into the Body of the Lord until proper provision is made for the Biblical and cultural education of Jewish youth. When there are enough messianic synagogues, enough Jewish parochial schools, enough messianic Bar and Bat Mitzvahs to insure a sufficient number of Jewish believers for an adequate Jewish messianic marriage market, then a Jewish people movement in the Body of Messiah will begin, and will probably increase as has never been seen before in the history of the Jews.

Therefore, a celebration of Shabbat in light of the New Covenant really presupposes more than a minor liturgical adjustment. Masses of Jewish people must be exposed to the Good News through all possible means of communication. The Church must be educated and mobilized into action. Jewish Bible classes and fellowships must be multiplied. Messianic Jewish congresses must convene. Messianic synagogues must be organized. Jewish parochial schools must be founded. New structures must be formed and old structures in the Jewish community must be leavened with Jewish believers.

Much work lies ahead. But God will lead the way and use all these means to build bridges whereby hundreds of thousands of Jewish families can come into the Body of the Messiah and can come to know their true Sabbath rest in the New Eternal Covenant of God. May the formation of many messianic Yeshivas in the United States and around the world hasten the day!

PART II

A Messianic Yeshiva

SUBJECT MATTER
RESOURCES
POSSIBLE MODELS

7

A Messianic Yeshiva

By Joseph Shulam

One would think that with all the different institutions of higher learning that exist within the framework of Evangelical Christianity, we would not need a hybrid referred to by nature and by name as a "messianic yeshiva." However, the need for a messianic yeshiva arises intrinsically from two basic presuppositions:

(1) Jewish people who accept the New Testament and Yeshua as their personal savior need to study the Good News of the New Covenant in a Jewish setting.

(2) The traditional interpretation and approach to the New Testament has not taken sufficiently into account the *Jewish* background of the Scriptures. Granted, in the last two thousand years, Christian hermeneutics study has taken into account the Greek, the pagan, the mystery religion background of the New Testament. However, we must not forget that the New Testament was written in its major part *by* Jews and *for* Jews in a Jewish context (namely, the conflict between the believers and the synagogue). A messianic yeshiva would be a fertile academy for further study in this area.

Returning to the first presupposition, within the traditional Jewish upbringing, the educational method of learning has been a dynamic and a Socratic method of learning. Learning in the rabbinical colleges (which are called yeshivas by the Jewish community) was and is today basically according to the Socratic method of questions and answers. This aspect will be expanded later in this article, but first let us define and understand the concept of "Yeshiva."

"Yeshiva" basically comes from the Hebrew word for "sitting, sitting and meeting together." This concept is derived from the fact that people gathered, usually on the Sabbath day, to study together at their leisure the tradition and the law. Originally, in the first century context, there was no term as Yeshiva. The term used for the rabbinical schools was Bet Midrash, "the house of learning." In these institutions, the pupils gathered together to discuss and to define the Jewish law mainly by reflecting it one from another. This method was called "havruta" which means "get together of friends." It comes from the root of the word "haver" which means "to join or to become friends." This is clearly defined in the tradition of the early Tannaitic rabbis that were called the "zugot" or the "pairs," because the great rabbis were "paired" in polemics. From their polemics came the great teachings of the Scriptures. This, then, is the yeshiva method, which comes from questions and answers.

If one will forgive the over-generalization, there is within our Jewish character a certain argumentativeness, an impetuousness. I would offer the theory that this quality of character has developed as a result of the traditional yeshiva method of study, which was designed to be a mind-sharpening experience by the questions and answers.

Now, what advantage would such a thing be for people who are born-again believers? The first advantage that we have in using the yeshiva method to train men of God is to understand the Jewish background of the New Testament and at the same time be effective witnesses of Yeshua as our personal Saviour even within the Jewish setting of our studies. In the messianic yeshiva we would learn to encounter in a very Jewish way the questions and the objections the Jewish people have to believing in the New Testament.

The second benefit that such a method of learning would have is in the materials that would be learned in the yeshiva. We are not talking about a place in which only the Bible would be learned. We are talking about a place in which the traditional Jewish body of literature would also be given general attention, *with special emphasis* of how to use this Jewish literature to present a better and more *Jewish* approach to win to the Lord the Jewish people cognizant of this literature.

The objective of a traditional Jewish yeshiva is what is called "Talmud Torah." Talmud Torah, "the learning of the Torah," is considered an end in itself. However, as a messianic Jew, I don't see in my vision room for an institution of higher learning that would delve strictly (for the sake of intellectual exercise only) into this vast body of Jewish tradition. But I *do* see that, because of two thousand years of the wrong kind of Christian witness to the Jews, we need to revise our witness and use good sense and tactics in preaching the Good News to the Jewish people from within the structure and the tradition which they are well acquainted with. In addition to this, I feel that through the study of this Jewish literature and the use of it for witnessing, we can get a better grasp of certain of the issues and relationships of Biblical doctrine that would not only enable us to witness, but also give us a deeper understanding and a closer walk with Yeshua.

Now, what do people study in an Orthodox Jewish yeshiva normally? In an Orthodox yeshiva, first of all, in the early ages, emphasis is put on the Mishnah, mainly on memorizing the Mishnah and not really delving in depth into every possible interpretation.

In the higher classes and high school, emphasis is put on the Talmud and mainly on the passages of the Talmud which deal with halakhah. Not a great deal of emphasis is put in the beginning years of Talmudic study on the subject matter itself but mainly on the method of study.

A knowledge of the Talmudic method of study is very important for us as students of the New Testament, because we must realize that especially in Paul's literature some of the same types of questions and answers in this Talmudic style were incorporated by Paul, the student of Gamaliel. Understanding how to study first century Jewish literature would assist us in understanding Paul and his writings. See, for example, such rhetorical questions which betray a clearly rabbinical style in Paul as these: Since we have grace, shall we sin more so that grace may abound? (Romans 6:1) Is there an advantage to the Jew?(Romans 3:1) Is the law unholy? God forbid.(Romans 7:7) Was Israel stumbling in order that they may be lost?(Romans 11:11)

Questions like this and their answers portray a clearly rabbinical and Talmudic style.

In the higher levels and after high school the Orthodox yeshiva concentrates on what is called the Midrashic literature, the different stories and legends (haggadot) in the Talmud and in the related Midrashic literature. These very old traditions are sometimes important because they have direct applications to the New Testament and its background.

In a messianic yeshiva, I would see the main purpose of the course of our study as being to train students in how to present Yeshua as the Messiah of the Jewish people and as an intrinsic part of God's revelation to Israel. That is, to present Biblical Judaism, not as it has been presented in traditional circles as *another* religion, an alternative to the Jewish religion of the first century, but as an outgrowth and an offshoot of that same root to which Abraham, Isaac and Moses belonged.

In the Orthodox Jewish yeshiva, we must understand that the objective of every religious Jew is to eventually study the law. It does not make a difference if he's a watchmaker, a cobbler or a tailor. He desires to study the law and God's Word and his tradition. This he desires to do, at least part-time, if he cannot dedicate himself full-time to this great commandment and calling. Remember, in Tevya's song from *The Fiddler on the Roof* it says, "If I were a rich man, I would sit and study the Torah all day long." This is the vision not only of the so-called Rabbi or Jewish clergy but of every Jew that is interested in delving deeper into the knowledge of God. So a messianic yeshiva could be a layman's school, as well as for clergy, and would be modified in a pragmatic way to equip the believer to give an answer for the hope which God has planted in him through Yeshua Hamashiach.

The teacher in any yeshiva, messianic or orthodox, is a very important figure. The teacher is important, not because he stands before the class and lectures, as professors in universities and in seminaries do, but because he is the one informed person who has the time to spent individually with people when they have questions. Basically, the teacher (rabbi) has his time multiplied by the fact that, as he presents the subjects and the difficulties and asks the questions from the students, they separate into groups of two-by-two to discuss the text, its intricacies and its solutions. Then, when they gather together again at the end of the day, the rabbi is able to ask his students the questions that would be relevant to bring forth the most dynamic and valuable lessons that they could learn from the text that has been discussed.

Now I have said this much in order to state that a yeshiva is not necessarily an institution which requires large facilities. Mainly, it is an institution which deals with a certain approach and method to learning. This is why it is important to realize that, in order to start a messianic yeshiva, the main thing one needs first is to have the people, the students who are willing and hungry to win souls for the Lord in the most effective and in the most convincing Jewish way. I would say that this is the first requirement for a yeshiva.

The second requirement for a yeshiva is to have the basic books and works with which Jewish people are familiar, and which contain in them the material that would best relate to the New Testament. Unlike a traditional Jewish yeshiva, I would say that studying a tractate of Babylonian Talmud Bezah is not the most important thing that a messianic yeshiva should be studying, although it is one of the tractates that is normally studied in an Orthodox yeshiva. On the other hand, a tractate like Sanhedrin has multiple passages that are dealing with the Jewish view of Jesus (and I'm using here advisably the name Jesus instead of Yeshuah because they don't want to use the name Yeshuah but Yeshu which is a derogatory sense of the word Yeshuah.) Therefore, a talmudic tractate like Sanhedrin would yield multiple passages dealing with the person of Jesus. These passages have been sometimes used as a stumbling block to prevent Jewish people from accepting the Lord as their Saviour. But, a careful analysis and study of these passages could reverse them and they could be used as an important tool to show the historicity, the validity and the true character of the teachings of Yeshua as the Son of God and as the Messiah. (Note the short bibliography at the end of this chapter which would help the student in looking through these vast volumes of Jewish literature and finding material that could be beneficial to this kind of a learning experience.)

What else is needed to start a messianic yeshiva? We said that first of all you need the people willing to become serious students and effective witnesses, made more credible by their familiarity with this Jewish literature. Secondly, we said the yeshiva needs to have the right books. In addition, we must stress that the learning of the Hebrew language in a messianic yeshiva would be imperative. Much of the Jewish literature we are talking about has not been adequately translated into English and is still not respected in its English version by the Jewish community. Therefore, one of the principal courses of study in a messianic yeshiva, in my opinion, would be the learning of the Hebrew and Aramaic languages to enable one to delve deeper into this vast Jewish literature.

In addition to the learning of the Hebrew language, the messianic yeshiva should offer its students a very close spiritual pattern of life. Messianic spiritual warriors have to have a very living faith which expresses itself in a devotional life that is unequivocally dedicated to Yeshua as the Messiah and to the discovery and the preaching of the New Testament as a Jewish book! A messianic yeshiva would not survive and will not succeed if there is no rich exercise of all the fruits of God's Spirit in prayer and in fasting and in a dedicated life that would be an example to any Orthodox Jew that would stumble upon such a yeshiva.

Some of the practical technicalities of the yeshiva as they are expressed in the messianic Jewish cultural context are these. First of all, an orthodox yeshiva is usually open from Sunday to Friday at noon. The study hours are twice during the day-time, when the rabbi addresses his students, once in the morning when he presents to them the chapter or the page in which they will be studying (and gives some direction to it), and once in the evening when the rabbi of the Yeshivah gathers his disciples to find out what they have learned (and to redirect their thinking in case they have strayed from what is right).

The messianic yeshiva, depending on where and when it is started, would probably have to make some adjustments because of the cultural difficulties in daily life. We in Israel have found that because of the fact that believers are scattered over a large part of the country and their numbers are limited, it is only possible for us to meet one day a week with three, four or five hours in straight intensive study. However, I realize that in a different context in America, it would be possible to give more time for such an endeavor. The question would be left to the local needs of the students or congregations participating.

In addition, I would say that a messianic yeshiva ought not to appear as a cultural-theological mongrel but ought to be authentically a messianic Jewish expression. This can be achieved by wearing some of the outward trappings whether it is in decorating the place, or in the clothes that we wear, the yamulke, the tallis, the fringes, which provide the feeling of being inside the Jewish community, and inside a true yeshiva. Now I realize that these are only outward trappings, but atmosphere is important for our credibility.

In all the discussions of a messianic yeshiva we are talking as if we are ignoring our Gentile brothers and sisters. It is true that a messianic yeshiva would be primarily designed for training Jewish believers to be better witnesses to their fellow Jewish brothers and sisters, but I would say that a messianic yeshiva is not only for Jewish believers but *any* believer, be he white, black, Gentile or a Jew, that has a burden for Israel and desires to see Jewish people saved and wants to understand the Jewish background of the New Testament. Any such believer would find interest and spiritual edification in studying in the same way that Paul studied from Gamliel, and with the same method, and even some of the same materials.

It is important for us to know that the Jewish people who have been educated in the Orthodox tradition are well aware of many of the passages in the Talmud dealing with Jesus. These passages reverberate over and over again in the mind of the educated Jew preventing him from seeing the New Testament as the Word of God. The average Jew looks at the New Testament as a Christian(Gentile) book. It is important for us in our witness to the Jewish people to establish not only the divinity of Jesus and his messiahship, but also to establish the very deep Jewish roots in the writings of the apostles of the New Testament. For this reason, I feel that anyone who wants to be more effective as a witness to Israel would by necessity have to deal sooner or later with some of this yeshiva material. Therefore, where is there a better place than with the fellowship of other Jewish and Gentile brothers who want to see the people of God return to their true spiritual heritage in Yeshua Hamashiach?

Now let us delve in the curricula and in to the material that is actually studied in the yeshiva. First of all, let us deal with the curriculum of a messianic yeshiva.

Every yeshiva, whether it be that of the believers or of the Orthodox Jews, starts with the studying of the basic mishnaic literature. I would think that in order to interest the students initially it would be important to study a tractate that has connections and implication to their faith. That, of course, is different than the average Orthodox yeshiva. The average yeshiva starts with the tort laws and the agricultural laws. But the messianic yeshiva, in my opinion, ought to start with something like *Pirke Aboth*, "the sayings of the Fathers," in English, or another tractate that would generate the initial interest and zeal required to attack this material. After one learns the character of the mishna and its background I would think that it would be time to delve into how to analyze and study the arguments of a Talmudic page. In Israel the yeshiva regularly started with Tort laws (which are usually found in Baba Metzia or Baba Kamma of the Babylonian Talmud) or in Kidushim, "marital laws." But any one of these tractates would be sufficient to teach a student how to study by himself a page of Talmud.

After the understanding and the analysis of this methodological application, I think it would be time to start to deal with some of the passages that touch on Jesus and to see if one could understand them. One should attempt to understand their background and their literary character, not only in order to refute them but in order to gain an insight into the minds of the Rabbis who actually thought that they would have an impact on the Jewish people and would serve as contraceptives to the powerful message of the Gospel.

After a course of dealing with the passages throughout the Talmud that touch on Jesus, I would think that it would be right for the believer to delve into some of the messianic concepts and problems that are discussed in tractates like Sanhedrin and Hagigah and in separate incidents in the different tractates of the Talmud. I think that the course of study of such dimensions would probably take as long as a year.

The second year I would suggest would be dedicated to the Midrashic literature and its parallels in the Biblical hermeneutics of the New Testament. The third year of the yeshiva study, I think ought to be dedicated to the text of the New Testament itself and to the application of the things that have been studied before in the direct witness of the New Testament to the Jewish community.

Of course, what I have said does not exhaust all the material that should be studied, but it would at least give to the person interested enough knowledge that he could pursue this study on his own as long as he lives.

Now, in order to achieve all this study, the yeshiva has to have some books. First of all it would be imperative to have the basic Biblical tools for study: that is, of course, the Concordances, the Dictionaries, the Biblical Encyclopaedias, that are general tools for examining the Scriptures. Second of all, I would say that the yeshiva ought to have the Babylonian Talmud, the Jerusalem Talmud, the set of the rabbinical commentaries of the Torah which are all included in the series called Mikraot Gedolot and all the books of Maimonides. These would serve as an excellent commentary on the Talmud and the Laws.

In addition to these, one could have of course the Hebrew and the English versions of all these books that are available and then the major midrashim of the five books of Moses and the five scrolls, Esther, Eccelesiastes, Song of Songs, Ruth and Lamentations. The major midrashim can be obtained in English by the Soncino Press. A messianic yeshiva should have an *Encyclopaedia Judaica*. If the people know Hebrew, then the *Talmudic Encyclopaedia*, which has been published in Hebrew, is important. Also, there is Marcus Jastrow's *Dictionary of Talmudic and Palestinian Aramaic*. There is also Rosenthal's *Aramaic Grammar*.

Now I realize that such books are costly. What we did in Israel to help was to type out and reproduce the lessons so that students didn't have to buy all the books, but could have available to them the particular lessons that they had to study during that day. I would suggest that a messianic yeshiva save by the employ of a full-time secretary to type out these lessons, both in Hebrew and in English.

There are additional works that would be helpful to the student of the Jewish background to the New Testament and which deal with the character of Jesus. Let me mention a few of them. First, there is Dr. Gustaf Dalman, *Jesus Christ in the Talmud, Midrash and Zohar and the Liturgy of the Synagogue*, published in 1839 in London and republished by Arnold Press of New York in the series of the Jewish People, History, Religion and Literature. Emil Schürer, *The History of the Jewish People in the Time of*

Jesus Christ which was published recently in two volumes. Also by Schürer there is *The Literature of the Jewish People in the Time of Jesus Christ* and also *Sider Toldot Yeshua,* (The Book of the Genealogies of Jesus) which was published in English. Then R. Travers Herford has written *Christianity and the Jewish Talmud.* Many of these can be found in libraries, such as Hermann L. Strack's *Introduction to the Talmud and Midrash,* a Temple Book, Atheneum NY 1972; David Daube, *The New Testament and Rabbinic Judaism;* W. D. Davis, *Christian Origins and Judaism,* both published by Arnold Press, reprints; W. D. Davis, *Paul and Rabbinical Judaism;* E. P. Sanders, *Palestinian Judaism and Paul;* E. P. Sanders' second book has just been published called, *Problems of Identity in Judaism and Christianity in the Second Century.* Hans Shoeps, *Paul.*

There are numerous other books which would be helpful to a person who is interested to know more about the Jewish background of the New Testament, but these would be some good suggestions to start with in building a proper source library for a messianic yeshiva.

In conclusion, it is clear to me that there is a real need both for the growth of the Jewish believers and for the witness to the Jews, to establish real schools of training for people who are interested in bringing the gospel to Israel and to the Jewish community throughout the world. In addition, I believe a model would be afforded to the non-Jewish Christians by these yeshivas showing the implications for cross-cultural communication of the Gospel. This model would enhance the effectiveness of those who are interested in reaching people of different cultures, namely, by showing that not only an outward adaptation of the gospel but also an adaptation in the very means of communications is a healthy imperative for an effective witness. I long to see the day when one or two such messianic rabbinical yeshivas will be established in the United States and in Israel in order to train Jewish believers to give a more effective witness on the one hand, and a deeper understanding and identity with their own heritage on the other hand, as well as an effective tool for the evangelizing of Israel that she may return to her true and natural Messiah, the Son of David who, in the name of Israel and the Jewish people, brought salvation to all mankind.

8

Rabbinic Writings

By Rachmiel Frydland

Basic to Talmudic and Rabbinic writings is the claim that their teachings have Mosaic authority. Thus one of the most important tractates in the Talmud begins with these words:

> Moses received the LAW from Sinai and handed it down to Joshua, and Joshua to the elders, and the elders to the prophets, and the prophets handed it down to the men of the Great Assembly.
>
> (Tractate Avot 1:1)

This was sufficient excuse for later rabbinic opinions and decisions to claim Mosaic authority. While the Lord Yeshua is aware of this claim, as seen in Matt. 23:2, "The Scribes and Pharisees sit on Moses' seat," he goes on to show the inconsistency of the Rabbis between their teachings and practice. Their claim to Divine origin, therefore, has no practical value.

THE PEOPLE OF THE BOOK

Nevertheless, the Jewish people are justly called "The People of the Book," for God called them to write down His Word for us, both Old and New Testaments, as the Apostle Paul says:

> Then what advantage has the Jew? ... Much in every way. To begin with, the Jews are entrusted with the Oracles of God. (Roman 3:1-2)

In addition, the Jewish people were primarily responsible in preserving for us intact the text of the Old Testament. From the time of Ezra, of whom it is said, "Ezra...was a *scribe* skilled in the law of Moses" (Ezra 7:6), until this very day, the religious Jewish scribe is extremely careful in copying and preserving the text of the Tenach (Old Testament).

The scribes not only carefully copied the Old Testament text, but also produced new religious teachings based on the Old, as the Lord Yeshua says: "Therefore, every scribe who has been trained for the Kingdom is like a householder who brings out of his teasure what is new and what is old." (Matt. 13:51)

TEN PERIODS OF JEWISH LITERATURE

Generally speaking, Religious Hebrew Literature can be divided into Ten Periods:

1. The Period of Holy Scriptures;

2. The Intertestamental Period, when the books of the Apocrypha were composed;

3. The New Testament Period, when as we believe, some of the New Testament books like Matthew and James, were originally composed in Hebrew;

4. The Talmudic and Midrashic writings;

5. The Gaonic Period;

6. The Kabbalah which is esoteric and mystic explanation of the Torah;

7. The Karaite Period, those who denied the Rabbinic authority;

8. The Jewish Religious Poetry. Much of it became part of the Jewish Prayer Books for the various Jewish Holidays and Holy Days;

9. The writings of the Decision Makers. The Codes of

Biblical and Jewish Law in the narrower ceremonial sense;

10. The writings of the Hassidim and their Rabbis.

Leaving out the first three periods, which we assume are familiar to our readers, we take up the Talmudic and Midrashic writings. Perhaps we should not have used the term "writings," for until at least 200 A.D., these teachings were handed down orally from generation to generation. (Nevertheless, even in this period, when it was officially forbidden to put these teachings into a book, there is strong probability that some of the students and Rabbis would at least have made some notes as *aide-memoire*.) Be it as it may, we are told that Rabbi Yehuda Hannasi, who died 212 A.D., composed the first part of the Talmud called "The Mishna," which simply means "The Teaching" or "The Learning." It has six parts to it, dealing with the following Laws:

1. *Zera'im*. Seeds, dealing with laws relating to Agriculture. To this section has been added, at the beginning, the laws of which blessings to say over the various foods and seeds. And, since one should not eat before one prays, also the laws for the Daily Prayers.

2. *Mo'ed*. Seasons, laws regarding the Sabbath and the Jewish Holy Days.

3. *Nashim*. Women, laws relating to marriage, divorce, marriage treaties, levirate marriage, suspicion of unfaithfulness, etc.

4. *Nezikin*. Damages. Criminal laws, also laws for the Court and Court Proceedings. In this tractate is also included Avot -- the Sayings of the Fathers from which we quoted the first Mishna at the beginning of this article.

5. *Kodashim*. Holy Things pertaining to Temple Services and sacrifices; also dietary laws, slaughter of animals, laws of meat and dairy dishes.

6. *Toharot*. Purification of Priests, people and women. It must have been a gigantic task to put all these laws in order. Rabbi Yehuda had the help of his many students to complete the task, who, as we surmised, must have had some notes to aid their memories.

THE GEMARA

The ink was hardly dry, and a new generation of scholars began to discuss and expound the Mishna. They recalled teachings which were not incorporated in to the Mishna called Beraitot (Aramaic for the text left outside). Others worked on a Tosefta (Additions to the Mishna), but the main body of scholars were occupied with discussing and exegeting the reasons that lie behind the final decisions of the Mishna. They could not contradict what was decided, but by far-fetched sophistication they could modify or explain things in spite of seeming contradiction with the Biblical text or contractions within itself or with a Beraitha or a Tosephta. The Palestinian Schools of Tiberias, Sephoris, and Lydda, suffering under persecutions of the Roman governors, especially one Ursicinos, were forced to complete their work by 400 A.D. The Babylonian schools had much more freedam to elucidate the teaching of the former Rabbis. They established far more academies. The most famous were in Nehardea, Sura, Pumbeditha, Mahoza, Naresh and Mata-Mehasya,, all in Babylonia which is now Irak. The Halakhic exegesis was usually accomplished by two famous Rabbinic leaders taking opposite views and each adducing reasons and Scripture to support his view. The most famous of these pairs are Rav (short for Rab Abba) (died 250 A.D.) versus Shmuel, and Rava (also for another R. Abba) (died 352 A.D.) versus Abaye. Rabba bar Nahmavi (320 A.D.) was called Oker Harim (Uprooter of Mountains because of his erudition) and R. Joseph (323 A.D.) was referred to as Sinai (because of his knowledge of the Law).

The larger Babylonian Talmud has 2½ million words consisting of one-third halakha (law) and two-thirds Aggada (religious and ethical stories and teaching).

The Babylonian Talmud was arranged and closed by the two great scholars Rabina and Rab Ashi at the Academy of Mata Mehasya.

THE GAONIM

The scholars following them were called Gaonim. To them were addressed Questions about the choice of a final decision in a matter of Halakha (law) about the order and the dates of each scholar mentioned in the Talmud. The answers to these questions were preserved in a literature which is called Responsae (in Hebrew *She'elot utshuvot)* which were studied and elucidated by subsequent scholars.

THE KABBALAH

The Talmud is aware of the mysticism that surrounds Moses' seeing God, the Schechineh, Ezekiel's chariots, the mysticism of creation, Daniel's vision of the Ancient of Days (Daniel 7), and the dates he gives about the coming of Messiah (Daniel 9, 12). Yet the preoccupation was with the Law, since this gives Life as it says in Lev. 18:5, "which if a man do, he shall live by them." To a certain degree there is even a warning in the Talmud not to meddle too much with esoteric matters. For, according to the Talmud, of Talmudic scholars who tried to find out the secrets of the hidden things, only one entered peacefully and came out peacefully -- R. Akiba. Of the others, one died, one went mad, and one lost his sound faith.

Yet others did attempt to find out the mystic secrets, and it was Rabbi Shimon bar Yochai of the Second Century A.D., who is known to have lived in a cave for many years and to whom God is said to have revealed many secrets. The Rabbis who dabbled in mysticism usually ascribed their findings to this revered saint and Rabbi. According to modern scholarship, the whole book of the *Zohar* (a mystic elucidation of the Pentateuch, ascribed to R. Shimon b. Yochai) was actually composed in Spain in the 13th Century by Leon Di Modena. Other mystics wrote in their own name. Especially famous are R. Isaac Luria and his disciple Hayim Vital. Be that as it may, these writings became the handbook of the Hassidic movement that started in the 18th Century with R. Israel Baal Shem Tov (the Master of the Good Name), and is still prospering today in the USA and in Israel.

THE KARAITES

The New Testament mentions often the Sadducees who did not accept the oral law and did not believe that the Torah speaks of supernatural angels, or the resurrection. Jesus opposed them and agreed with the Pharisees who believed in angels (Matt. 18:10) and in the resurrection (Matt. 22:29-32). He even had an attitude of respect toward the Oral Law (Matt. 23:2), except that he condemmed its promoters, the Pharisees, in that they didn't practice it themselves (Matt. 23:3), that the burden was too hard (Matt. 23:4), that it tends to ignore the weightier matters of justice, mercy and faith (Matt. 23:23), and that many of them were seeking recognition (praise) of their piety by other men.

With the destruction of the Temple in A.D. 70, the Sadducees lost their prominence but remnants kept up their faith and convictions. In the Eighth Century, Anan ben David who had a claim to the leadership of the Jewish people in the Diaspora, but was refused the position, revived the Sadducee movement. Now they called themselves Karaites (from the Hebrew Kara or Qara-Scripturalists). Now the stress was not on the supernatural, angels, or the resurrection, but the denial of the authority of the Talmud in ordering how every Jew must practice the law. This involved literalism. There was no fire, hence no lights, on Sabbath eve, based on a literal reading of Ex. 35:3. The tallit with the fringes was hanged only on the eastern wall of the synagogue, so that everyone could see it as it says in Numbers 15:39, "and ye shall see them."

The Karaite apologetic literature is extensive. Of the other Karaite writings, the most popular is *Hizzuk Emunah* by Isaac Troki of the 16th Century, a book that attacks the claims of Jesus' Messiahship and Divinity. This is adequately answered by A. Lukyn Williams in the *Manual of Christian Evidences* (Cambridge, London, 1911).

Remnants of the Karaite movement have found a home in the land of Israel in a town near Jaffa Tel Aviv.

RELIGIOUS POETRY

Needless to day, many of the books of the Old Testament are written in a poetic way. These books include Job, Psalms, Proverbs, Song of Solomon, Lamentations, and Ecclesiastes. The Prophets also gave many of their messages in a poetic style. Here we should mention the great poets of Israel and of the Spanish Golden Age of Hebrew poetry, the 8th to the 12th Century: Eliezer Ha-Kalir's poem was based on Isaiah 53, *Pana Mendo Mashiach Tsidkenoo* ("Our Righteous Messiah has turned from us -- the one who bore our sins and our iniquities upon His shoulders" -- which is found in older prayerbooks) has been quoted by Messianic Jews often in tracts and pamphlets. R. Yehuda Halevi of Spain, who went to Israel to die there and was apparently killed on arrival, pours out his love for his people and the land with the words of Psalm 102:15, "So precious your dust, so sweet your stones of Zion. How I would love to embrace your rocks and fall down to kiss your stones."

THE CODES OF LAW

With the conclusion of the Talmud it was necessary to make decisions as to which opinion is the stronger. Of the many Codes, probably the most popular is that of Maimonides of the 12th to 13th Century. However Rabbis today base their decision on the Great Code called Joseph Karo's Shulchan Aroch (16th Century).

This was commented on by Taz (Turey Zahav) and by Shakh (Rabbi Shabtai Cohen). A student who wants to receive Semicah (ordination) has to study the four large tomes, dealing with the House and Synagogue kashrut, court procedures, laws about relations with women and menstrual purity.

9

Training Messianic Jewish Leadership

By Daniel Juster

I. Training Lay Leaders.

Messianic Judaism presently experiences a vacuum of leadership. Small congregations grow up and seek adequate leadership to teach and to shepherd the new flock; they find this leadership hard to come by. Many are the new followers of the Messiah in the movement; few are seasoned, mature followers. Those Jewish followers of Yeshua who could provide leadership are often unwilling to sacrifice and to receive a small salary by the struggling congregation. "Tent-making" (that is, a willingness to make a salary by working in another profession) is often necessary at this stage.

Messianic Judaism thus faces these difficult problems, which by God's grace, will be solved:

1. The practical, spiritual, and intellectual preparation of Messianic Rabbis.

2. The development of strong elders (lay leaders).

3. Adopting congregational models which can most adequately fulfill these goals.

If we recognize the existence in the United States alone of over forty messianic congregations, recognize that nine or ten have full-time spiritual leaders, and of these leaders perhaps only half a dozen have adequate Biblical and Jewish backgrounds, we can recognize the intensity of the problem.

The training of adequate lay leaders is foundational for finding those who can be called to full-time congregational leadership. It is my view that the grass-roots nature of our movement is such that most full-time clergy leadership will be and should be drawn from the ranks of those who prove their maturity on a lay level. Certainly some will train for leadership from a strictly academic level, college and seminary, but such people are poor risks if they can give no congregational proof of pastoral qualities. In the next section, we shall look at the strictly academic model of training and speak of the pros and cons. Here are some of the crucial factors in developing lay leaders:

First, fellowship, prayer, and work with present leadership. This first step is crucial. This is the model Yeshua provided in choosing twelve "to be with him." It is crucial to identify potential and aspiring leadership. The present leadership should gather aspiring or potential leaders for prayer, sharing, fellowship and teaching of the central principles of Biblical servanthood, humility, spiritual life and stability. As a trust and love relationship grows, these potential leaders can be given various responsibilities according to their spiritual gifts and interaction with others. A potential elder will demonstrate involvement in caring for others, good council, and an ability to learn and convey the Word. A potential shamash (or deacon) will demonstrate coordinating ability as well as dealing with the material and physical needs of the congregation as a whole and its members. If the Biblical requirements of eldership or the diaconate are fulfilled, a person may be ordained to this office according to the congregation's system of choice.

There are unlimited opportunities to prove potential leadership and fellowship times can enable discussion of leadership problems and performance. Here are some suggestions we have found useful:

1. Building coordinators to assist the messianic rabbi.

2. Training lay counselors by the Biblical counseling methods developed by Dr. Jay Adams, Hatfield, Pennsylvania.

3. Leading cell groups which include Bible study, prayer, personal ministry and fellowship. Cell leaders should be part of a cell serving as assistant leaders before assuming head leadership (see Ron Trudinger, *Cell Life*, Logos).

4. Discipling new believers through a series of Bible study lessons.

5. Committee chairpersons for fellowship, outreach, etc.

6. Teachers of various Bible classes.

7. Coordinators of transportation, tape ministry, book ministry.

Those proven as humble servants, teachers and shepherds become elders, since they have proven themselves functionally.

The growth of a person does not stop upon being ordained into the eldership or diaconate. Each elder should seek to better equip himself according to the Biblical ideals of shepherding, recognizing the heavy and holy responsibility laid upon him (See Ezek. 34, I Pet. 5, Titus 1). Meeting with the messianic rabbi for continued fellowship, prayer, and growth is essential. Also, the elder should seek to equip himself spiritually by regular study. Here are some essentials:

1. Regular times for Bible study and prayer . . . learning to use good tools for help (Bible dictionaries, encyclopaedias, and commentaries, e.g., Intervarsity, New Bible Dictionary, and New Bible Commentary).

2. Reading the best of great spirit and faith building literature.

A. The Books of Watchmen Nee.

B. Biographies of the greatest men of New Testament faith such as Norman Grubb, C. T. Studd, Rees Howells, and also Hudson Taylor's *Spiritual Secret*. These are only starts. The principles of faith and of reaching the lost exemplified by these men are models for us.

C. Books on doctrine and teaching of a systematic nature.

(1) Charles Finney on Revival;
(2) J. O. Buswell, *A Systematic Theology of the Christian Religion*;
(3) Bernard Ramm, *Protestant Christian Evidences;*
(4) Books and tapes by Derek Prince;
(5) Mark Bubeck's *The Adversary* on Spiritual Warfare.

D. Books to broaden an understanding of Jewish history and literature.

(1) Abraham Cohen, *Everyman's Talmud*;
(2) C. G. Montifiore, *A Rabbinic Anthology*;
(3) Buber, *Tales of the Hassidim*;
(4) S. Grazel, *A History of the Jews*;
(5) Parkes, *The Conflict of the Church and the Synagogue*;
(6) Franklin Littell, *The Crucifixion of the Jews*;
(7) Hertz, *Authorized Daily Prayer Book*.

E. Books to increase our Jewish witness.

(1) A. Fruchtenbaum, *Jesus Was a Jew;*
(2) Arthur Kac, *The Messianic Hope*;
(3) P. Liberman, *The Fig Tree Blossoms*;
(4) Sid Roth, *Something for Nothing*;
(5) R. Frydland, *When Being Jewish was a Crime*;
(6) Juster, *Jewishness and Jesus--Foundations of Messianic Judaism* (forthcoming).

Leaders who do not give themselves to study may be narrow in mind and spirit, dogmatic, intolerant, and unable to discuss with understanding. The above is a small beginning to life-long study and development.

As the elders meet together, they may discuss their personal needs, and their problems and concerns in shepherding those in their charge. Some among the eldership will show special desire and ability for training to be messianic rabbis. We turn now to that concern.

II. Training Messianic Rabbis.

1. The Professional Model.

In this model, usually a young person senses the desire to train to be a spiritual leader. He therefore goes off to college and chooses a major that coincides with this call. After graduation he goes to a seminary and at the end of approximately seven years of training seeks to find a one year student internship before finding a congregation of his own. What are the pros and cons of this arrangement?

In favor of this arrangement we should note that such a program may maximize ability to think and perform academically. If the right schools are chosen, the student can learn to interact with the arts and sciences. He may gain insights from the very best Biblical scholars. The potential for developing a broadness of mind and heart can be enhanced in the environment of Biblically oriented schools. Furthermore, interaction with students and professors produces some very valuable growth in personal areas.

However, there are several negative factors in this model. In my experience, students in colleges and seminaries far from their home congregation are little involved in the body. They learn in an artificial atmosphere. Not only does the messianic congregation lose their gifts for years, but they lose the practical ministry-training which is crucial to pastoring and can only be gained in congregational life. And who says it must always take seven to ten years to train a congregational leader?

As far as the congregation is concerned, calling an academically-only trained person is a real risk. Perhaps he has the gifts; perhaps not. He will perhaps develop in the hard knocks of the ministry; perhaps not. However, the final tragedy might be a disillusioned person leaving his ministry *and* a disillusioned congregation. Most messianic congregations are not of a size to hire such formally trained students to the positions of assistants so as to prove them, and a one year internship, if available, may not be adequate.

Perhaps developing as a lay elder *after* the academic training could prove such a person. However, as Saul writes "knowledge puffs up," and the pride of strictly academic training may blind a person to his need for spiritual and practical growth in the areas of ministry.

Secondly, there is not as of this writing one academic school which gives the balance of courses in Bible, Jewish studies and practical areas which a messianic Jewish leader would desire. Perhaps after Christian academic training such a person could enter a Jewish training program. This is indeed a long haul.

2. The Congregational Model of Training.

In this model of training, it is the current spiritual leadership of the local congregation that trains the new leadership. Out of such training, it is hoped, will come solid leaders. Those who espouse this model argue that the most valuable training takes place in the context of the practical experience to be gained in congregational life. Furthermore, the spiritual leader is the one called to disciple new leaders, just as Yeshua trained the twelve disciples.

The above arguments speak well for this model of leadership development. This thinking fits extremely well with our reasons for developing a leadership-fellowship in the local body. There is a direct accountability and evaluation as increasing responsibilities are given. This maximizes the personal, spiritual, and practical development of the future leader. However, this model also exhibits weaknesses.

First of all, let us note that when the Twelve trained under Yeshua, they trained under the perfect Son of Man! The Scriptural teaching he gave was the best, the moral and practical experience gained in following him was without comparison! In other words, training on a totally local level can only be as adequate as the one who is the trainer. How many leaders provide the trainee with adequate spiritual modeling, administrative ability to provide for the trainee's practical experience, and a broadness of mind sufficient to provide adequate development in Biblical theology and Jewish studies? Who can, in addition, exemplify the ability to apply insights from these studies to the complex situations we face in modern life?

Although this model maximizes the truth that leadership training is a function of one's growth in leadership responsibilities, there are dangers. They are:

A. Producing disciples who are mirror images of the discipler. Do I really want future leaders to be just like me, or do I want them to develop uniquely so our strength together will be broad and complementary? Do I want them to preach just like me, think just like me, and act just like me?

B. The danger of narrowmindedness: Even if the leader is broad in his understanding, the strongest development of a student comes in getting firsthand exposure to various viewpoints. He may not be able to develop intellectually to the highest degree because he is precluded from learning from the best scholars in the areas of their expertise.

C. The danger of "ingrown" attitudes: This model maximizes the possibility that the student will not be able to respond to other traditions either in Chrsitianity or Judaism. Without fighting through to his own convictions through direct exposure to these traditions, he either appears foolish in his interaction or must "bury his head in the sand" so as to not be threatened by unknown possible opponents. Our primary goal is the production of leaders who are spiritually strong and exhibit the broadest possibility of interacting with various human beings. An isolationist mode of training is not helpful toward this end.

3. A New Pastoral Training Model.

The solution to the above dilemma is to recognize that the above models are not the only ones possible. Rather there are models that can combine the best of models 1 and 2 while avoiding their worst pitfalls. Most messianic congregations are located in large urban areas. The academic resources of these areas are great. Let us note some of them:

A. Christian colleges, bible schools, and seminaries;

B. Colleges of Jewish Learning;

C. Local leadership training Institutes;

D. Libraries for Independent Study Courses;

E. Jewish Community Centers for training.

Beyond this is an array of tapes, possible correspondence courses, and even an independent study reading program developed by Phil Goble for training messianic rabbis.

This new pastoral training model leaves the training of future leaders in the hands of the local congregation while combining with it the best academic training. Each congregational leader can tailor a curriculum for his aspiring future leaders. It can be flexibly tailored to the resources available. It may even combine a prescribed time away, say six months to a year, for study in Israel, at a seminary or at Betzel Shaddai Yeshiva, which we shall mention.

In this model, the student still is under the care of the spiritual leader, and gains the best practical experience through increments of leadership responsibility in his own local body according to his own rate of spiritual development.

A few years ago Betzel Shaddai Yeshiva was formed in Chicago. This provides the best example of the kind of thing we are speaking of. A student of Betzel Shaddai remains in his local congregation in Chicago. He takes the best and most relevant courses in Jewish studies from a local college of Jewish learning. He takes the most relevant Biblical Studies courses from Trinity Evangelical Divinity School, and takes integrative courses at Betzel Shaddai. There is a four year messianic rabbinic curriculum which offers an M. Div. from Trinity, a Bachelors of Jewish Studies from the local college of Jewish Studies, and a certificate from Betzel Shaddai Yeshiva. Moody Bible Institute also offers a Jewish Studies program under Dr. Louis Goldberg. Degrees are offered by independent enrollment in these schools; there is no cooperative arrangement and there does not need to be. However, the Betzel Shaddai Yeshiva certificate is offered on the basis of adequate study in the areas of Biblical and theological studies, Jewish studies and practical theology. There is also a one year and summer program.

Not everyone can be a student at Betzel Shaddai in Chicago, but similar programs can be tailored in most large cities and some Betzel Shaddai courses will be on tape.

At Beth Messiah in Rockville, we have sought to use the facilities of local seminaries, a local college of Jewish Studies, a local training Institute called New Life Training Institute, and courses taught by myself as an extension of Betzel Shaddai. Each student is given practical involvement in the local body and the congregation oversees his spiritual development.

We are not so concerned about the degree itself from the local institutes, although some will gain such degrees. We are more concerned about a record being kept of the students' course work and practical work to reflect his capability in prescribed areas. Perhaps someday the Union of Congregations will certify adequacy of training on this basis. Of course, any local congregation that seeks to be independent of this model can follow its own way and forego official recognition, but we think some standards are important and that a demonstration of proficiency is significant. Instead of academic institutionalization, the model of "equivalency in training" by recorded independent study under the spiritual leader and course work taken at various schools can fully suffice. This gives us a flexibility to enable training to take place in as rapid a pace as individual capability allows. Even while one leads a congregation he can continue training. To help the spiritual eldership of various congregations, we list the Betzel Shaddai curriculum. A similar one can be tailored in your area and Betzel Shaddai Yeshiva can perhaps help you.

Courses to be integrated into a full messianic rabbinic training course, a one-year intensive study program, and a special summer study program. Most courses are three quarter hours.

CORE COURSES TAUGHT BY THE YESHIVA

Theology

- Messianic Jewish Theology - covering covenants, law, grace, and other central theological issues.

History

- The New Testament Against Its Jewish Background - understanding the New Testament in its original setting.
- Messianic Judaism and Jewish Christianity - historical survey from first century to the present.
- Anti-Semitism - survey from biblical times to present (2 quarters).

Apologetics

-Messianic Jewish Apologetics - general course geared to Messianic Jews (2 quarters).

Biblical Studies

-Crucial Biblical Issues and Messianic Judaism.
-Epistle to the Hebrews.

Talmud

-The Talmud and Messianic Judaism (2 quarters).

Practical Theology

-Cross Cultural Communications.
-Sharing Our Faith.
-Spiritual Life of the Messianic Leader - includes personal spiritual life, power of the Spirit, gifts of the Spirit, spiritual warfare and deliverance, establishing and leading a Messianic synagogue; above coordinated with internship involvement at Adat HaTikvah or Congregation B'nai Maccabim in areas of preaching, teaching, counseling, etc. (3 quarters).
-Contemporary Issues in Jewish-Christian Relations.
-Messianic Drama and Music.
-Liturgy - learning the traditional chants and prayers.

Summer study in Israel strongly recommended.

RESOURCE COURSES FROM AREA SCHOOLS

Theology

Survey of theology - 3 quarters (TEDS)

Languages

Greek - 6 quarters (TEDS)
Modern Hebrew - 3-6 quarters (SCJ)
Biblical Hebrew - 3 quarters (TEDS)

Biblical Studies

Survey of Tenach - 3 quarters (TEDS)
Survey of B'rit Hadasha - 3 quarters (TEDS)
Theology of Tenach - 1 quarter (TEDS)
Critical Introduction to Tenach - 1 quarter (TEDS)
Critical Introduction to Gospels - 1 quarter (TEDS)

Talmud

Survey and courses totalling 5 quarters (SCJ)

History
Intertestamental Period (TEDS)
Jewish History - 3 quarters (SCJ)
Church History - 2 quarters (TEDS)

Practical Theology - each one quarter
Counseling (TEDS)
Homiletics (TEDS)
Hermeneutics (TEDS)
Education (TEDS)
Administration (TEDS)

For Students Lacking College Background
Jewish Studies curriculum (MBI)

III. Models of Congregational Authority.

A messianic congregation is a New Covenant congregation. Its structure is based on the teachings of the New Covenant Scriptures. However, various groups throughout history have come to different conclusions in their study of Biblical passages. It is not our purpose to give an exhaustive exposition of the Scriptures on this topic. We only desire to put forth the models, and then to give some comments on each so an intelligent choice can be made.

MODEL #1: The final authority for spiritual direction *is vested in the spiritual leader of the congregation.* Under this model, the spiritual leader may have an advisory board of elders, but when push comes to shove, he makes the final decision. He may seek the input of congregations and other leaders, but this is on a solely voluntary basis.

1. Basis of the Model.

There are Scriptures that are used to show the final authority of leaders chosen by God. Moses in the book of Exodus appoints the leadership (Ex. 18:25); Timothy, as Spiritual leader, is told to teach, reprove and rebuke. Timothy was appointed by Paul. There is no appeal in this passage to a board of elders. Paul appoints elders in Ephesus and Timothy is told to appoint men (II Tim. 2:1, 4:2). The conclusion is thus drawn that (1) leadership is by God's appointment through other leaders and (2) that individual leaders have final authority in their own sphere.

2. Positive Features of This Model.

A. It fully recognizes that God's annointing upon a leader is the historical way of his great working throughout Scripture.

B. It recognizes that God does vest real Scriptural authority for leadership in selected individuals.

C. It enables future leaders to be chosen by mature leaders who have greater wisdom in choosing.

3. Negative Features.

A. It tends to overlook the response of the people as a criteria of leadership. I Timothy and Titus teach that a leader chosen should be of good reputation and well thought of by the believers.

Moses in Deuteronomy speaks of similar criteria for leaders, and the people acclaiming a prophetic choice seems to produce the King (Deuteronomy 17:14-17).

B. It places power of a very absolute type in the leader. There is no check on his power from other leaders, and the only recourse for individuals and other leaders who believe the head leader to be wrong, even to the point of sin, is to leave the congregation. The head leader may keep his operations secret or open and may or may not receive council or correction. When we remember that leaders are also fallible sinners saved by grace, is it a good idea to put this level of trust in any single individual, or to test an individual's life so radically by yielding all power to him?

MODEL #2: The congregationalist model holds that final power is vested in the congregations. The person who holds to this model emphasizes those passages which speak of the necessity of the leader's being well thought of and approved by the people. Leaders hence serve to inspire direction and to carry out the will of the people. Submission is a voluntary matter conditioned by whether the leaders carry out their prescribed tasks. Hence leaders are elected by the congregation and are subject to recall by them. Furthermore, major decisions should require congregational approval.

1. Positive Features.

A. Recognizes the dangers of the abuse of power in leadership and provides a check.

B. Seeks to develop in congregants the capability of hearing God.

2. Negative Features.

A. Although every soul is of value, should everyone have an equal say in the direction of the congregation? Are the wise and mature to be *outvoted* by a large contingent of new, baby believers. Our hearts recoil at such an idea.

B. Does not recognize the clarity with which the New Covenant Scriptures speak of the appointment of leadership and their authority. Also, this model imposes too literally a formal democratic election procedure, and all the "politics" that involves, on the manner in which the house of God is managed.

THE ELDER PLURALITY MODEL: In this model, the eldership of the local congregation serves as the ultimate spiritual authority. The spiritual leader is respected in his position, inspires direction and leads the meetings of the elders board. Under this model, however, the elders must come to a sense of unity in the spirit (at least a majority) before moving forward in major decision areas. The elders, in this model, are mutually accountable to one another. No one person can assume total power.

Some congregations in this model are given the opportunity to affirm and reaffirm elders periodically after the nomination or renomination of such a person by the elders board.

1. Positive Features.

A. Recognizes the dangers of vesting a level of almost final trust in human beings.

B. Recognizes that no one ever outgrows a need for a level of accountability and mutual submission in their lives.

C. Recognizes the spiritual power of the group coming to *Unity in the Spirit* and hearing from God together.

D. Leaves recourse to congregants to bring charges against leaders in sin and to not reaffirm those leaders who do not perform as unto the Lord.

E. Recognizes the Scripture's teachings of an authority and wisdom vested in the leadership so that the mature and immature do not equally define direction.

F. Fully gives room to those passages which teach submission to leadership (Heb. 13:7 and 17) as well as indicating the value of leaders having the approval of those they lead.

G. Gives full weight to those passages which give a sense of leadership acting in plurality such as (1) Acts 15, The Jerusalem council; and (2) Peter's address to the elders as acting as a plural center of authority (I Pet. 5:1-5).

2. Negative Features.

A. There is a chance of congregants not adequately responding to the leaders of God's choice.

B. The Plural Elders board may become a closed cliquish circle, neither letting in new capable mature leaders or adequately hearing from the congregants.

This discussion is not exhaustive, and does not treat, for example, the presbyterian or episcopal models of congregational authority. However, there are comments which I believe are important for whichever model is chosen.

1. Be open and direct concerning the model of leadership followed in your congregation. Prospective members have a right to know what they are opting for, and should be able to make an informed choice.

2. Have an open system of leadership.

A. Disclose finances; operating secretly creates suspicion and rightly so. First, the fear of criticism should not lead us into a closed style, for it is the place of congregants to show a proper submission in love, and it is the job of leaders to deal with criticism head on, not to adopt a secretive style.

Secondly, where money is spent is an index of the congregation's vision and direction, for which all should pray and work. Thirdly, secret finances can be a temptation to some men who are not capable of handling such in times of difficulty and dip into the reserves in injudicious ways! This has been a downfall of many.

B. Create channels for congregational input and do not dismiss those who disagree in the right spirit.

We have included the Beth Messiah Constitution as an example of this last model (see Appendix).

IV. Planting and Establishing Congregations.

One of the central areas requiring clarification is on how to move a congregation from the planting stage to the full congregational stage.

The planting stage is one in which either a leader or a group senses a call of God to birth a congregation. In this context they begin to study the Scriptures in regard to the structure of congregational life and come to clarity on the issues we discussed above. The very first step, if a planter-leader is not the initiator of the congregation, is to find an adequate leader. Experience has shown that most efforts are bound to dry up if there is not adequate leadership. A leader of a messianic congregation should have a solid knowledge of Scripture, an ability to motivate others, an ability to teach and train, a positive discerning appreciation and understanding of the basics of the Jewish heritage, and a willingness to discipline and exhort. His life should be a positive spiritual example.

At this stage, the leader encourages and gives on-the-job training to others to reach out to the unsaved. He also teaches concerning the vision and direction of the congregation and seeks to disseminate the Word among those who come to his meetings. Numbers should not be the main concern at this point. Rather the concern should be to make soul-winning disciples who are deeply committed to the Lord.

After a time, the leader should identify those with elder potential and give himself to them for special training. They can be given minor responsibility as well. Charles Coleman's *The Master Plan of Evangelism* is helpful in giving the Biblical foundations of this model.

At the time of discerned readiness, when adequate eldership has developed to care for the fledging flock, an organization meeting should be called. The nature of this organization meeting will vary depending upon the congregational model being followed.

Some will choose to have the congregants affirm the constitution as well as the leader's proposed elders. In other settings, the congregation will affirm elders but not the constitution which would become effective through its adoption by the leader and his chosen elders. However, it is important that the congregants be continually informed of the direction of the leadership so as not to feel that any subterfuge has taken place. All should know what they are opting for, and there should be no hidden agenda.

Once this has been accomplished, the leadership as constitutionally stated now seeks to develop the full orbed life of the congregation, bringing forth new leaders as well as the gifts of the members.

V. Growing and Dividing versus the Large Congregation.

A messianic congregation, as with any other congregation, can follow several models of growth. The most common model has been to grow as large as possible. Even numbers in the thousands are considered desirable. This model of growth has several advantages.

1. It minimizes the need for messianic rabbis.

2. It provides a large group for all ages and hence can meet those specific needs.

3. It can provide through a larger pool of people:

A. Excellence in a variety of educational offerings;

B. Excellence in a large music program;

C. Excellence in finding adequate numbers for committees, boards, etc.

4. It provides a powerful visible testimony to the Jewish community.

There are disadvantages, however. As largeness grows, one's sense of personal significance and intimacy with the larger body begins to suffer. Largeness also creates an organizational bureaucracy which is hard for the individual to penetrate. It also requires the building or rental of larger and larger facilities for the work and a heavy emphasis must be given to these concerns.

Large churches have sought to minimize these procedures by dividing the larger group into smaller ministering cells. This is an excellent idea which we greatly encourage. The classes and programs for various groups also break down the anonymity. The gifts of the Spirit may also be practiced at the more intimate level of the cells with the elder leadership providing oversight for such practice. However, we do not want to minimize the difficulties of a large congregation. A large group of lay shepherds must be trained, and it is possible that some of these could lead a congregation in their own right; so the large model may stifle their potential.

The second model is the house group model. Those who perfect this model point to the fact that the New Testament congregations met in houses. They see the house group as maximizing intimacy, the sense of welcome in real fellowship. The gifts of the Spirit in the home atmosphere, Bible study, and prayer are deeply personal. The model has many advantages.

However if each house group is an independent congregation, there are several problems with this model.

1. Each group will need to have adequate leadership. Without adequate leadership, these groups will die. This will require a massive number of leaders, since if a house group grows beyond a certain point it must divide to maintain the ideal.

2. A structure must be developed to create such leadership; will each leader always seek to groom the next leader? Or will there be a cooperative effort under an agreed-upon area leadership.

3. How will the needs of various groupings and ages be met? We have often found single adults and

couples enjoying the house group for a time, but many singles and families with children eventually leave for a fellowship that can provide more adequate programming.

4. How will the house group adequately provide for the cultural expressions of Jewish worship? There is the question of Bar Mitzvahs, messianic weddings, social affairs, the Ark and scrolls, High Holy Day services, etc. We might forego all of this, but do we want to? In our geographical and cultural context such aspects of our congregation have been a great blessing.

The third model is the ideal which we espouse. Through our cell groups, we could survive without a building if necessary, but there are things we desire to do beyond the purely house-group model. Hence our ideal is a moderate congregational size from one to three hundred. Such a congregation is a feasible administrative load. It is large enough to have adequate programs for most groups. However, if broken into smaller ministry groups, it is still an intimate congregation. In this model, there would be few enough cell groups that the leadership could adequately oversee them. Those programs requiring larger numbers could be done in cooperation with a sister congregation. We have found that our congregation is large enough (100 members, 175 attendance) to have a full program of education including a messianic Jewish Day School for grades 1-9, six ministry cells, a Yeshivah extension, a Bar Mitzvah program, a building of our own, etc. Yet we are small enough to be personal. Such a congregation can be looking to train an adequate leader to take over a spin-off sister congregation at a near future time. In their mutual cooperation they can help one another.

Studies of congregational life and growth have shown that most people are on an acquaintance "first name" level with a maximum of fifty people. Therefore, a fellowship of under one hundred is usually intimate. However, many have found one hundred to be a stagnation point because of the limit of recognition, marriage market, etc. Unless a congregation then breaks into smaller ministry groups and trains for outreach and growth beyond one hundred, it will stagnate. Some break into such groups via education programs, etc. without realizing it. The goal of the New Testament is a ministering body, not a weekly rally.

The model we espouse has the following disadvantages:

1. It cannot provide the larger groups for various ages like the bigger congregation, unless it cooperates with a sister congregation.

2. It requires adequate leadership to take control of the spin off congregations (but we believe this is a feasible goal).

We believe that growing and dividing is a healthy model just as bodily cells strengthen the physical human body in growing and dividing. Where the size of the Jewish population warrants it, there should be several messianic congregations in every area.

Some may feel that at a stage in which most messianic congregations are small, we need not concern ourselves with these issues. Yet they are crucial if by faith we expect supernatural growth in the near future.

VI. Four Extremes in Messianic Judaism -- A Section for Leaders.

Messianic Jewish leaders are liable to attack from various sectors in congregational life. A balance of authority and open channels of communication are very important. Our perception has been, however, that rebellion and division has primarily come from four quarters. For want of better terms, we shall describe them as Legalistic Judeans, the Anti-Jewish Jews, the Super-Charismatics and the Anti-Charismatics. Common to all these groups is an attitude problem. We are not speaking against any style of worship or against the variety of viewpoints within Messianic Judaism concerning identification with tradition. We are rather speaking of attitudes which, for various reasons, exhibit lack of love and narrowmindedness.

1. The Legalistic Judeans.

These people parallel that group of pharisees which constantly derided Yeshua and engaged him in debate. In this group, the error is not so much that they hold a strong identification with tradition, as it is their *attitude* in holding it.

A. They get angry and cause strife whenever things in services are done in a new way.

B. They show marks of hypocricy; for example, they may themselves work on the Sabbath while at the same time become outraged at a Jew-Gentile marriage or another minor change from traditional style.

C. They are offended at songs and choruses which they take to be "gentile" even if these songs have a neutral folk style and wouldn't be associated with "churchiness" by Jewish visitors.

D. They constantly criticize the congregation for its level of traditional Jewishness, even if that low level compares favorably with many synagogues.

These people can be a great thorn in the flesh. Remember, we are speaking of a negative attitude and not a view. There are friends who are messianic Jews who live a very Jewish traditional life, but do not exhibit this attitude problem.

The source of this problem is parental harshness and criticism. Through insecurity the person in this mold very often is threatened by whatever is contrary to this parental childhood model. Perhaps as a child he was severely disciplined for minor mistakes in traditional observance. Hence his response to adult freedom in approach to tradition is fear and anger. Yet the same person mistakes being able to do something well in terms of tradition as a mark of real spiritual merit or piety. It is a throwback to parental approval. These reactions are rote copies of childhood response and experiences. This is why there is such hypocrisy and irrationality. The Sabbath-breaker will often be the most vociferous critic in minor traditional areas! Yet it is hard to penetrate such a person. What can be done?

A. Make sure such a person is not put in leadership until he is healed.

B. Seek to counsel such a person with love and to enable him to receive inner healing from his wounds and the idiosyncrasies in behavior that they cause.

C. Help him to understand such key teachings as "freedom in the spirit" and the spirit and truth of the law.

D. Help him to seek repentance and forgiveness for dogmatic judgmental attitudes copied from parental models.

2. The Anti-Jewish Jew.

An equally difficult but opposite problem is the anti-Jewish Jew. Such a person finds Jewish practice and observance to be dead and finds himself or herself bored and angered whenever there is a piece of traditional music, prayer, or teaching on loyalty toward the Jewish heritage. Such a person is displaying something more subtle than the modern "lawless" imbalance which seeks complete amoral "freedom" and total hedonism in the spirit of our age. You might say, regardless of that, what is such a person doing in a Messianic congregation? We shall answer shortly, but unless they are soon helped they won't remain in a Messianic congregation.

In its least severe case, such a person seeks a constant emotional high in entertainment and exhibits no patience for things which require depth in thinking or quiet reflection. Such a person needs to be counseled in regard to the "meat of the word" and the dangers of shallowness.

The worst case is the Jew who was brought up with harsh disciplines and inconsistencies in the home. Jewish things bring memories of a very painful childhood. There is rebellion against the harsh parents and the synagogue teacher who cracked the knuckles. This underlying bitterness and rebellion thwarts spiritual life, leads to self-rejection, and leads to the rejection of Jewish things. There are cases in between as well, where, as a child, Jewish things were boring, empty and externally enforced.

Such persons come to a Messianic congregation because they are from physically Jewish origins. Hence, despite all the above, they are threatened in non-Jewish congregations by the fact that they alone are Jewish. Though they have no patience to appreciate Hebrew, the language of their people, they are uneasy at "First Baptist" too.

Unless these people are kept from leadership and given counsel in love so as to seek God's healing touch, they will continue in an unhappy, "up-down" spiritual roller coaster until they end up rejecting all Jewish identities.

3. The Super-Charismatic.

The Super-Charismatic is one who rebels against all form, discipline, and order. Such people are disruptive and will not hear sound teaching. To subject their prophecy to the body is for them "quenching the Spirit."

There is no patience for the deeper teachings of the Word, of history, or heritage. The bottom line for these folks is very often rebellion against parental authority. They will thus not be under authority in the body either, but will rail against "deadness" in a constant quest for "spiritual highs" and emotional entertainment. Such people may make common cause with the anti-Jewish Jews in opposing authority, discipline, and any traditional identifications in the body.

If such people are willing to receive counsel, there will often be noticed an almost manic-depressive dimension to their spiritual life. It is crucial that they understand their syndrome and repent, seeking the inner healing that is necessary for continued growth.

4. The Anti-Charismatic.

This person fears all expressions of freedom and the gifts of the Spirit in the body. They are horribly offended by any of the immature manifestations which are necessary for the body to grow in Spiritual maturity. Such a person would outlaw *all* spiritual manifestations of freedom altogether to avoid embarrassment.

Perhaps this person was embarrassed in younger years and now cannot tolerate any breach of decorum. He was embarrassed in youth and will not again be so embarrassed either by his own actions or by association. Safety from embarrassment comes from having a tidy and neat and logical plan that can be fully anticipated with no surprises; this means a totally formal approach to worship. Furthermore, such a person often is distant from God. Upon questioning, it is discovered that a real, deep and intimate love between God and the person is absent. Quiet time is a rarety and prayer and faith are not effectively exercised. God is the great but distant "watchmaker" who determines all, so, why pray?

The charismatic, on the other hand, challenges such a person to confront the personal reality of God in his own life. This is too painful!

Often such a person had distant, cool, formal-acting parents. Keep in mind that we are describing the extreme type of anti-charismatic, no one else.

Their need is for counsel, prayer, and healing as in the other cases. The anti-charismatic may often make common cause with the Jewish legalists.

May these thoughts help the Messianic Jewish leaders of congregations to be gentle and kind with all, having a healing objective (see II Timothy 2:22-26; also I Timothy 1:3-11).

10

Practical Help in Congregation Planting and Preaching

By Phillip Goble

CHAVER FELLOW IN BIBLICAL JEWISH STUDIES (FIRST YEAR) TEXTS

BIBLIOGRAPHY

1. Goble, *Everything You Need to Grow a Messianic Yeshiva-Leadership Training for Messianic Judaism*, William Carey Library.

2. Goble, *Everything You Need to Grow a Messianic Synagogue* (William Carey Library, 1705 North Sierra Bonita Avenue, Pasadena, CA 91104, (213) 798-0819, $2.45)

3. Goble, *The Rabbi From Tarsus*, Tyndale Publishers

Recommended

4. Rosen, *Share the New Life With a Jew* (Moody Press, 1977)

5. Adler and Van Doren, *How to Read a Book* (Touchstone Books, Simon and Schuster)

6. Donin, *To Raise a Jewish Child* (Basic Books, 1972)

7. Dimont, *Jews, God and History* (Signet, 1962)

8. Buksbazen, *The Gospel in the Feasts of Israel* (Christian Literature Crusade, Fort Washington, PA 19034)

9. Rosenbaum, *To Live as a Jew* (KTAV Publishing House, 1969)

10. Wittman and Bollman, *Bible Therapy: How the Bible Solves Your Problems: A Guide to God's Word* (Simon and Schuster, 1977)

11. McGavran and Arn, *Ten Steps for Effective Church Growth* (Harper & Row, 1977)

12. Chandler, *The Kennedy Explosion* (Elgin, David C. Cook, 1971. Order from Evangelism Explosion, P.O. Box 23820, Ft. Lauderdale, FL 33307, 781-7710)

13. McIntyre, *Big Ideas for Small Sunday Schools* (Baker Book House, 1977); also Word of Life Catalogue, GPH, 1445 Boonville Ave., Springfield, MO 65802

Recommended Reference Books

14. Strong's *Exhaustic Concordance of the Bible* (Abingdon, Nashville, New York)

15. Jay Green, Sr.'s *The Interlinear Bible*, 4 volumes (Religious Book Discount House, P. O. Box 1161 C, Evansville, IN 47713 (812) 464-2569)

Also Required

12 Book Report forms completed

12 Biblical Survey entries completed

12 Visitation forms completed

10 Symposiums attended

CHAVER FELLOW IN BIBLICAL JUDAISM (SECOND YEAR)

Bibliography and Requirements

Prerequisite: Certification as *Chaver Fellow in Biblical Jewish Studies.*

Required

1. Gartenhaus, *Winning Jews to Christ* (Sword of the Lord Publishers, Murfreesboro, TN 37130)

2. Chill, *The Mitzvot: The Commandments and Their Rationale*, Keter Publishing House, Jerusalem, 1974

Recommended

3. Heilman, *Synagogue Life* (University of Chicago, 1977)

4. Towns, *The Successful Sunday School and Teacher's Guidebook* (Creation House, Carol Stream, IL)

5. Kitov, *The Jew and His Home* (Shengold Publishers, 1963)

6. Coleman, *The Master Plan of Evangelism* (Fleming H. Revell Company, New Jersey, 1963)

7. R. C. Sproul, *Objections Answered* (Gospel Light, Glendale, CA, 1978)

8. Green, *Why Churches Die* (Bethany Fellowship, 1972)

9. Tanenbaum, Wilson & Rubin, eds. *Evangelicals and Jews in Conversation* (Baker, 1978)

10. McNair, *The Birth, Care, and Feeding of a Local Church* (Canon Press, 1971)

11. Green, Michael, *Evangelism in the Early Church* (Eerdmans, 1970)

12. Aron, Robert, *The Jewish Jesus* (Maryknoll, New York: Orbis Books, 1971)

13. Donin, *To Be a Jew*, Basic Books, 1972.

Recommended Reference Books

New International Version Bible

The Open Bible, Nelson Bible Publishers

Also Required

12 Book Report forms completed

12 Biblical Survey entries completed

12 Visitation forms completed

10 Symposiums attended

CHAVER FELLOW IN BIBLICAL RABBINIC STUDIES (THREE YEAR SUPPLEMENTAL READING TO COINCIDE WITH ORDINATION REQUIREMENTS)

Bibliography

Prerequisites: See *Chaver Fellow in Biblical Jewish Studies* and *Chaver Fellow in Biblical Judaism.*

Recommended

1. Engstrom and Dayton, *The Art of Management for Christian Leaders,* (Word Books, 1976)
2. Gordon, *Leader Effectiveness Training* (Wyden Books, 1977)
3. Bower, *Solving Problems in Marriage* (Eerdmans, 1972)
4. Turnbull, *Baker's Dictionary of Practical Theology* (Baker Book House, 1967)
5. Martha Zimmerman, *Celebrate the Feasts of the Old Testament in Your Own Home or Church,* (Bethany House, 1981)
6. Goldberg, Louis, *Our Jewish Friends* (Moody Press, Chicago, 1977)
7. Goldin, Hyman, Hamadrikh, *The Rabbi's Guide,* (Hebrew Publishing Company, 77-79 Delaney Street, New York)
8. *New Bible Dictionary* (Eerdmans)
9. *New Bible Commentary* (Eerdmans)
10. Adler and Van Doren, *Great Treasury of Western Thought* (R. R. Bowker Co., New York, 1977)
11. *The Jewish Catalogue*
12. *The Second Jewish Catalogue*
13. Hertz *Authorized Daily Prayerbook*
14. Hertz *Pentateuch and Haftorahs*
15. Strong's *Exhaustive Concordance*

16. Jay Green, Sr., *The Interlinear Bible,* 4 volumes

17. Englishman's *Hebrew and Chaldee Concordance*

18. New Brown, Driver and Briggs, *Hebrew and English Lexicon*

19. New Englishman's *Greek-English Concordance*

20. New Thayer's *Greek English Lexicon*

21. *Thompson Chain Reference Bible*

22. *Information Please Almanac*

23. *The Doubleday Rogets Thesaurus in Dictionary Form,* Doubleday, New York, 1977

24. Webster's *New Collegiate Dictionary*

25. Abraham Mayer Heller, *The Vocabulary of Jewish Life*

26. Idlesohn, *Jewish Liturgy and Its Development*

27. Werblowsky and Wigoder, eds., *The Encyclopedia of the Jewish Religion*

28. Keil and Delitzch, *Commentaries on the Old Testament*

29. Robert Nicoll, *The Expositor's Greek Testament*

30. *The New Testament in Hebrew and English*

31. Coopersmith, *The Songs We Sing*

32. A. Dana Adams, *Four Thousand Questions & Answers on the Bible,* A. J. Holman Co., Phil., PA

33. Lawrence Crabb, *Basic Principles of Biblical Counseling,* Zondervan, 1977.

34. Lawrence Crabb, *Effective Biblical Counseling,* Zondervan

35. Tracy D. Connor, *The Non-Profit Organization Handbook,* McGraw Hill, 1980

36. William Proctor, *The Born-Again Christian Catalog,* M. Evans, 1979 distributed to Christian Bookstores by Fleming Revel

37. Harry Gersch, *Sacred Books of the Jews,* Stein & Day, 1972

38. Eric Werner, ed. *Sacred Bridge: Liturgical Parallels in Synagogue and Early Church,* Schocken, 1970

39. R. J. Zwi Werblowsky and Geoffrey Wigoder, *The Encyclopedia of the Jewish Religion,* Holt Rinehart and Winston, 1966

40. D. Stern, *Jewish New Testament,* Box 1045, Pasadena, CA, 91101

41. Donin, *To Pray As A Jew,* (Basic Books)

BOOK REPORT FORM -- ANALYSIS

1. What kind of book is this? Describe the nature of the subject matter (Interpretation, Congregation Growth, History, etc.). ______________________________
____

2. Very briefly, state what the whole book is about. ____
____

3. Study the table of contents or the chapter headings. Very briefly, state what each chapter or major division is about. ______________________________
____
____

4. Define the unsolved problem that the author may have believed created the need for his writing this particular book. ______________________________
____

INTERPRETATION

1. What are the author's key words in the heart of the book's message and what do these words mean to the author? ______________________________
____

2. What are the leading propositions (truths the author intends his book to demonstrate) in the author's most important sentences (the heart of the book's message)?
____
____

3. Where are the key arguments in the book? Give page numbers and quote briefly. ______________________
____

4. Which problems did the author solve? ______________
____

5. To your knowledge, was the author's treatment of his subject uninformed, misinformed, illogical or incomplete at any point? What page? Quote briefly.
____
____
____

6. What did you gain from the book in terms of your own cultural credibility in Jewish ministry or in your own Biblical knowledge that will help you minister to Jewish people? ______________________________________
____
____

A PRELIMINARY CONGREGATIONAL DESIGN

BE IT RESOLVED THAT the fellowship called ____________ has the following purpose for being: to call out and build up for service the chosen people of God in the true Biblical Judaism of our Fathers in order to fulfill the Great Commission, locally and world-wide; to propagate in the community of __________(city), __________(state) the spiritual values of Israel in order that our children will not depart from our God-given heritage as Jews.

BE IS RESOLVED THAT the fellowship called ____________

HAS THE FOLOWING GOALS:	HAS THE FOLLOWING STRATEGIES FOR THE GOALS:
To cooperate with like-minded synagogues in creating a viable Jewish people movement for the spiritual and cultural survival of our Jewish people;	To participate in a monthly inter-Temple function and an annual inter-Temple Passover service as well as such other activities that may seem productive (inter-Temple School of Rabbinic studies, youth camp, young singles retreat, etc.) for the creation and sustenance of a Jewish people movement;
To increase our constituency at the rate of at least ____ a year (____ a month);	To institute a program of Jewish lay training and visitation ministry;
To achieve financial sovereignty within five years so that funds can be available to raise up a daughter synagogue before that time;	To institute a stewardship lay committee and to cooperate with it in implementing a specially designed stewardship program for our synagogue;
To contribute prayer and tangible support to the work of the Great Commission in the diaspora and in the nation of Israel;	To institute a congregational and inter-Temple strategy to effectively implement strategies for synagogue planting in both the diaspora and in the nation of Israel and for non-Jewish Messianic people movements in our local area, the U.S. and abroad;

To provide a program to meet the needs of the whole man and the entire family as well as the special purpose needs of the Jewish community.

To implement strategies for meeting the social, physical, recreational, and spiritual-liturgical needs of our local community.

HOW TO USE THE BOOK
EVERYTHING YOU NEED TO GROW A MESSIANIC SYNAGOGUE

The chapters of the book, *Everything You Need to Grow a Messianic Synagogue*, are written as tracts to be distributed to people individually rather than the entire book at one time. The underlying idea is that people come to growth in spiritual matters gradually, that a person who is first interested and oriented into Biblical Judaism can then be taken step by step all the way until he is a worker in Biblical Judaism. Therefore, the first chapter is intended primarily for inquirers; the second chapter, for seekers.

The third chapter, "The Cost of Commitment in Messianic Judaism," is intended for people who are actually preparing to make their decision ceremonially, that is they are ready to take the mikveh. Before they are taken into the water they are read the first part of the chapter, and after they get out of the water they are given the last part of the chapter, which contains a membership application and explanation. This part of the chapter should be supplemented by the message, "Building with Silver and Gold."

The fourth chapter, "A Messianic Synagogue Member's Manual," should be given to the new member in a binder bearing the name of the Temple when he comes forward to be formally received into membership in the congregation through extension of the right hand of fellowship. This binder should also contain the appendix because members of the Temple should know something about the types of materials used to train members to become workers (teachers, prayer group leaders, bus ministers, phone ministers, and visitation ministers).

In the appendix there is a section on how to conduct a Jewish Home Bible study and a bibliography for a Home Bible study teacher. It should be emphasized that a Jewish Home Bible study is not an end in itself but a means to a larger end which is that of a congregation. In other words, the Bible studies should be satellites of congregations or a larger fellowship rather than independent entities. The reason for this is that little groups that have no connection to larger groups tend to go off on tangents and even can fall into error. Therefore, the Bible teachers and prayer group leaders of these smaller groups should have meetings on a monthly or frequent basis with the leaders of the larger fellowships in order that there will be a measure of coherency in the Biblical truth that is being disseminated. If these group leaders want the privilege of teaching and having others teachable to them, they should also accept the responsibility of being teachable to others who are over them in the Lord.

The book, *Everything You Need to Grow a Messianic Synagogue,* is a library of tracts that can be given one by one to people so that they can move as the Holy Spirit leads them through the continuum from inquirer to worker. That is why page 178 in the book explains how to set up a file so that people can be processed through from inquirer to worker as they are led by the Holy Spirit. The reason for this file is that it's very important to keep careful records of people. The Lord has required of us that we be good stewards not only of our time and of our money but of *His people!* This is why attendance sheets are so important for the Bible studies and even for congregational meetings, so that when someone is absent, their absence is noticed and they are contacted via post card, telephone, or visitation. Only in this way will they know that people care about them. If they do not know this, they will not come back.

That's why it's important to keep correspondence going between the leaders and all the people, which involves regular letters, post cards, newsletters, phone calls, etc.

Obviously, no one man can visit all the people. However, if he is a good executive and if he has cooperation, a leader can help to coordinate other people to help him do visitation by having a regular weekly night of visitation in which he goes out with perhaps just one person in the beginning, but later on, goes out training people to train others to visit people. Also, he can sit down at different times during the week and do phone ministry with other people that he is training to do this so that he can then delegate to them people to telephone. Also, he can sit down with other people and deal with them about how to help him with correspondence, post cards, newsletters, or whatever he may be sending out. It's extremely important in starting a Bible study to spread the word around via the mail and phone and also to remind all the people who came to keep coming. This is why attendance records, guest sheets, addresses, zip codes, and phone numbers are extremely important, probably as important as anything that is taught or studied, since there can be no follow up without this information.

On page 178 in the book there are two types of files that are described. There is a file in which all the names can be put under one of five divisions: Wait, Transfer, Personal Visit, Letter, or Already Committed. When a name comes into the file, it is processed through to either Letter or Already Committed after so many times of Waiting or Transferring or Visiting. This way a person has a real opportunity to get committed before he is passed over. All the names can be put in this file and all the names can be moved through these five file divisions on individual file cards.

The other type of file is the Binder Index File which is a record of a particular individual's binder, which document he has read, when they were assigned to him, and which documents he has not read. In helping to spiritually educate someone from Inquirer to Worker, a binder can be set aside and assigned to him or her by number, which is recorded and filed in the Binder Index Files. Each time he is given a new portion to read, it is checked out of his binder and notated on the file, because each binder can be given a number and that same number can appear on all the sections of the binder. If Joe Schwartz is given binder #53 and #53 is put on all five of the sections of the book, *Everything You Need to Grow a Messianic Synagogue,* when the Binder Librarian looks at his card, she can see that he still has chapter 1 of #53 and has had it for three weeks. Someone can then be assigned to call him or visit him to get him to return it and either drop out or keep reading, beginning at the next section.

It's important to be very consistent and very thorough in dealing with cross-cultural persuasion where there is a prejudice barrier. Without this thoroughness and care about details there are many people who will be carelessly slipped over and will not be given the attention that the Word of God would have us give people for whom the Messiah died.

PREPARATION FOR VISITING PEOPLE

A. RECRUITMENT OF VISITORS (SURVEYORS) should be done by individual invitation, rather than general announcement, and in terms of a planned program of regular visitation.

B. TRAINING OF VISITORS (SURVEYORS) has three aspects.

1. Instruction:

   Workers must be trained on a regular weekly basis in how to relate the Word of God to the needs of people by means of the Holy Spirit.

2. Homework Assignments:

   An outline and a list of accompanying Scriptures must be learned along with supplemental Scriptures for refutation and ministry to special needs.

3. On-the-Job Training:

   Yeshua said, "Follow me." He did not only lecture or exhort in the synagogue or temple; he *took* trainees *two* by *two* and little by little reproduced himself in them as a "playing coach." Then in the Great Commission of Mt. 28:19, he commands his followers to go and do likewise. The gross failure in much congregational growth and in much of our educational models is at just this point. *We lecture, we don't train on-the-job.* James Kennedy took two observers with him once a week for three months. Then each became a leader taking two more observers for another three months. This pattern worked because it follows the Scriptural principles that Yeshua taught in the New Covenant for his workers to use in training other workers, namely: selection, association, consecration, impartation, demonstration, delegation, supervision, reproduction. For an excellent explanation of these, read Robert E. Coleman's, *The Master Plan of Evangelism* (Fleming H. Revell Company, Old Tappan, New Jersey, 1963).

   All workers must have a system of reporting the results of their labors to a coordinator who can oversee their total effort and insure that every visit or contact is properly prayed over, reviewed, followed up and moved forward as far as possible on the continuum of Inquirer-Seeker-Disciple-Member-Worker.

C. POTENTIAL PEOPLE TO CONTACT:

1. Those who visit the congregations

2. Those who see the drama programs

3. Those who attend the Passover and other special affairs

4. Parents of children contacted

5. New residents in the community (see listing of those buying new homes)

6. Family and friend referrals of people known to the congregations

7. Jewish names in the geographically arranged telephone book via telephone survey

8. House-to-house survey

9. Bus worker survey

10. Campus survey

11. Prayer group invitations

12. Bible study invitations

13. Street literature distribution

Visitation ministry cannot be done by worldly people or methods, but only by people whose hearts are sensitively and prayerfully full of the love of the Lord. When speaking to a person about spiritual matters, always remember that he was created by God and God loves him. Therefore, no matter what he says, we must still treat him with love, courtesy, respect, and consideration.

Before we can help another person move forward in spiritual matters, we must first know where the Lord has brought him so far. If he is only a casual inquirer and has not yet given his heart to the Lord, we should not discuss the deeper teachings that only a member or worker would be ready to handle (like tithing, supporting outreach projects, etc.). Therefore, we must listen and ask questions to determine the point of spiritual apprehension the person has already attained before we endeavor (prayerfully) to minister to that person. Otherwise, we may try to deal with a person in an area where God has not yet prepared him to receive our words. The questions on the survey on page 175 will help you determine something about the person's degree of spiritual apprehension.

TERMINOLOGY

Always consider the area of Jewish sensitivities when sharing the Messiah. Many words should often be substituted to avoid offense or wrong interpretation. Keep in mind that many of the people to whom you will be witnessing may have at one time or another been accused of killing Christ. It is not easy for them to overcome bad impressions that were created in their childhood by insensitive people who did not understand God's plan for the Jewish people. Remember, too, that the Jewish person with whom you are sharing the Messiah is not used to your gospel vocabulary. The word, church is stereotyped among most Jews and they think of only one church -- the Catholic church. Use the word, congregation, instead. The term, Holy Spirit, is something Jewish people think the Gentiles invented. Use the term, Spirit of God, in place of it. Your aim is to make the Good News clear, to express it in fresh words untainted with old, embittered concepts. A euphemism is a less offensive term. Here are a list of some euphemisms that may be helpful to you in expressing your faith to a Jewish person.

OFFENSIVE PHRASES (FOR JEWISH PEOPLE) AND POSSIBLE EUPHEMISMS

Cross - The tree of sacrifice

Christian - Bible believer, messianic believer

The Jews - Some of the Jewish people (watch anti-semitic suggestion in over-generalization about the Jewish people)

Christianity - The true messianic faith, true Biblical Judaism, Judaism for all peoples, the true Scriptural faith of the Jews, the true Jewish faith

Christ - Messiah, Mashiach, the Holy One of Israel, the Anointed One

Church - Local congregation, or (if used in the universal sense) the world-wide congregation of the Messiah's people, or the messianic assembly

Denomination - fellowship

Saved - rescued

Deacons - Shamashim

Pastor - Spiritual leader

Jesus - Yeshua

Old Testament - Tenach, Old Covenant

New Testament - New Covenant

Gospel - Good News

Missions - World outreach

Missionary - World outreach minister

Evangelist - Minister of proclamation

Christian friends - Messianic brothers

The Christian Church - The messianic community (local or universal)

John the Baptist - John the immersionist, Jochanan Ha Matbeel (Hebrew)

Saviour - Redeemer, Messiah

Bible - Jewish Scriptures (the Bible is often thought of as a Gentile-distorted book because it is not understood that the New Testament is a Jewish document)

Jehovah - The Lord (considered irreverent to say "Jehovah")

Conversion - Change of heart toward God

To be converted - Have a change of heart toward God

Christian Gospel - Messianic Good News

Gentile - Non-Jew

Baptize - Immerse or give a mikveh of repentance

Baptism - Immersion, mikveh of repentance

Lord's Supper - Lord's Seder

New converts - Adherents, new believers

Evangelize - Take the Good News to

Saints - Messianic believers

The Christian message - The messianic message, the Word of God

Jesus Christ - Yeshua the Messiah or Yeshua ha Mashiach

The blood of the cross - The death of God's paschal lamb

Sunday School - Religious school

Such a list may at first seem overwhelming. So much to remember! It's so difficult to witness to a Jewish person! Not really. Most people believe that Jewish people are all Bible experts, but the truth is that -- like most Gentiles -- many have never read the Bible, or at least have never studied it. If they ask forceful questions, it may be that they really want to know, and are not merely arguing. Many of the old walls of prejudice and resistance are crumbling, and Jewish people are more open to the claims of Yeshua of Nazareth now than ever, especially in these fearful times! One does not have to be eloquent in terminology or an expert in Judaism to gain an interested hearing for the Good News from our Jewish friends in these last days. Therefore, the following section on answering objections and the Good News presentation we have outlined should be especially useful in sharing our very Jewish faith.

APOLOGETICS (DEFENSE OF OUR FAITH)

OBJECTION #1: *What about the Crusades and the Spanish Inquisition and all the hurt that has been perpetrated against the Jewish people in the name of Christ?*

ANSWER: Not all Christians in name are true believers in fact. Not all Gentiles are truly followers of the Messiah. Those who follow the Messiah ought to live as he lived (I John 2:6). The fact that religious men have failed only proves that religion is not enough.

We must be born again, into a new spiritual existence, become new creations.

The Messiah died to *save* his Jewish people -- he has proven his love in this irrefutable way. Nothing anyone, even one of his ignorant followers, can do will ever change such proof. Those in whom the Messiah fully lives cannot hate or intentionally hurt our Jewish people. In Galatians 3:13 Paul makes it clear that Messiah's death is a curse *for* the Jewish people, not a curse *against* them.

OBJECTION #2: *I don't need it, and I don't buy it.*

ANSWER: It's not for sale, it's a gift. But we must renounce self righteousness, self sufficiency, and self centeredness or we will never realize our unfelt need until it's too late. (Ps. 53:3; Isa. 53:6, 11; Jer. 8:20; Dan. 12:2; Isa. 55:1)

OBJECTION #3: *Death is only a natural phenomenon, not also the result of sin.*

ANSWER: Ezekiel 18:4 says, "The soul that sins, it shall die."

OBJECTION #4: *Then why don't our teachers believe this?*

ANSWER: The Bible is well aware of their unbelief, which the Scripture predicts (Isaiah 53:1-3). You must seek the truth yourself and not allow yourself to be misled or you -- like them -- will be responsible (Isa. 43:27; Ezek. 34:2).

OBJECTION #5: *I'm already Jewish.*

ANSWER: Yes, but not Jewish enough to please God, who has the criteria you must meet. To be truly Jewish, you must be in good covenant standing with God. Since the Old Covenant (contract) can no longer be kept now that the Temple sacrifices have ceased, you cannot be a true covenant-keeping Jew in God's sense of the word "Jew" without the New Covenant prophesied by Jeremiah. Read Jeremiah 31:31-34 and Deuteronomy 18:19.

OBJECTION #6: *I don't believe in hell.*

ANSWER: Neither did Adolf Hitler. Are you putting yourself in his company -- forever? Daniel 12:2 says that God says there is a hell. One of the surest ways of going there is to call God a liar. Your belief about hell won't help you escape it.

OBJECTION #7: *We believe in one God, not three.*

ANSWER: We believe in one God, who sent his Word as the Messiah to heal us (Ps. 107:20; Isa. 42:6-7) and his Spirit to give us a new birth (Ezek. 18:31-32). The Trinity is found in the Jewish Bible in Isa. 48:16 and Gen. 1:26. The Holy Spirit is mentioned in I Samuel 10:6; Micah 3:8; Psalm 51:11; Isaiah 63:14; the Son of God in Psalm 2:7 and Proverbs 30:4.

OBJECTION #8: *The virgin birth is impossible.*

ANSWER: Jeremiah 32:27. Do you not believe the story of Isaac's birth, either? The Messiah's way of entering life was no more supernatural than his way of overcoming death. The Jewish Bible predicts his return will also be supernatural (Daniel 7:13-14). The Hebrew word for "virgin" in Isaiah 7:14 (almah) was certainly understood by the orthodox rabbis who translated the Old Testament into the Greek Septuagint 200 years before the New Testament times. These Jews translated the Hebrew word into the Greek word for virgin. Can anyone in the 20th century claim to know the original meaning of the Hebrew word better than these ancient and revered orthodox rabbis?

OBJECTION #9: *If this is true, why are we blamed for the death of Jesus?*

ANSWER: The New Testament teaches that Gentiles killed Yeshua (Matthew 27:27-32) but that we *all* are sinners, Jews and Gentiles alike, and the sins of all of us have required his death to pay the penalty for our sin. So we are all responsible (Acts 4:27; Isaiah 53:6) and cannot be cleared of our guilt until we obey the Lord and become his students (disciples).

OBJECTION #10: *But what about all the hypocrites?*

ANSWER: They will get theirs (Luke 13:26-27). But we must make sure we won't be with them. This means we must turn from ourselves and trustfully obey the Lord. If we rebel, we are hypocrites, too, and will share their fate.

OBJECTION #11: *Sorry, I'm orthodox.*

ANSWER: You are not orthodox enough. Read Leviticus 17:11 and tell me how you can be orthodox without a blood sacrifice. Who is more orthodox, the one who obeys Leviticus 17:11 or the one who does not? The one who has a high priest (Psalm 110:4) or the one who does not? The one who has a kaporrah (guilt offering of blood) or the one who does not? You are by no means orthodox enough in the Biblical sense which is more important than the Talmudic sense of orthodoxy.

OBJECTION #12: *How can you say you are Jews when you don't follow the Talmud?*

ANSWER: We are not Talmudic Jews, we are Biblical Jews. We do not believe in Talmudic Judaism, we believe in Biblical Judaism. We don't believe in burdening men with man-made teachings (Matthew 23:4) or making void the doctrines of God by the precepts of men (Isaiah 29:13; Matthew 15:8-9). But our religion has not changed. It is still Judaism, though Biblical and not Talmudic.

OBJECTION #13: *All my friends will be in hell, and we'll have a good time.*

ANSWER: You won't see them. Hell is a place of outer darkness, pain, and torment (Matthew 8:12; Isaiah 66:24).

OBJECTION #14: *Whoever came back from heaven or hell to tell anyone what it is like?*

ANSWER: Yeshua. See John 8:42; 14:2; I Peter 3:19.

OBJECTION #15: *I don't believe in God.*

ANSWER: God's existence is seen in the order of nature (Romans 1:19-20). The Bible says that only fools would jump to the unreasonable conclusion that Chance caused the order of the world (an absurd, foolish conclusion that is obviously impossible). See Psalm 14:1.

OBJECTION #16: *I don't believe the Bible is God's Word, it's only a book written by men.*

ANSWER: It's clearly a supernaturally inspired book, whose human authors demonstrate by their agreement that their common source was God. There is no other book like the Bible in the world, because no other supposedly "divine" book is able to actually produce what the Bible is: a book in which God makes his will infallibly known by predicting history through prophets and confirming history through eye witnesses and written records (Isa. 53; I Cor. 15:1-8). What other God can do this but the God of the Jewish Bible (Isaiah 41:23)? Look at the predictions that have come true in our own time regarding the nation of Israel (Isaiah 11:12; Jer. 16:14, 15).

OBJECTION #17: *Isaiah 53 is not talking about the Messiah, it's talking about Israel.*

ANSWER: Can Israel die for Israel? The Scriptures say that everyone must die for his own sin (Ezek. 18:1-4).

OBJECTION #18: *That's right. I must die for me, not some mediator. No mere man can die for another man* (Ps. 49:7-9).

ANSWER: He was no mere man (Isa. 9:6).

OBJECTION #19: *We Jews do not worship men. You've turned a man into an idol. You're no longer a Jew.*

ANSWER: We Jews worship God through his Word, which is the way to God. And his Word became the Messiah who is the way to God. We are told to worship his Word with praise (Ps. 56:10).

OBJECTION #20: *What about the good and innocent people who never heard about the Messiah?*

ANSWER: The Scripture specifically states that no people are good and innocent. "There is no one who is righteous, no not one," according to Psalm 14:3. But if a person has never heard of the Messiah, he will not be judged guilty for that, but for rejecting the Father of whom he has heard. "The heavens declare the glory of God; and the firmament showeth his handiwork." (Psalm 19:1). Creation and conscience speak to every person of the glory and the holiness of the Father, but all people invariably tend to exchange the truth for a lie (Romans 1:19-25; John 8:42) and by going their own way, deserve death. Absolutely no one deserves, for any reason, salvation. However, the rejected Father has mercifully sent his Son (also rejected) who sends us (and we are often rejected, too). But the Great Commission (Matthew 28:19-20) is that all believers do all they can to help the proclamation of the Good News reach every person in the remotest part of the earth. For it is not God's will that any should perish (II Peter 3:9), and God takes no pleasure in the death of the wicked (Ezekiel 33:11).

OBJECTION #21: *How can there be a God, or how can he be good, when there is so much evil? Why does God let evil go unpunished?*

ANSWER: God has already punished all the evil of all men by mercifully directing his fury against part of himself that he sent among us as a man to take our punishment in our place and give us a way of escape from God's anger against evil. This one is Yeshua, who fulfills all these Messianic prophecies in the Tenach predicted hundreds of years before Yeshua was born!

Messiah to be the Son of David	Psalm 132:11
to be a prophet like Moses	Deuteronomy 18:15, 19
to be the Son of God	Psalm 2:7; Proverbs 30:4
to be raised from the dead	Psalm 16:10; Isaiah 53:10
to be crucified	Psalm 22; 69:21
to be betrayed by a friend	Psalm 41:9
to be rejected	Psalm 118:22-23; Isa. 8:14-15; Isaiah 28:16
to be born of a virgin	Isaiah 7:14
to minister to Gentiles	Isaiah 42:1
to pay the penalty for sins to make men whole	Isaiah 52:13-53:12
to bring in a New Covenant	Isaiah 42:6; 55:3-4; Jer.31:31-34
to be called "the Lord"	Jeremiah 23:5-6
to come before the Temple & Jerusalem are destroyed (70 A.D.)	Daniel 9:24-26
to be born in Bethlehem	Micah 5:2
to bring the coming of the Holy Spirit	Isa. 11:2; 42:1; Joel 2:28

God has not allowed the evil of this world to occur without warning his people. In Deuteronomy 18:18-19, God warns that when a law-giver-prophet like Moses comes, the people will be "cut off" (punished) if they do not listen to him. In other words, to disobey the Messiah is to reap eternal disaster. Then, in Deuteronomy 28:15-68 all the horrors of the Holocaust are predicted if God's people do not obey him. THE BETTER QUESTION IS NOT: WHY DOES GOD LET EVIL GO UNPUNISHED, BUT IS, WHY DO PEOPLE INSIST ON DOING EVIL AND TAKING THEIR OWN ETERNAL PUNISHMENT FOR IT WHEN THEY COULD STOP DOING EVIL AND LET YESHUA TAKE THEIR PUNISHMENT? CAN YOU THINK OF ANY GOOD REASON WHY YOU WOULDN'T WANT YESHUA TO TAKE YOUR PUNISHMENT RATHER THAN FOR YOU TO HAVE TO SUFFER ETERNALLY YOURSELF?

GOOD NEWS PRESENTATION
(THE ROMANS OUTLINE IN THE JEWISH BIBLE---CONDENSED)

LEAD-IN QUESTION: "Let me ask your opinion...God forbid, but if you passed on tonight and met your maker, do you know for sure that his judgment of you would be favorable?"

PERMISSION QUESTION: "Would you like me to quickly tell you how the Jewish Bible answers that question?...it's really wonderful!"

THE GOOD NEWS IN THE JEWISH BIBLE IS THIS:

1. ALL OF US WILL INDEED LIVE AGAIN TO MEET OUR MAKER (DANIEL 12:2).

> Many of those who have already died *will live again:* some will enjoy *eternal life* and some will suffer eternal disgrace. (Daniel 12:2)

2. HOWEVER, ALL OF US DESERVE GOD'S PUNISHMENT FOR REBELLIOUSLY GOING OUR OWN WAY INSTEAD OF GOD'S WAY IN HIS WORD (ISAIAH 53:6).

> All of us were like sheep that were lost, each of us going *his own way.* But the Lord made the punishment fall on him (the Messiah), the punishment all of us deserved. (Isaiah 53:6)

3. THE GOOD NEWS IS THIS:
OUR JEWISH BIBLE PREDICTED THAT THE MESSIAH WOULD TAKE OUR PUNISHMENT SO THAT WE CAN BE SET FREE FROM THE PUNISHMENT WE DESERVE (ISAIAH 53:5)

> But because of our sins he was wounded, beaten because of the evil we did. *We are healed by the punishment he suffered,* made whole by the blows he received. (Isaiah 53:5)

> By the Word of the Lord were the heavens made...(Psalm 33:6); God sent his Word (the Messiah), and healed them, and delivered them from death (Psalm 107:20).

4. OUR JEWISH BIBLE PREDICTED THAT THE MESSIAH WOULD RISE FROM THE DEAD SO THAT WE CAN KNOW HIM, THE RIGHTEOUS ONE, AND BE JUDGED RIGHTEOUS BY GOD (ISAIAH 53:8, 10, 11).

> He (the Messiah) was put to death for the sins of our people...when he makes himself an offering for sin...the Lord shall prolong his life...*and the righteous one (the Messiah) will make many to be judged righteous by knowing him* and he shall bear the penalty of their guilt. (Isaiah 53:8, 10, 11)

5. YOU CAN KNOW FOR SURE RIGHT NOW THAT GOD WILL JUDGE YOU FAVORABLY WHEN YOU PASS ON--NOT BY YOUR OWN RIGHTEOUSNESS (PSALMS 14:3), BUT BY FAITH IN THE MESSIAH, GOD'S RIGHTEOUS ONE (HABAKKUK 2:4).

> There is none righteous, no not one. (Psalm 14:3)
>
> The righteous shall live by faith. (Habakkuk 2:4)
>
> Behold the days are coming, says the Lord, when I will make a new covenant with the house of Israel and the house of Judah...I will put my law within them, and I will write it upon their hearts. (Jeremiah 31:31, 33)
>
> Behold, I stand at the door and knock; if any one hears my voice and opens the door, I will come in to him and dine with him and he with me. (Revelation 3:20)

6. YOU CAN PRAY THIS PRAYER:
GOD OF ISRAEL, I AM JEW AND I AM GOING TO DIE A JEW. BUT I ADMIT THAT I--LIKE EVERYONE--HAVE SINNED AND GONE MY OWN WAY, INSTEAD OF YOUR WAY, IN YOUR WORD. I HAVE RELIED ON MY OWN UNDERSTANDING RATHER THAN ACKNOWLEDGING YOUR WILL. I HAVE RELIED ON MY OWN RIGHTEOUSNESS, RATHER THAN TRUSTING YOUR RIGHTEOUS WORD. I THANK YOU, LORD, THAT THE WORD THAT CAME TO MOSES CAME IN THE

MESSIAH FROM NAZARETH TO OVERCOME DEATH AND LEAD ME TO GOD. COME INTO MY LIFE, RIGHTEOUS MESSIAH. FORGIVE MY SINS THROUGH YOUR DEATH IN MY PLACE. MAKE ME RIGHTEOUS BY KNOWING YOU, LORD YESHUA OF NAZARETH, MY MESSIAH. AMEN.

KEY QUESTION: "Does that prayer make sense to you?"

CLOSING QUESTION: "Don't you want to pray this prayer with me right now?"

ASSURANCE QUESTIONS (AFTER YOU PRAY THE PRAYER TOGETHER):

"IS MESSIAH YESHUA TRUSTWORTHY WHEN HE PROMISES HE'LL COME INTO YOUR LIFE IF YOU ASK HIM TO?"

"DIDN'T YOU JUST ASK MESSIAH YESHUA TO COME INTO YOUR LIFE?"

"IS MESSIAH YESHUA IN YOUR LIFE RIGHT NOW?"

BEHOLD, I (YESHUA) AM WITH YOU ALWAYS, EVEN UNTIL THE END OF THE AGE. (MATTHEW 28:20)

NOW WHAT ???

7. IF YOU WISH TO GROW AND REMAIN IN YOUR KNOWLEDGE OF THE RIGHTEOUS ONE MESSIAH YESHUA (IN ORDER THAT GOD WILL CONTINUE TO JUDGE YOU RIGHTEOUS), YOU MUST BE FAITHFUL IN STUDY AND FELLOWSHIP IN A CONGREGATION WHERE THE JEWISH BIBLE IS BELIEVED AND FAITHFULLY TAUGHT (PSALMS 84:4; HEBREWS 10:25-27).

> Happy are those who dwell in thy house, ever singing thy praise! (Psalm 84:4)
>
> Do not stay away from our meetings, as some do, but rather come encourage one another; for if we willfully persist in disobedience after receiving the knowledge of the truth, no sacrifice remains: only a fearful prospect of judgment and a fierce fire which will consume God's enemies" (Heb. 10:25-27).

> We know that we have passed from death unto life, because we love the brethren (other believers in Yeshua). (I John 3:14)

SOME THINGS TO DO: 1) Meet other Jewish believers and stay in touch with sincere Bible believers whose godly lives reflect their true faith in our Jewish Bible. 2) Realizing you are a new believer who may not yet know fully what has happened to you, walk softly and do not criticize Judaism or your family's beliefs and practices. 3) Understand that your life will not be easy and perfect always just because you are a believer. 4) Keep your eyes on the Lord and not upon people, whose failings would steal your joy. 5) Avoid every kind of evil, even the appearance of evil. 6) Worry about nothing, but involve yourself fully in meditation on and study of God's Word in order to find wisdom and strength to participate in God's Work. 7) Watch in prayer that you would not fall into temptation or into an unfruitful life.

WHAT SHOULD I PRAY FOR?: Some of the things to pray for are: 1) the peace of Jerusalem (Psalm 122:6); 2) that more Bible believers would become in some sense zionists--since God is, according to His Word (Amos 9:15); 3) that the World--wide body of believers in our Messiah would regularly intercede for our Jewish people--especially on all the Jewish holidays--and would educate all people against anti-Semitism and callousness toward Israel by supporting ministries that serve the Spiritual and physical best interests of God's ancient people (Romans 15:27).

SURVEYOR'S NAME __________
DATE SURVEY TAKEN ________

BIBLICAL LITERACY SURVEY

Whom the Surveyor Represents: A JEWISH STUDIES INSTITUTE

Why the Information Is Needed: FOR A SHORT SURVEY

Why the Survey Is Being Taken: TO DETERMINE THE NEEDS OF THE LOCAL JEWISH COMMUNITY

PERMISSION QUESTION: YOU WOULDN'T MIND GIVING US A QUICK BIT OF INFORMATION WOULD YOU? (MAY I COME IN AND CHAT WITH YOU FOR A WHILE?)

(Circle One)

1. WHAT IS YOUR RELIGIOUS BACKGROUND - ARE YOU JEWISH? Yes No

2. DO YOU BELIEVE OUR JEWISH RELIGIOUS SCRIPTURE SHOULD BE STUDIED TO STRENGTHEN HUMAN VALUES IN OUR SOCIETY? Yes No

3. HAVE YOU EVER READ THE JEWISH BIBLE IN ENGLISH IN ITS ENTIRETY? Yes No

4. WHAT IS YOUR NAME? ________________

5. HOW LONG HAVE YOU LIVED IN THE AREA - ARE YOU A FAIRLY NEW RESIDENT? Yes No

6. IS YOUR PHONE LISTED? Yes No

7. WOULD YOU BE INTERESTED IN RECEIVING A FREE JEWISH COMMUNITY NEWSPAPER TO KEEP INFORMED ABOUT EXCITING LOCAL EVENTS? Yes No

   YOUR ADDRESS AND ZIP CODE (APT. NUMBER)

   Street ________________________________

   City, Zip ______________________________

8. DO YOU BELIEVE IN GOD? Yes No Uncertain

9. AN OPINION QUESTION: GOD FORBID, BUT IF YOU SHOULD PASS ON TONIGHT, DO YOU THINK YOU WOULD MEET YOUR MAKER? Yes No Uncertain

10. FOR THE PURPOSE OF THE SURVEY... IF TONIGHT YOU DID PASS ON AND DID MEET YOUR MAKER, WHAT DO YOU SUPPOSE HIS JUDGMENT OF YOU WOULD BE - DO YOU THINK IT WOULD BE A FAVORABLE JUDGMENT? Yes No Uncertain

SURVEYOR'S NAME _________
DATE SURVEY TAKEN________

BIBLICAL LITERACY SURVEY
RESULTS*

		(circle one)	1	2	3	5	6	8	9	10
	4									
1.	(Name) ____________		y	y	y	y	y	y	y	y
	7		n	n	n	n	n	n	n	n
	(Address) ____________							u	u	u
	(City-Zip) ____________									
	(Date-Phone?) ____________									

		1	2	3	5	6	8	9	10
	4								
2.	(Name) ____________	y	y	y	y	y	y	y	y
	7	n	n	n	n	n	n	n	n
	(Address) ____________						u	u	u
	(City-Zip) ____________								
	(Date-Phone?) ____________								

		1	2	3	5	6	8	9	10
	4								
3.	(Name) ____________	y	y	y	y	y	y	y	y
	7	n	n	n	n	n	n	n	n
	(Address) ____________						u	u	u
	(City-Zip) ____________								
	(Date-Phone?) ____________								

		1	2	3	5	6	8	9	10
	4								
4.	(Name) ____________	y	y	y	y	y	y	y	y
	7	n	n	n	n	n	n	n	n
	(Address) ____________								
	(City-Zip) ____________								
	(Date-Phone?) ____________								

*(y for Yes, n for No, u for Uncertain)

FLOW CHART

To develop a "flow chart" to help you clarify your thinking, place the goal and the necessary enabling steps in some sequential order. Think through and assign necessary persons, methods and programs, remembering that people must be motivated, equipped, and trained on-the-job, as well as frequently encouraged and renewed if they are to succeed in anything, whether it be in a youth group or a visitation group or a Bible study. Below is an example of a flow chart found on p. 155 in *Everything You Need To Grow A Messianic Synagogue* for co-ordinating phone, bus, and visitation ministry. If each new name is placed on a 3" x 5" card in a file and prayed over daily, with several workers in the congregation each having a file, the information on the card (name, address, phone, referral's name, any background information) will be invaluable in assigning phone, bus, and visitation ministry for the new comer.

FLOW CHART

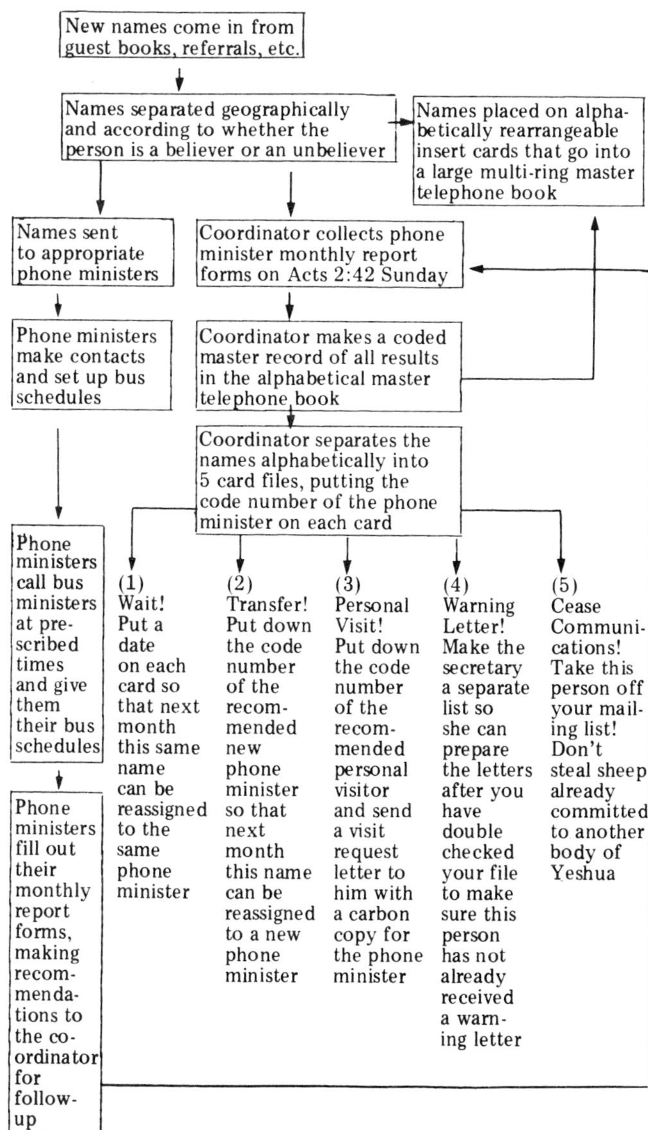
New names come in from guest books, referrals, etc.
Names separated geographically and according to whether the person is a believer or an unbeliever
Names placed on alphabetically rearrangeable insert cards that go into a large multi-ring master telephone book
Names sent to appropriate phone ministers
Coordinator collects phone minister monthly report forms on Acts 2:42 Sunday
Phone ministers make contacts and set up bus schedules
Coordinator makes a coded master record of all results in the alphabetical master telephone book
Coordinator separates the names alphabetically into 5 card files, putting the code number of the phone minister on each card
Phone ministers call bus ministers at prescribed times and give them their bus schedules
(1) Wait! Put a date on each card so that next month this same name can be reassigned to the same phone minister
(2) Transfer! Put down the code number of the recommended new phone minister so that next month this name can be reassigned to a new phone minister
(3) Personal Visit! Put down the code number of the recommended personal visitor and send a visit request letter to him with a carbon copy for the phone minister
(4) Warning Letter! Make the secretary a separate list so she can prepare the letters after you have double checked your file to make sure this person has not already received a warning letter
(5) Cease Communications! Take this person off your mailing list! Don't steal sheep already committed to another body of Yeshua
Phone ministers fill out their monthly report forms, making recommendations to the coordinator for follow-up

PHONE MINISTER'S REPORT FORM

Phone Minister's Name ____________ Month and Year _____

1. Is there any reason why you couldn't come this week?
A. Too busy
B. Afraid of converting
C. Too much to give up
D. I have my own ideas
E. Not now . . . maybe later
F. Involved in a cult
G. Back-slidden baptized believer
H. Yeshua was just a man
I. Won't explain
J. Other (write on back)

2. How much probability is there you could come if I should call you later?
K. Don't call me again ever!
L. Don't call us — we'll call you.
M. You can call again, but I probably will not be able to come
N. I'll come later once in a while
O. Other (write on back)

3. Do you have any needs you would appreciate prayers for?
P. Illness
Q. Depression
R. Financial
S. Spiritual
T. New believer needing nurture
U. Other (write on back)

Recommendation
V. Wait before contacting
W. Transfer this name to __
X. Have someone make a personal visit (recommend who on back)
Y. Send friendly warning letter (put address on back)
Z. Already committed to another Body of believers

Note: If the person is not home or is unreachable by phone, write absolutely nothing here but instead make your own notes on the back of this page. Remember, too, if Yeshua needed a quiet time before he ministered, how much more do you! Before you send this to the outreach coordinator on Acts 2:42 Sunday (the last Sunday of the month), save a carbon copy for your own records.

	Name	Phone	Day/Time Called	#1	#2	#3	Recom-mendation
1.	_____	_____	__/__	_____	_____	_____	_____
2.	_____	_____	__/__	_____	_____	_____	_____
3.	_____	_____	__/__	_____	_____	_____	_____
4.	_____	_____	__/__	_____	_____	_____	_____
5.	_____	_____	__/__	_____	_____	_____	_____
6.	_____	_____	__/__	_____	_____	_____	_____

(On a larger page there will be reporting room for more names.)

VISITATION FORM

NAME ______________________ DATE OF CALL ______________

NAME OF TEMPLE AND TEAM MEMBERS ________________________

____

NAMES OF PEOPLE VISITED _______________________________

____

STUDENT'S ROLE: OBSERVER __________ PRESENTOR __________

SUMMARY REPORT OF CALL: WHAT HAPPENED?

EVALUATION OF CALL: STRENGTH, WEAKNESS, ETC.

WHAT DID YOU LEARN IN THE EXPERIENCE?

BUS MINISTER'S FORM

BUS MINISTER'S NAME ____________________

ADDRESS, ZIP ____________________ PHONE __________

1. WHO DO YOU PRESENTLY BRING TO A MEETING?

   ____

   ____

   ____

2. HOW MANY MORE PEOPLE DO YOU HAVE ROOM FOR IN YOUR VEHICLE?

   ____

3. WOULD YOU BE WILLING TO BRING THE FOLLOWING PEOPLE IN YOUR VEHICLE? ______ (YES) ______ (NO)
   (NAMES, ADDRESSES, AND PHONES TO BE FILLED IN BY THE LEADER)

   ____

   ____

   ____

   ____

4. WOULD YOU BE WILLING TO BE RESPONSIBLE TO SEE THAT THESE PEOPLE ARE BROUGHT EVERY WEEK?

   ______ (YES) ______ (NO)

   A. TO WHICH SERVICES WILL YOU BRING THEM? (CHECK ONE OR MORE)

      FRIDAY __________

      SUNDAY __________

      MIDWEEK __________

   B. WILL YOU ALSO TAKE THEM HOME?

      ______ (YES) ______ (NO)

C. WILL YOU CALL THEM AT LEAST TWO DAYS BEFORE EACH MEETING TO CONFIRM THEY WILL BE PICKED UP AND AT A CERTAIN PLACE AND TIME?

______ (YES) ______ (NO)

D. WILL YOU PRAY FOR AND WITH THESE PEOPLE AND WILL YOU PRAY THAT GOD WOULD GIVE YOU MORE LOVE FOR THEM, SINCE ONLY AS WE HAVE THIS TYPE OF FAITH ACTIVE IN LOVE WILL OUR FELLOWSHIP GROW?

______ (YES) ______ (NO)

RELIGIOUS EDUCATION STAFF REPORT

DATE ____________________

NAME OF TEACHER ____

NAME OF CLASS ____

*ATTENDANCE LAST SUNDAY ________________________________

*HOW MUCH TIME DID YOU SPEND IN PREPARATION? ______HR(S).

*DID YOU PERSONALLY PRAY FOR EACH STUDENT OF YOUR CLASS THIS WEEK?____

*HAVE YOU SENT A POSTCARD TO EACH ABSENTEE?______________

*DID YOU VISIT OR TELEPHONE EACH ABSENTEE? ______________

*DID YOU ISSUE ALL TIMELY BIRTHDAY, ANNIVERSARY, GET-WELL CARDS? ____

*DID YOU RECONTACT ALL NEW VISITORS SUBSEQUENT TO SUNDAY?____

*HAVE YOU ENCLOSED ALL VITAL INFORMATION REGARDING NEW VISITORS? ____

*WHEN IS YOUR NEXT CLASS ACTIVITY FUNCTION AND WHAT IS IT? ____

*PLEASE LIST ANY IMPORTANT DEVELOPMENTS RESULTING FROM THIS WEEK'S MINISTRY:

1. ____

2. ____

3. ____

4. ____

5. ____

*PLEASE LIST ANY PROBLEMS YOU ENCOUNTERED THIS WEEK:

1. ______________________________

2. ______________________________

3. ______________________________

*PLEASE LIST ALL STUDENTS YOU MINISTERED TO (IN PERSON OR BY PHONE) COUNSELLED, VISITED, ETC., DURING THE PAST SEVEN DAYS: (USE BACK AS NECESSARY)

1. ______________________________

2. ______________________________

3. ______________________________

4. ______________________________

5. ______________________________

6. ______________________________

7. ______________________________

8. ______________________________

9. ______________________________

10. ______________________________

HOME TORAH SECRETARY REPORT SHEET

FOR THE WEEK OF ______________ SECRETARY'S NAME ____________

TORAH STUDY __________________

1. DID YOU ATTACH THE GUEST SHEET WITH ALL FIRST TIMER'S NAMES, ADDRESSES, PHONE NUMBERS AND ZIP CODES?

______ (YES) ______ (NO)

2. DID YOU LIST BELOW THE NAMES OF ALL ABSENTEES SO THE PHONE MINISTER CAN CONTACT THEM? (YOU MUST HAVE AN ATTENDANCE ROSTER.)

__________________________ __________________________

__________________________ __________________________

__________________________ __________________________

__________________________ __________________________

3. LIST BELOW THE PEOPLE AND THEIR COMPLETE ADDRESSES WHOM YOU FEEL ARE INTERESTED ENOUGH TO READ DOCUMENT 1 OF "EVERYTHING YOU NEED TO GROW A MESSIANIC SYNAGOGUE" AND WE WILL MAIL IT TO THEM.

__________________________ __________________________

__________________________ __________________________

__________________________ __________________________

__________________________ __________________________

4. PLEASE MAKE SURE THAT ALL NAMES AND ADDRESSES ARE *PLAINLY PRINTED* ON THE VISITOR SHEET.

5. PLEASE MAKE SURE THAT THIS INFORMATION IS MAILED IMMEDIATELY AFTER THE TORAH STUDY SO THAT WE CAN MAKE USE OF THIS INFORMATION THE SAME WEEK.

SOME TOOLS FOR INTERPRETATION AND TEACHING PREPARATION (II TIMOTHY 2:15)

We cannot persuade anyone to believe the truth until we have first discovered and understood the truth. Rhetoric is the art of persuasion. Exegesis is the discipline of probing the meaning of a written passage to lift out the truth that is there and expose it. We will deal with rhetoric in the next section. Here we are primarily concerned with exegesis (interpretation), the science of which is called hermeneutics.

THE HERMENEUTIC PROCESS

The systematic discipline of interpreting the real meaning in a text is called hermeneutics. The 12-Step study preparation method given in this section involves the student in Exegesis, New Testament and Old Testament Theology, Systematic Theology, Hermeneutics, Classical Rhetoric, Homiletics, Evangelism, and Creative Writing.

Suppose your text is from the Hebrew Bible -- say Jer. 3:15: "And I will give you pastors according to mine heart, which shall feed you with knowledge and understanding." You look up some of the key words in Strong's Concordance after you check the verse in Green's Interlinear Bible -- if you own it -- as well as a familiar translation like the King James. On page 774 in Strong's, the key word "pastors" is listed along with the Jer. 3:15 text and the *7462 number of the Hebrew Lexicon. You turn to the Lexicon in the back of the Strong's Concordance to 7462 on page 109 in the Hebrew Dictionary, and you find that the Hebrew word is transliterated "raw-aw" and means literally "the one who tends the flock" and, figuratively, "the one who tends the Lord's flock, the believers."

Now, suppose your passage is in the New Testament. Take I Cor. 3:10. If possible, look up the text in the Interlinear Bible. Then look it up in Strong's Concordance by checking out key words like "foundation," which is located on page 369 in Strong's. The number *2310 tells you the place to look in the Greek Dictionary in back. But before you turn, notice the same Greek word number 2310 is also used in Eph. 2:20 where it speaks about "the foundation of the apostles and prophets." On page 36 in the Greek Dictionary in the back of Strong's, you see that *2310 is the Greek word for "foundation" meaning "something put down." By asking obvious questions (who? what? when? where?), you are led to ask *who* puts it down. And the answer in the larger context is: the Lord's workers (see I Cor. 3:9) or laborers. This leads us to ask who are the Lord's workers? How do they build effectively? How are they prepared and recognized? What standards are they given in the New Testament and the Old Testament? A teaching or speech is germinating here. But much study is left to be done. To begin, we must know the resource books that will help us pursue our questions throughout the Bible.

The difficulties and obscurities of Scripture can be understood through a number of means. Hebrew and Greek Lexicons (dictionaries) and Interlinears (word by word translations accompanied by the original Hebrew and Greek of the Old and New Covenant Scriptures) can help us understand the words of the Bible more clearly. Comparing translations is useful, but equally helpful is Concordance word studies, where the original word is given to the reader as it appears in every verse of Scripture in the Bible, so that every shade of meaning the word can contain becomes apparent.

12-STEP STUDY PREPARATION

1. Select the brief portion of Scripture which will become the basis for your Bible study, Sunday School lesson, discussion, or message. For example, take I Cor. 3:10.

2. If possible, look at this text in an Interlinear. In any case, study its key words in Greek or Hebrew. In Hebrew, turn from Strong's to the back of Strong's to the new Brown Driver, Briggs Hebrew Lexicon and Concordance. In Greek, turn from Strong's to the back of Strong's to the Thayers Greek Lexicon and Concordance. (If you only have Strong's, use the Hebrew and Greek Dictionaries (Lexicons) in the back.)

3. Read about the text in the New Bible Commentary to check your initial understanding.

4. Look at the Thompson Chain Reference Bible to get topical ideas that are implicit in the passage and read these Scriptures.

5. Do a little systematic theological study by reading New Bible Dictionary article, "ministry" and some of these topics or closely related subjects on the pages, 195-196, "Labels for Starting A Filing System."

6. Begin asking the questions regarding the Introduction, Explanation, Argumentation, Refutation, and Summing Up on the Audience Analysis page, 192.

7. Begin creating arguments using the "Building with Silver and Gold" sample sermon as a model, especially referring back and forth from its text to its Glossary, pages 198-246.

8. Look through the portion of *Great Treasury of Western Thought* dealing with the main ideas of this passage and start looking for illustrative quotations. For example, look up "responsibility" (an important idea in the text being studied -- I Cor. 3:10) on page 1698 in *Great Treasury of Western Thought* where you will get from the index where to find a great supporting quotation such as the one by George Barnard Shaw on page 897 (13-1-60).

9. On separate 3 x 5 cards, write down each separate argument, figure of speech, quotation, or Scripture verse that comes to you. (These can be filed in your Speech Preparation File later for future use.) This is a good time to consult your Almanac for a statistical argument.

10. After sorting all material into thought groups so you have a crude outline of your whole argument, force yourself to reduce your argument to a short declarative sentence (proposition) like "Privilege requires responsibility." Write it on a 3 x 5 card. (Consult Topics on pages 53-55 in Charles Kollers, *Expository Preaching Without Notes*, Baker Book House, 1962.)

11. It will help you in revising and refining your proposition to state your raw argument formally (syllogism) and informally (enthymeme). Use a dictionary and thesaurus. See the terms you don't understand in the Glossary following the sermon, "Building with Silver and Gold."

    Syllogism: Being a presbyter, a minister, or a voting member is a privilege. This privilege requires the responsibility of keeping Scriptural standards. Therefore, presbyters, ministers, and voting members should keep the standards.

    Enthymeme: Presbyters, ministers, and members should keep Scriptural standards, since privilege requires responsibility.

12. Using your dictionary and thesaurus, select only your best material and refine it until it is ready to be presented orally or in written form. Remember, the words you choose should fit you as the speaker, your hearers as the audience, and your occasion as the total set of circumstances to which you are called to speak.

Special note on the greatest book of quotations ever assembled: *Great Treasury of Western Thought*, edited by Mortimer J. Adler and Charles Van Doren, R. R. Bowker Co., New York and London, 1977, $29.95. This book is a complete liberal education in one volume.

Two ways to use this book of quotations: 1) Look up your text in the index in the back of the book under New Testament or Old Testament on pages 1442-1443. If your text has been included as a quotation, you will find it plus quotes by several other sources and famous writers on precisely that subject. For example, if I were teaching on Gen. 3:16 which is about parents and children, I would notice that it is included on page 1443 and can be found in the second section of Chapter 2, Family (2.2). There I will find other Bible quotes on parents plus quotes from everyone from Homer to Freud. If Gen. 3:16 has not been quoted, I could still find my illustrations by looking under the topic "Parents" in the index on page 1660. Therefore, this book affords me a vast wealth of human wisdom I can use to illustrate and teach God's divine wisdom.

RHETORICAL RESOURCES FOR MESSIANIC PERSUASION

Needed Books

Interliners Vol. I, II, III and New Testament

Strong's Exhaustive Concordance

Englishman's Hebrew Concordance

New Brown, Driver and Briggs Hebrew Lexicon

Englishman's Greek Concordance

Thompson Chain Reference

The Doubleday Roget's Thesaurus in Dictionary Form (Sidney Landau, Editor, Doubleday, New York, 1977)

New Bible Dictionary

Great Treasury of Western Thought

Information Please Almanac

Webster's Dictionary

New Bible Commentary

Thayer's Greek Lexicon or Ardt & Gingridge

New International Version

The Open Bible

Charles Kollers, *Expository Preaching Without Notes*, Baker Book House, 1962

AUDIENCE ANALYSIS AND PRELIMINARY MEDITATION ON THE DISCOURSE

But this is not just an exposition of a text. It is also a speech or teaching or discussion *with* someone. Therefore, the way the material is presented must take into account the audience. Here are the questions I asked myself as I prepared the discourse for an audience:

1. What is my purpose?

2. What is the occasion or the urgencies of the hour? (I knew that a membership meeting was only a month away -- the annual January business meeting of the congregation where I was asked to speak, Temple Aron Kodesh.)

3. What is their purpose? What do the people for whom I must speak need or expect?

4. Who exactly will be in the audience?

5. How will they feel about what I'm going to present?

6. Where will the sensitive points come, probably?

7. What do they need to hear?

8. What do they expect to hear?

9. How can I make what I have to say most memorable and most persuasive to them?

10. What will they already understand about what I need to say?

11. What will I need to explain?

12. What will they probably agree with me on?

13. What are the points on which they probably have to be persuaded to agree with me?

14. Where am I leading them? When I've finished speaking, what do I want them to have changed their mind about? What decision do I want to bring them to?

15. What about organization?

Before I worry about the exact words I want to use -- to get their attention at the beginning and to stick in their memory at the end -- let's think about organizing the content of the discourse. I know that a good start is to be able to put the point I'm trying to make into a simple sentence (a proposition). Then everything I say has to be related to that proposition (I must not digress from the point). A good format is to interest and orient my audience to the proposition (this is the job of the INTRODUCTION.) Then I must provide them with any preliminary background details they need to follow my argument. (This is the job of the EXPLANATION). Then I must present my arguments (this part of the discourse is called the ARGUMENTATION). Then I must disarm all the counterarguments that may be popping up in my audience's mind (this part is called the REFUTATION). Then I must sum up the case and leave the audience with a clear conclusion that neatly ties together all the loose ends so there won't be any confusion left in their mind as to what I was talking about for the past few minutes. Finally, I must give the audience the opportunity to actually do what I've been asking them to do.

Oh, yes, now there's the other thing -- the time. Can I cover all this in the time allotted? How can I cut it down? What material will go over well with this audience? How can I cut it down to the briefest possible time and still get in the best strokes to move this audience to follow me all the way to the point I want them to go? How can I use humor and all the other things at my disposal to keep them with me, both in their attention and in their emotions? How can I use explanation (what), argumentation (why), illustration (how) and application (how in regard to you and me), to drive home the *one* point that I'm trying to make as I go through the various aspects of that one point?

Let's see. What about my own life? How does this passage relate to me? Let me search my memories. Then let me go to my books, my files, etc. Let me begin to pray. God will put it all together if I mull over it for awhile.

PURPOSE		GENERAL PLAN:
PART:	INTENDED TO:	MATERIAL TO DO THIS:
INTRODUCTION	GET ATTENTION AND	
EXPLANATION		
ARGUMENTATION	KEEP ATTENTION AND	
REFUTATION	KEEP ATTENTION AND	
SUMMING UP	KEEP ATTENTION AND	
OPENING SENTENCE*	GET ATTENTION AND	
CLOSING SENTENCE*		

*THE OPENING AND CLOSING SENTENCES ARE SO VERY IMPORTANT YOU WILL WANT TO GIVE SPECIAL ATTENTION TO THEM.

LABELS FOR STARTING A FILING SYSTEM

- Abraham
- Adam
- Angel
- Apostasy
- Ascension
- Assurance
- Atonement
- Authority
- Baptism
- Brotherly love
- Call
- Clean & Unclean
- Chanukah
- Communion
- Confession
- Conscience
- Conversion
- Covenant
- Creation
- Cross
- Crucifixion
- Day of the Lord
- Death
- Devil
- Disease & Healing
- Divination
- Eden
- Education
- Election
- Eschatology
- Ethics
- Evil
- Evil Speaking
- Evil Spirits
- Expiation
- Faith
- Fall
- Fasting
- Fear
- Feasts
- Flesh
- Forgiveness
- Glory
- Gnosticism
- God
- Names of God (cf Name)
- Good
- Gospel
- Government
- Grace
- Hell-Heaven
- Holy Spirit
- Hospitality
- Humility
- Immanuel
- Incarnation
- Inheritance
- Inspiration
- Israel of God
- Israel
- Jesus Christ, Teaching of
- Jewish Arbor Day
- Judaism
- Justice
- Justification
- Kingdom of God
- Knowledge
- Kol Nidre
- Lamb of God
- Law
- Lawgiver
- Life
- Light
- Logos
- Longsuffering
- Lord's Supper
- Love
- Lust
- Maccabees
- Magic & Sorcery
- Man
- Marriage
- Mediator
- Meekness
- Mercy
- Messiah
- Messiah's Birthday (Christmas)
- Ministry
- Miracles
- Missions
- Moses
- Mother's Day
- Neighbor
- New Year's Day
- Ordination
- Passover
- Patience
- Peace
- Pentateuch
- Pentecost
- Perfection
- Persecution
- Perseverance
- Pharisees
- Possession
- Poverty
- Power
- Praise
- Prayer
- Predestination
- Pride
- Priests & Levites
- Prophesy
- Propitiation
- Proselyte
- Providence
- Purim
- Purity
- Reconciliation
- Redeemer
- Regeneration
- Religion
- Repentance
- Reprobate
- Resurrection
- Resurrection Day (Easter)
- Revelation
- Reward
- Righteousness
- Rock
- Rosh Hashanah
- Sabbath
- Sacraments
- Sacrifice & Offering

Sadducees	Salvation	Sanctification
Satan	Seal, sealing	Sermon on Mount
Seven Words	Shame	Shekinah
Shepherd	Sign	Sin
Slave	Sons of God	Spirit
Spiritual Gifts	Steward	Stumbling Block
Suffering	Synagogue	Tabernacle
Feast of Tabernacles	Talmud & Midrash	Temperance
Temple	Ten Commandments	Temptation
Text & Version	Thanksgiving	Time
Tithes	Tongues, gift	Tradition
Transfiguration	Trial of Jesus	Tribes of Israel
Tribulation	Trinity	Truth
Unbelief	Vanity	Virgin
Virtue	Vision	Vow
Wages	Watchman	Wicked
Widow	Wilderness Wandering	Wine and strong drink
Wisdom		
Work	World	Wrath
Yom Kippur		

Most of these words plus Biblical Books and Characters are given full treatment in the *New Bible Dictionary*. An additional file section for previous Sunday School lessons taught or Bible Studies, too, would be helpful.

THE RHETORIC OF HOMILETICS

Homiletics is the science of faithfully expounding the Scriptures; rhetoric is the art of the effective use of language to accomplish persuasion. What follows is the speech that was written on I Corinthians 3:10 with a glossary of the rhetorical devices, figures of speech, lines of argument, and other language means used to accomplish the end of persuasion.

It should be noted that a knowledge of figures of speech is necessary because the Bible is full of them and assumes their familiarity by the reader. My analysis, it should be emphasized, was set forth in this detailed manner *after the fact*, and the Holy Spirit was the chief analyst prior to my giving the speech. That is not to say that I just got up without preparation and spoke. No, there was preparation, but the Holy Spirit put so much more into what I said than I realized, that the post-speech analysis brought forth much that I was only subconsciously aware of (or totally unaware of) as I spoke. This is not surprising since the Holy Spirit was the chief author of the discourse, as he should be in all homiletical discourses.

We study only to show ourselves approved as good students of the Word, who follow the Lord's thoughts after him. Study the speech and then go back and let the glossary take you through the speech again, teaching you how to use the art of rhetoric in your religious discourses before audiences of 1 or 1,000. Your repertoire of rhetorical devices, figures of speech, and lines of argument will expand with practice and imitation. Your aim is Paul's in Colossians 4:4, to make the Good News clear, as you ought to speak.

BUILDING WITH SILVER AND GOLD (I COR. 3:10) TITLE
A Sermon on Standards for Ministers & Voting Members SUBJ.
Preached at Temple Aron Kodesh on December 4, 1977.

> You are also God's building. Using the gift that God gave me, I did the work of an expert builder and laid the foundation and another man is building on it. But each one must be careful how he builds. For God has already placed Yeshua the Messiah as the one and only foundation and no other foundation can be laid. Some will use gold or silver or precious stones in building on the foundation; others will use wood or brass or straw and the quality of each person's work will be seen when the Day of Messiah exposes it. For on that day fire will reveal everyone's work, the fire will test and show its real quality. *If what was built on the foundation survives the fire, the builder will receive a reward.* But if anyone's work is burned up, then he will lose it. But he himself will be saved as if he had escaped through the fire.

INTRO

1. I'm not going to be preaching a salvation message this morning. I'm not talking about salvation. Did you notice that last verse? Even if you blow it, you can still be saved from God's wrath, because it's not by works that we are saved, it's by grace. So there's hope for Goble even if he blows it. ASSON

2. However, since you are the builders of this congregation, (Neil Lash, Randi, and I would look a little stupid here by ourselves this morning, wouldn't we?) since you are the builders, you have an interest in this verse, because it says, "*if* you build with silver and gold, your work will remain and you will get a reward." So this is what the sermon is all about this morning, how to get a reward, a reward made possible by certain golden standards PAREN

in the ministry which are God's insurance policy
for our work, that these congregations will
remain after our death. PUR

EXPLAN

3. But first let's look in the future. Let's look
at 1984, George Orwell's date. Wouldn't it be
terrible if there was an announcement read at
Temple Aron Kodesh like this:

> We're having a theatre party Saturday SAT
> night for all our Temples. We're going
> to see "Lust Pigs" starring sexy Burt
> Reynolds and foul-mouthed Richard Pryor. CURR EV
> Then after the show we're meeting for
> cocktails, cigarettes, bingo, and bar-
> room dancing at Big Daddy's. A good time
> will be had by all. The next morning ANASTRO
> we stalwart members of Temple Aron Kodesh IRONY
> will meet for a business meeting to vote HUM
> on the holy matters of God.

4. No way. It's not going to happen. *Privilege* PROP
entails responsibility. We're going to set
standards so that won't happen. Those people DEDUCT
might as well sleep in on Sunday morning,
because they're not going to be the voting
members of Temple Aron Kodesh. They are not
going to have control over the holy matters
of God.

5. "We are God's house," it says in I Cor. 3:9.
What is God's house? Haggai 1:4 says this:
"My people, why should you be living in well EXEG
built houses while my temple lies in ruin?" DIFF
You know your house and my house is not God's
house. That's the reason why a privately
owned corporation or house is not a congregation. My house is not God's house. One of EPAN
the real temptations we have is to make "my
house" God's house.

6. I was tempted this week. I put new carpeting ANEC
in and it looked so beautiful, and then a PER EXP
little voice turned on in my head and said, EXAMP
"Hey, why don't you get an extra job, don't
do quite so much visitation, don't work quite

so hard, start socking it away and fix up the whole house. Take care of Number One, like the best-seller says." AUX

7. I knew who that voice was, friends, and I think you know too, I clicked off that little voice quite quickly and got back out into my bus and made myself keep going, because, you see, your house and my house are not God's house. ONOM

8. Now sometimes we do things for people, and our homes are important: like, for instance, this week I helped move a lady from Temple Aron Kodesh into her new apartment. So we need to be concerned about our homes, but a materialistic worldliness can turn a home into an idol, so that we neglect the House of God. EXAMP

9. Now here's the question: How can we make sure that God's House remains? There are structural weaknesses in the House of God and we have to be very sure that we know what they are. There are structural weaknesses in Temple Aron Kodesh and we have to be aware of them so that Temple Aron Kodesh will remain. Q-A

10. Let me mention some of these. These are some possible structural weaknesses that could rear their ugly heads in the years to come. DEF.
One structural weakness in God's House is a kind of Seventh Day Adventist disdain for Sunday as the Lord's Day. You know, we start Torah services on Saturday morning -- which is fine -- but then we go one step further and declare that only the stupid Christians go to church on Sunday morning, we're messianic Jews, we don't have anything to do with that. On Sunday morning you find us lounging around the pool or at the golf course hobnobbing with other people who think Sunday is really not an important day. That would be bad, wouldn't it? Particularly when even many temples have Sunday programs! But we take our Jewishness from the Bible and not from anything else, correct? DIV.

11. Another type of structural weakness would be to develop a kind of Roman Catholic awe of dead

unscriptural ritualism, a kind of Talmud- ANTHIM
idolatry. You know about the Talmud, how we
could get so wrapped up in rituals that we KEN
really lose the substance and get hopelessly C-E
bogged down in form. Then we become a very
formal place where there's no real on-going
personal relationship with God. Where we don't
break through that incessant ritualism to have ELLIP
a real on-going relationship with God. That
could be a problem. Now that's not to say ANTITH
that we throw the Jewish holidays and traditions out the window, but we keep an eye on
them, because this could become a structural COND.
weakness if the substance gets lost in the
form. It's already happened once in Judaism
and we don't want it to happen again. Keep PFFF
it all Biblical. In our quest for liturgical
credibility let us not lose the spontaneity
of the Spirit and the fire of the Word of God.

12. Another structural weakness would be a kind of anti-Gentile exclusivism where we become a kind of Jewish club, for Jews only, an elite with a proud pedigree. That could be very bad, because after all, aren't we supposed to be "or olam," the light of the world? Don't we have a commission, the Great Commission, to go to all the ends of the earth to make messianic peoples out of Indians and Chinese and everybody else so that they all can become spiritual Jews?
And doesn't that require a world-embracing CLIM
organization as well as world-embracing
mentality? We can't ever get so enraptured
with ethnicity that we become ethno-idolaters.
We've got to remember that the ecclesia, the
Body of the Lord, is a world-embracing fellowship under a divine discipline to reach out to
fulfill the Great Commission, which is to make
disciples of *all* peoples. POLYPT

13. There's a fourth structural problem and this
one is very important. It's called nominalism. To be a nominal is to have a commit- ETY
ment "in name only." Let me tell you about
three types of nominalism we have to look out DEF
for. Some of this might come a little close
to home, but remember, it's kind of close to my PUN
home too, and I have to watch myself, too and

keep Goble in line. I'm tempted to make God's house my house, so I'm preaching to myself here too.

ARGU

14. One kind of nominalism is what we call "Second Generation Nominalism." That's when some of the children in our service become 16 or 17 years old and we can hear conversations something like this: "You know I was bar mitzvahed at Temple Aron Kodesh. But I don't believe Yeshua thinks there's that much wrong with smoking a little pot. And of course, my big brother, he was bar mitzvahed there too. But he doesn't believe there's all that much wrong with living with your girlfriend at the University. I mean, everybody does it and they do love each other. Now come on, God is love." You see? That's "Second Generation nominalism." Mom and Dad got saved from the world at Temple Aron Kodesh but the kids grew up taking the Temple for granted -- ("Great for Mom and Dad," you know.) Nominalism sneaked into the house. Mom loved the Lord, but she let the kids bring acid rock records into the house. And the little kids grew up and they're not quite following Yeshua with Mom and Dad, and their experience with God is never really personal. Second generation nominalism is a phenomenon that you've got to watch out for because ten or twenty years from now this place could be a completely different place if the children don't have a heart-felt experience with Yeshua the Messiah.

DIV

PERSON

GEN-SPEC

CONCLU

15. A second kind of nominalism I call "the seven month itch." I suffered from this in December of '76. It's when you lose that first love for the work. Look at Rev. 2:4.

DIV

> But this is what I have against you: you do not love me now as you did at first. Think how far you have fallen. Turn from your sins and do what you did at first. If you don't turn from your sins, I will come to you and take your lampstand from its place.

16. The lampstand here is talking about the TEST
congregation. I suffered from the seven
month itch nominalism in December of '76.
I *loved* Miami Beach, I was going to *serve*
Miami Beach, I was going to *finish* the Lord's SEQ
work in Miami Beach. But after the Devil
got finished clobbering me for about five or
six months, and after I went through some very
bad experience with some people that I thought
should have been a little more mature as
spiritual leaders, I was itching to leave.
My feet were badly infected. I had itchy C-E
feet. I was beginning to flirt with maybe
going to a little greener grass on some MAX
other side of the fence. And the Enemy was
dangling carrots. And then I was wavering PERSON
and my thoughts were fluctuating something F-I
like this while I was rationalizing: "Oh
well, at least I've accomplished something
here. I've pioneered a little something
here. If I left now I'm sure something
would remain -- no I'm not so sure something
would remain -- I really haven't done all
that much here -- maybe I'd better hang on."
Because you see, we can lose the pioneer
spirit very quickly. We can stop being
pioneers. But let me tell you something,
Paul never stopped being a pioneer. He knew
he was in warfare from the day he started on
the road to Damascus until the day they cut
his head off, and he never retired, never DESCRIP
went to part-time service, to a nominal half-
hearted commitment that looks for the easy
way out. He said, "Forgetting what lies
behind, I press on to the upward calling in
the Messiah Yeshua."

17. Now let me tell you something: You've only
just begun at Temple Aron Kodesh. If anybody
thinks that "Oh well, things are in pretty
good shape here, we can more or less pack up
and leave, " I've got news for you. You ANAD
haven't got a real Temple yet. You've got
something that's starting to look like one,
but you haven't arrived yet. You need to
have a messianic Jewish Day School. You've
got to have a way to raise the children to
know they're Jews but to also know they're ANAPH

saved from the wrath of God because they've
turned from the world and repented. You've
got to have more than you've got here now, and
it's going to take time, it's going to take
work. But praise God, if the job was over it
would be a little boring, wouldn't it? So let's
keep that in mind, because it's very easy after
the honeymoon is over, to pack up and get a
divorce without working through to the mature
thing God intended. That's the danger of the
Seventh Month Itch type of nominalism: it's
so subtle and so well rationalized that you
don't realize you've quit before you get CONCLU
started.

18. All right, the other type of nominalism is the
worldly variety, and I've got to talk about DIV
it now because it is very subtle. You see,
it can even creep into the ministry. Now
I hope everyone here can hear what I'm saying
without it being a stumbling block to you.
It's pretty heavy and you've got to really
know the Lord to be able to hear what I'm
saying and accept it and understand that it's
true. When we build with silver and gold, we
have to have high standards for everybody who
makes decisions and controls the work of God.
Basically this boils down to three types of DIV
people in the work of the Lord.

19. We have the presbyters, the ordained ministers
and we have the voting constituency of the DEF
membership. Now when I use the word
"member," I'm not talking about the member
of the Body of Yeshua in the general sense.
I'm using the word in the special sense of
the "voting member." I'm not just talking
about the "member" of the Body of Messiah
who comes regularly and who considers this
Temple his place of worship. I'm talking about
the voting member, the one who can call the
shots by the way he votes at the business meeting. He is very important and I'm going to
get to him in a minute. But before I do, I've
got to talk about the ministers.

20. Because, you see, worldliness can creep into the
ministry, too, and you need to know about this.

We have to have high standards for the ministry,
because if we don't -- what does it say in BIB
I Timothy 4:12? It says, "Set the believers
an example in speech and conduct, in love, in
faith and in purity." And what if the man who's
leading the congregation doesn't do this? Now
this may come as a surprise to you, but there
have actually been ministers who have been
caught guilty of adultery. Are you ready for
this? Adultery! Are you ready for this? A EMOT
minister! It can happen -- some lady comes
into a man's office for personal counseling
and begins to cry on his shoulder -- the next
thing you know she has him in a head lock --
and one thing leads to another. Now this is F-I
terrible. And there has to be the power to
defrock an immoral, or heretical or adulterous minister. There has to be that power.
And this is why an independent you-don't- REPET
tell-me-what-to-do-and-I-won't-tell-you-what- KEN
to-do type of organization is not going to
work. Because, you see, to have order, there
has to be police, and they have to have real METAPH
clubs, and they've got to be able to go in
there and make arrests and indict, try, and
convict people and get rid of them when they
are no longer fit for the ministry. You see
what I mean? And that's the reason we have
elders or presbyters.

21. Now some of you may not even know what a
presbyter is. But he is a pastor's advisor. DENOT
And if ministers get out of line and have to RESTA
be defrocked (stripped of their right to
minister), there have to be men (elders or
presbyters) who can do this. Let me tell you EMOT
something: *there are going to be men who can
do this!* And we're not going to have that kind
of problem. That problem exists, but we're
not going to have it. And if we do have it in
the years ahead, it'll be taken care of, because
we're not playing around here. Can you imagine
what would happen if a man committed adultery EMOT
and people in his congregation began to backslide
because of this? Can you imagine? We are going
to have to stand for eternity for what we do!
We're going to have to stand for eternity and
give an accounting for souls that weren't saved

because of us. That's why James says, "Not many of you should be teachers." Because it's a very high responsibility.

22. Now what does this mean? It means that the ministers have got to measure up to high standards. This means that the doctrine they teach -- the trinity, the virgin birth, that hell is real and no myth, that salvation is through Yeshua alone, that the Holy Spirit infilling is for today, and so is divine healing -- all these teachings, (which many people are not preaching and many ministers don't even believe) have got to be believed by our ministers. APPOS PAREN

23. Let me tell you what I don't want to see in the future. Suppose a novice took over this congregation. Suppose he decided to do away with all home meetings and began preaching strictly orthodox rabbinic sermons, mere pedantic lectures on the Talmud and anti-semitism, no Good News, no life, no Yeshua. Suppose a spirit of megalomania and paranoia entered him because of his proud, bitter heart and he began culture-shocking and alienating Gentile Christian leaders and even many messianic Jews. Suppose he tried so hard to impress the Jewish religious establishment and other rabbis that he removed the messianic content from all the services and legalistically, belligerently required all members to keep the law while he turned the services into dead, predictable, dry liturgical treadmills. Suppose, further, he stopped winning Jewish souls and drove off everyone who disagreed with him, while at the same time he tolerated immorality in the temple leadership. Can you imagine that? It could happen. All you need to have it happen is a novice who doesn't know Biblical theology and doesn't have his heart right with God.

24. The ministers must be submitted to the presbyters or elders. Now this is important, because when it says in Hebrews 13:17, "Obey your leaders," it's not just talking to laymen, CONTRAD LAW

it's talking to ministers, too, you know!
We've got to obey our leaders. A pastor is SAR,
not a little tin pope. He is not a law unto PAR T
himself, so that if he commits adultery or
falls into immorality or heresy as long as
he's got his board hood-winked and the little
immature people -- they don't know what's
going on -- then he's got everybody fooled.
Oh, no! He's got the elders to reckon with.
Obey your leaders! That means Goble, too.
Goble has got to be obedient to people over
him. Goble is not a law unto himself, and
neither are you! Members should submit
themselves to their pastors and pastors should ANAD
submit themselves to their presbyters -- as
unto the Lord! None of us are free-wheeling SAR
independents -- or does anyone here think
Hebrews 13:17 doesn't apply to such a free- FAL. CON.
spirit as himself!

25. Now I think this should be a relief to all
of you, because we are submitting to offices
ordered by the Lord, not to free-wheeling SYNON
independent personalities. There is nothing
more frail or fickle than human personality, ALLIT
but if we have Scriptural checks and balances
to keep us in line, and if we are under the
discipline of being submitted to the offices
of our leaders, then we're going to become
good disciples, and the work of God will ENTHY
be protected by the Lord's insurance policy
that I was telling you about, which is in
the epistle of Titus in the New Covenant
Scriptures.

26. Please read the letter to Titus. You'll
find that this book in the New Covenant
gives to the presbyters the power to
excommunicate pastors -- to defrock them
and to excommunicate them. And that's very
important. Presbyters are the Lord's bishops
to checkmate the Devil and their Office is ALLEG
part of the rock upon which Yeshua has built METAPH
His ecclesia so that the gates of hell will
not prevail against it.

27. Now let me tell you something. All of this is
a gift from God! Praise the Lord. It's Good

News! He has given us the offices of presbyter
and minister to help us! It's all a kind of SIMILE
insurance policy to keep the work of God
going. Individual ministers come and go, and
congregations run hot and cold, come in
multitudes today and fall away tomorrow,
but the offices we have will remain to pick
up the pieces after any attack of Satan. Is
this a relief to anybody? It is to me, because
believe me, I'm working hard and I don't want METAPH
to see a house of cards based on personalities
collapse. I'm not building a house of cards.
I'm building with silver and gold, with offices
and standards, and so are you. Take care that
you are! That's my text, I Cor. 3:10.

28. Now let's talk about the high standards for the
voting membership. You know, the Jerusalem
Council -- where that very critical decision HIST
about new believers (proselytes to Biblical
Judaism) was made that they must not be
circumcised according to the Law of Moses,
that they could become just spiritual Jews and
not have to become practicing Jews under the
full yoke of the Torah -- that Council in
Jerusalem was not a smoke-filled room! Peter
and James were not drinking buddies! When LIT
Paul was working he did not interrupt some of
his activities in this way: Can you imagine
Paul saying to Timothy if he were alive today,

> Say, Timothy, Lust Pigs is playing down HUM
> at the Bijou. And listen, after I finish
> dictating this Romans thing, what say we R.P.
> get a six-pack and pack of cigarettes and
> catch the flick this afternoon.

And Timothy says: PARODY

> But wait a minute, Paul, you know Tuesday, APOST
> Wednesday, and Fridays are my bridge days.
> Besides, wouldn't you rather play the HUM
> horses and maybe make some dough before
> we go to Las Vegas next week?

Can you imagine Peter spending time off at the
Circus Maximus? Can you imagine that? PUN

29. And let me tell you something. The voting membership -- the people who make the decisions of this Temple -- are in a very critical and important position, too. They can determine a lot of things in the future, too. *And wherever there is privilege there must be responsibility!* Now the person who wants to come here and be a member in the sense of "Boy, I'm regular and, man, I'm here, and you can count on me" and all like that -- that's fine, and praise God, we want people to come and feel members in that sense. But now I'm speaking in a very technical sense. I'm speaking in the technical sense of the *voting* member, the person at the business meeting who raises his hand "yea" or "nay" on the holy matters of the Lord. Now that person has got to be sanctified. That means, he's got to turn from the world. The scriptures say that "whoever loves the world or the things in the world, the love of the Father is not in him." And it also says, "Lay hands suddenly on no man." — APPOS; EXCLAM

30. Now let me tell you something. There are two ways of laying hands on a man. You can, as the presbyter, lay hands on a man to ordain him for the work of the ministry, to preach the Good News, and to get out and to make disciples and start congregations. You can do that. All right? That's for the clergy. — DEF; DIV

31. There's also this other kind of "laying hands" recognition of responsibility, and that is when you extend the *right hand of fellowship* to this voting member who will be making decisions at the congregational business meeting. This voting member must be sanctified and sensitive to the Holy Spirit because if he's carnal and nominal, he will destroy the work of God. And all you have to do is look at certain expressions of "Christianity" in the last two thousand years of Church History and you'll see this phenomenon occuring time and time again. Nominal believers who are really not true believers tear down (from within) the work of the Lord. And they make the House of God into a pig pen, a den of thieves and hypocrites. — POLYSYN; P.F.F.F.

32. You know there were a couple of demons speaking in *The Screwtape Letters* by C.S. Lewis. They were trying to decide how to best ensnare a man. And here's what one of these demons said, "Murder is no better than cards if cards can do the trick. Indeed, the safest road to hell is the gradual one." And let me tell you friends, you're looking at a guy who was on a very safe road to hell. When I was a little boy in the congregation, I didn't really know Yeshua. "While the minister was speaking, I was doing what some of the children may be doing right now, dreaming -- counting the number of light bulbs on the cross. And when I got up so high I started across counting this way. But unfortunately I would lose count about right here and have to start all over again. And I did that for 500 sermons for thirteen years, and after it was all over with, all I really knew about the New Testament was that there were 26 light bulbs on the cross. — AUTH, QUO, C.P., FAR, DESCRIP, JEST

33. Let me tell you something, friends. The safest road to hell is the gradual one! When I was thirteen, I started smoking cigarettes; and I won't go on and tell what else happened in my life, but believe me it was gradual, and believe me I was headed straight for hell. I know what it is to be a nominal believer. I almost spent eternity being tortured forever in hell fire because of nominalism. And this is one man you're not going to find being a nominal believer again. — STA

34. Now at the same time I am not a legalist. And the thing that I'm going to be saying here I'm going to be qualifying, because these are just principles, they are just standards, they're not laws, they're not legal ways of earning righteousness or salvation. But a believer is someone who is born again and a voting member is someone who is *also* a number of other things. He's open to the infilling of the Holy Spirit (he doesn't quench the Sprit but desires to be filled); he has been immersed; he believes — ASYND, ANTITH

in the sound doctrine of an infallible, divinely
inspired Bible, one God, the trinity, the virgin
birth, water immersion, the Lord's Seder, divine
healing, salvation through Yeshua alone, a real
hell for unbelievers, a Final Judgment and the
New Heavens and the New Earth. In this way the
doctrine doesn't get watered down, because if
it gets diluted, then the voting constituency
votes in a liberal, and then the liberal CLIM
doesn't preach the Gospel any more, and then
the whole house of cards collapses. METAPH

35. Furthermore, this voting member has separated himself from secret unbelieving, unregenerate
societies. I'm not going to name names about AMBIG
what some of those societies are, but you ASYND
know what they are. They come together,
they have a kind of Ku Klux Klan "Grand CON-ABS
Master, Honorable Matron" ritualism, it's
all from the Bible they say, it's all PERIPH
wonderful, it's a mighty social aid for making
business contacts, and there's all kinds of IRONY
reasons to learn the mumbo-jumbo. The only AUX
problem is that the Scriptures say we are to
separate ourselves from unbelievers, and
secret societies are fellowships comprising
nominal believers or unbelievers.

36. With secret societies, the voting member also
avoids Hollywood pornography. For him or her,
theatrical pornography is bad news. Let me tell
you something, Goble has said "goodbye" to PERIPH
Burt Reynolds. You see? And it's very
important for me to say "goodbye" to him for
good and not get involved in that. Because
I was almost sucked into hell via the CONNOT
Hollywood pornography palaces once, and
that's enough. While I was counting those
light bulbs I was also dreaming about leaving
Indiana and going to Hollywood. And I know
all about the carnality and demonic control
in that type of worldliness. A believer who
goes to those types of films is as big a
hypocrite as Paul would have been if he attended
the gladiatorial orgies in Rome. SIM

37. The voting member has also renounced gambling
and bar-room dancing. (I'm not talking about ANTITH
dancing the Hora, I'm talking about dancing the

Hustle.) I'm talking about the general type of thing that the heathen are involved in. This is bad news and we've got to say no to it. I'm talking about deliverance from drugs of all kinds.

38. Finally, the voting member has a willingness to tithe to the local body. Malachi 3 says this: "Bring ye all the tithes into the storehouse that there might be meat for my house." It's the responsibility of the members who have the privilege to decide for the congregation to put their money where their mouth is. MAX

REFUT

39. Everything I'm saying, I'm saying with fear and trembling because I know I'm stepping on toes. If I had preached this sermon to SYNEC myself a few years ago I couldn't have handled it because I wasn't spiritually mature enough to agree with the Lord on these touchy personal matters. It's tough stuff I'm talking about, and it's not salvation I'm talking about -- ANTITH I'm talking about responsibility, that adult responsibility we must have to be good stewards for God. It is this principle, not a mere PUR list of laws or do's and don't's, that I'm exhorting you to respect, so that we would not use our freedom as a cover-up for evil.

40. Now what does this mean? This means that for Goble and each one of us Yeshua has got to become our social director, our entertainment CON-ABS advisor and critic, our censor, our dancing instructor, our dietician, our disc jockey, our conscience, our tour guide, our escort -- He has got to come into our life and take control of it, and get into our home and turn off the boob tube and have devotions with our children and make them into disciples and train them up the way they should go. It's going to mean a total consecration of our lives to Yeshua. We're not playing games, this is ANTITH not social religion. This is life or death reality and many people may or may not come to know Yeshua as their Messiah because of what we do and the decisions we make.

41. What does this mean? This means that if any of
you have been thinking while I've been talking, ANAD
"Wait a minute. Is Goble saying 'I can't do
this, and I can't do that and what if I want
to do this once in a while, does this mean I
can't do it? Wait a minute! Wait till he gets
off that podium and I get a chance to talk to
him after the service. I'm going to tell him
a thing or two. If I want to do this any time
I can and that's it, etc.'"

42. Now I'm not saying that you should battle me. COMM
Battle yourself! *I've* got to keep control
over Goble. I pommel my body and subdue it,
lest preaching to others, I myself should
fall short of the prize. I'm the guy who LOG
doesn't want to drive the bus. I'm the guy
who doesn't want to pick up the people. I'm
the guy who maybe would like to get lazy once
in a while. I've got to keep Goble under
control and keep him in the bus. My battle
is against the old man within me. The battle
is within you and you've got to win it. It's ANTIM
within me and I've got to win it. And you know
why? Because I've got to keep blood off Goble's EPIS
hands. Because let me tell you something, SYNEC
people are going to hell. And if I don't
straighten up and fly right, their blood is
going to be on my hands. And I've got to
keep Goble under control. And so do you.
So don't come up here and grab me by the tie.
Grab yourself by the tie, because we're in
warfare. And this is real tribulation we're
going through. But praise God, we don't
have to get on a guilt trip because God loves
us and He's helping us and if you say you can't
quit the Klu Klux Klan, it's true you can't be HUM
a voting member until you drop your membership. HYPER
Okay, don't have a nervous breakdown-- we'll
wait for you. We're not going anywhere. Keep
hanging in here, you'll become a voting member
some day. P-I

43. And when I say that, I don't mean that by becoming a voting member, you join an elite.
I don't mean that, and please don't interpret
me that way, because everything I've said can
be misinterpreted and distorted if you want

to, but it's not that. I'm not saying that.
It's responsibility. If Goble has a problem
and he's guilty of immorality, Goble's got to ANTE-
get out of the ministry. And pray that someone CON
else will come in and take over so that what
has been started will remain. And if a person
is toying with some cult-practice or the occult,
he'd better not become a voting member. It's
that simple. Because people will come in and
look at us and if we lower the standards, then
we'll really let the dike down and other people
will take over. There are people who would
like to come in and make this a Jewish social
club and they'd like to bring all this worldly CONN
garbage in with them. They're going to say,
"Well, look if the leaders do this and the DEG
voters do this, then why can't I do that?"
And pretty soon you'll have just exactly what ADVIS
you don't want. And this is what we cannot
have. And this is what I'm trying to say. SYNEC
Get the blood off your hands, because the INDUCT
blood of all the people who'll be lost is on ENTHY
our hands if we don't straighten up.
(Numbers 32:15; Ezekiel 33:8)

44. Let me ask you something. Would you go to a hospital with a doctor who had not been properly screened? Where they haven't been properly schooled? And tested and approved by the high standards of a competent medical school? Would you risk your physical health
with people like that? No, you wouldn't, ELLIP
would you? This is more important than that DEG
because this is spiritual well-being for eternity. What we're going to ask people to do is to trust God and to come with us. And when we say us, we're talking about *all* of us, but we're particularly talking about the decision makers: the ministers and voting members among us who are consecrated and sanctified. Hear this now: *We will not lower the standards*. We will not lower the standards for the ministry or the voting members. We will not lower the standards,
but we will by God's help *raise the people to* ADVIS
the standards. And so they'll start to grow. And if we don't help them to grow, if we don't give them standards, if we just say, "It's

all right, if you enjoy gambling, praise God,"
then we've made a real mistake. ADVIS

45. Let me tell you something. I don't miss the PERIPH
world. I don't miss Burt Reynolds. You know
why? Because I get so busy seeking the
kingdom first, I don't have time to worry
about whether I'm unhappy or not. I don't
have time for Hollywood nonsense because I'm
too busy serving God. Now if you're into some
kind of inner psychological turmoil where BATH
you're dealing with yourself as a psychoanalyst
trying to understand this unhappiness you're
going through, what I would say to you is very
simple: Pick up your sacrifice tree, forget
about yourself and follow Yeshua. Get so busy EUPH
working for God that you don't have time to
worry about worldly happiness. Because, let
me tell you something, there are going to be
a lot of people who are going to be eternally
unhappy if you don't get busy. And if you do ANTITH
get busy, God will give you joy the world can
never know. Lose your life in Yeshua and you
will find it. Die to the world and rest in
the Lord!

46. Now there are certain rebels who are not going ADVIS
to like what I'm saying. But rebels don't build
lasting congregations. They burn their bridges
and cut themselves off from their supply lines. ALLUS
We're not going to do this. We're going to
have Bible colleges where we can draw a steady
supply of trained Jewish leaders. We're going
to have congregations like the congregation in
Ft. Lauderdale where we've already gotten so
many good leaders. We're going to have congregations all over the world where these Jewish
people are coming in off the street and getting
saved and then they're going to want to go to
their own people and we're going to be able to
tap into them. We're not going to be rebels
that cut off that source of supply. Now anyone
can become a rebel. That's what we were before ADVIS
we were saved, but a rebel only hurts himself
when he's dealing with the Lord and the Lord's
work.

SUM

47. We weren't called to be rebels. We were called to put to death, to crucify the old rebel that used to be us, and let the submitted humble One, Yeshua, take over in the rebel's place. "Take no part in the unfruitful works of darkness, but instead expose them." This is what I've tried to do in this message. I've tried to expose the unfruitful works of darkness. They are all rebellion. A minister who won't listen to his presbyter or elder can be just as rebellious as a layman who won't stop cursing and gambling. And remember, the sin of rebellion is as the sin of witchcraft (I Sam. 15:23). Now I'm sure that maybe on this little point or on that little point maybe somebody may have disagreed with me as I went through this material. But what I'm asking you to do even if you don't agree with every little dot and tittle of what I've said, is to agree with the basic point: which is my concern that you haven't been wasting your time for the last year, my concern that if you drop dead tomorrow this thing will go on, that every time you came to one of these services it meant something and it will continue to mean something long after you're dead. Agree with me about God's insurance policy that if your monthly payments are silver and gold, your dividend will be collectable because your work will remain. If the payments bother you, at least agree with me on the soundness of the policy because it's the Lord's. Don't compromise the high standards, don't become proud, suspicious, unsubmissive, unteachable and rebellious. Others have done it before you. Expressions of Judaism have done it. Expressions of Christianity have done it. We have no excuse because history has warned us. God has warned me and I'm afraid of God. I'm warning you in love as a brother. Don't build with wood or grass or straw. If you do, the quality of your work will be revealed for what it is. Build with presbyters and elders and ministers and voting members, with fellowship loyalty rooted in sound doctrine and high moral standards. Build with silver and gold. If you don't respect me, respect the blood, sweat and tears I have given before you. Respect the

CONTRAR

OBSERV

ANAL

PARAL

ETH

the hard work with silver and gold that has gone before you. Respect it enough to hear me. God bless you. (See Ezra 9:11-13; James 4:4; II Cor. 6:14-18; Romans 6:1-2) SYNEC

FORMULA-SUMMARY OF SERMON OUTLINE

PROPOSITION (*x*, not *y*, is true about *z*)

(1) INTRODUCTION (The fact that *x*, not *y*, is true about *z* is introduced)

(2) EXPLANATION (*z* defined and magnified)

(3) ARGUMENTATION (*x* defined and recommended)

(4) REFUTATION (*y* defined and indicted)

(5) SUMMATION (*x* particularized and applied)

CALLED TO BELONG

One of the deepest desires each of us has is to have fellowship with others. This is especially true of new believers who seek to walk in newness of life. Such fellowship can be found through membership in the local congregation. Congregational membership means mutual benefits and responsibilities for both the congregation and the member.

The Congregation Should Expect Me to:

-- faithfully attend its services.
-- be aware of the total congregational program at home and abroad and to support it by prayer.
-- live a consistent life as a believer.
-- serve in the congregation and its outreach according to my abilities.
-- share my faith by word and life on a person-to-person basis.
-- support its work by the methods of tithing (giving a tenth of my income) and offerings.

I Should Expect the Congregation to:

-- minister to my spiritual needs, especially through the preaching of the Word.
-- assist me with godly counsel especially in times of decision, stress, and difficulty.
-- provide me with opportunities for fellowship.
-- serve me and members of my family in matters of religious instruction.
-- sustain me by the prayers and concern of leaders and fellow believers in any of the distressing circumstances of life.
-- be a sound steward of my financial and personal investments in the kingdom of God.

WE BELIEVE:

-- the Bible is the inspired and only infallible and authoritative Word of God. (2 Tim. 3:16)
-- there is one God, eternally existent as God the Father, God the Son (the Devahr Adonoi -- the Word of the Lord), and God the Holy Spirit. (2 Cor. 13:14)
-- in the deity of our Lord Yeshua the Messiah, in His virgin birth, in His sinless life, in His miracles, in His vicarious and atoning death, in

His bodily resurrection, in His ascension to the right hand of the Father, and in His personal future return to this earth in power and glory. (Matt. 16:16; I Cor. 15:3, 4)

-- in the blessed hope, which is the rapture of the believers at Messiah's coming. (Titus 2:13)

-- the only means of being cleansed from sin is through repentance and faith in the precious blood of Messiah. (I Pet. 1:18, 19)

-- regeneration by the Holy Spirit is absolutely essential for personal salvation. (John 3:3-5)

-- the redemptive work of Messiah on the tree provides healing of the human body even today by God's grace. (I Pet. 2:24)

-- the infilling with the Holy Spirit is for now, even today manifest by speaking in unknown languages as in Acts 2:4; 10:44-46; 15:8, 9 since God has not changed (Hebrews 13:8).

-- in the sanctifying power of the Holy Spirit by whose indwelling the believer is enabled to live a holy life. (Gal. 5:16)

-- in the resurrection of both the saved and the lost, the one to everlasting life and the other to everlasting damnation. (John 5:28, 29)

APPLICATION FOR MEMBERSHIP

Having personally experienced the new birth through faith in the atoning blood of the Lord Yeshua the Messiah, and being in agreement with the doctrines and practices of this congregation and desiring to be associated with those of like precious faith in fellowship, I hereby apply for membership.

Mr.
Mrs.
Miss ______________________________ Phone ________

Address ________________ City ________________

State ________________ Zip ________________

Occupation ______________________________

Business Address ________________ Phone ________

Date of Birth ____________ Place of Birth ____________

Date first believed ______________________________

Mikvahed in Water?________ Infilled with Holy Spirit?_____

Marital Status:

Single ______ Married ______ Widowed ______ Remarried _____

Names and Birth Dates of Children:______________________

____

I am applying for: Adult Membership ___ Associate Membership

(age) ___ Junior Membership (under 12 years of age) ____

(age classification determined by congregation)

My membership has previously been in congregation ________

Address ________________ City ________________

State ________________ Zip ________________

( ) Please send for a letter of transfer from the above congregation.

Date ____________ Signature ______________________

ENLISTMENT FOR SERVICE

To help provide opportunities for meaningful ministry through your congregation, please check areas in which you have experience or interest in serving. What positions of service have you held in the past?

____

____

____

Check all areas where you have experience or would be willing to serve:

____ Religious Education

____ Temple Office

____ Transportation

____ Greeting

____ Visitation

____ Women's Sisterhood Council

____ Junior Sisterhood

____ Youth

____ Men's Brotherhood

____ Junior Brotherhood

____ Prayer Ministry

____ Telephoning

____ Nursery

Music:

____ Song Leading

____ Choir

____ Special Music

____ Instrumental Music

____ Instrument (s) __________

____

____ Other ______________

I am available: Days _________

Evenings _____ Saturdays _____

Other ____________________

Action of Temple Board ____________________

Date ______________________________

GLOSSARY

Below are a list of terms describing the types of rhetorical devices, lines of arguments and figures of speech that are to be found in the discourse. You can find the section of the speech that the term refers to by looking at the paragraph number given in the section. For example, if something is found in paragraph 13 it will be designated 13. There are some kinds of support that are not used in the speech although it is replete with most of the kinds of support used, omitting a few such as poetry, hymns, commercials, epitaphs, atheletics, nature, biography, word studies, editorial cartoons, prayers, and audio visual aids.

ADVIS. - ADVISORY ARGUMENT

This is the kind of argument that exhorts someone to do something or not to do something, that advises an audience to adopt a certain line of action in the future and generally employs four kinds of persuasion: do it (or don't do it) because of the good, the unworthy, the advantageous, the disadvantageous. To see these kinds of arguments employed in the speech, study 43, 44, and 46. An advisory argument is applied when we speak to the lost about salvation or when we speak to believers about getting involved in something in the future, from a bake sale to a building program.

ALLEG. - ALLEGORY

An allegory is the figurative treatment of one subject under the guise of another subject, such as in *Animal Farm* or in *Pilgrim's Progress*. There is no allegory in this sermon; however, because an allegory is an extended metaphor, the comparison of presbyters to "chess bishops" in 26 is a metaphor which I could have extended into an allegory in this way: On the chess board of God's kingdom, you and I were not intended to be pawns of Satan. For we have an ivory king -- Yeshua -- that God has already played to checkmate the devil. But that match is not all the contest, since God intends to play not only us, but also his bishops which we call presbyters. God intends us to use all his pieces to win the contest, but some silly players -- not following God's rules -- think they can win just as well without playing the bishop! They can't, and neither can we. (A Scriptural example of allegory is Galatians 4:21-31.)

ALLIT. - ALLITERATION

The repetition of initial consonant sounds in consecutive words or words close together such as"Pretty as a picture," or "dead as a doornail." An example is "frail or fickle" in 25.

ALLUS. - ALLUSION

A means of colorful language by indirect reference such as "supply line" in 46 which is a military allusion reminiscent of Ephesians 6:10-20.

AMBIG. - AMBIGUITY

An intentional vagueness such as my refusal to specify clearly the lodges I am referring to in 35.

ANAD. - ANADIPLOSIS

The repetition of the last word of one clause at the beginning of the following clause such as in the statement, "children need parents, parents need pastors, pastors need presbyters." You will find this in the first line of 41 and toward the end of 24.

ANAL. - ANALOGY

A partial resemblance between two unlike things which points up meaning in one or both of them. An analogy can also show similarity in proportional relationships, so that as A is to B, so C is to D. Or as A is in B, so C is in D. In 47 I draw an analogy between an insurance policy and its premiums and dividends, and building with presbyters, members, and ordained ministers.

ANAPH. - ANAPHORA

The repetition of the same word or group of words at the beginnings of successive clauses or sentences. See the repetition of "you've got" in 17. Winston Churchill used this stylistic device when he gave a speech saying, "We shall fight on the beaches, we shall fight on the landing grounds, we shall fight ..."

ANAST. - ANASTROPHE

The inversion of a natural or usual word order so that something occurs in the sentence in a backward way.

An example of this is in 3 where I say, "A good time will be had by all" instead of, "All will have a good time."

ANEC. - ANECDOTE

A short little story with a ring of truth to it or actual truth to it, such as is found 6.

ANTE-CON. - ANTECEDENT AND CONSEQUENCE

A loose kind of cause and effect argument where the persuader argues, "Given this situation or cause (the antecedent), a certain effect (the consequence) follows." This type of argument is found at the top of 43 with the sentences beginning "If Goble" and "If a person."

ANTHIM. - ANTHIMERIA

The substitution of one part of speech for another, such as the word "Talmud" in 11 which is normally a noun but has been changed into an adjective in a coined word. We use this figure of speech when we say a sentence like, "Turn it off before you *television* me to death."

ANTIM. - ANTIMETABOLE

The repetition of words in successive clauses in reverse grammatical order. I did not actually employ this figure of speech, but it would have been very appropriate in 42 where I say, "My battle is against the old man within me." I could have also added the antimetabole, "You win over the evil within you, or the evil within you will win over you."

ANTITH. - ANTITHESIS

A figure of speech in which irreconcilable opposites or strongly contrasting ideas are placed close togehter and in sustained tension, such as when Abraham Lincoln said in the Gettysburg Address, "The world will little note nor long remember what we say here, but it can never forget what they did here." Antithesis is when you say a negative and a positive together, such as "I'm not saying this, I'm saying this." Examples of antithesis are in 11, 34, 37, 39, 40 and 45.

APOST. - APOSTROPHE

This is the device of addressing an absent person or a personified abstraction such as in I Cor. 15:55. I could have used apostrophe in 28 if I had said, "Paul, you don't mind if I have a cocktail, do you?"

APPOS. - APPOSITION

The placing of one word or expression next to another in order to explain it. Appositions are normally set apart by dashes and commas. Notice the use of apposition in 22 and 29.

ARGU. - ARGUMENTATION

In the five main sections of a discourse (namely Introduction, Explanation, Argumentation, Refutation and Summing Up), Argumentation is the portion where all the arguments and the complete presentation of one's case is presented in the speech. My argumentation goes from 14 to 38.

ASSON. - ASSONANCE

The repetition of similar vowel sounds, preceded and followed by different consonants, in the stressed syllables of adjacent words, such as in "hope for Goble, even if he blows it" in 1.

ASYND. - ASYNDETON

The deliberate ommission of conjunctions between a series of related clauses, such as in "I came, I saw, I conquered." Notice this in 34 and 35.

AUTH. - AUTHORITY

An argument from authority is an argument stating the opinion of a respected or well known man. In messianic persuasion the opinion of a famous Jew that is favorable to Jesus or Christianity can be an important argument. I use this type of argument in 32 when I refer to C. S. Lewis.

AUX. - AUXESIS

This is the use of a dramatic term or name for something by which the very name carries an argumentative force.

For instance, to call pilfering embezzlement is to use auxesis. In 6 I use auxesis when I refer to "myself" as "Number One." I also use auxesis in 35 when I refer to the ritualism of lodges as "mumbo jumbo."

BATH. - BATHOS

An unintentionally or intentionally ludicrous attempt to portray grief or pity in order to ridicule or burlesque the emotions or to show their inappropriateness. It can also be used when one speaks in a straight-faced manner with elevated language in describing trivial subject matter with emotion. By the intonation in my voice I demonstrated bathos in 45 when I spoke about the soap opera-like turmoil that self-pitying believers go through.

BIB. - BIBLICAL QUOTE

The entire speech is seasoned with Biblical quotes that are used to make arguments. One example is 20 when I quote I Tim. 4:12.

C-E - CAUSE AND EFFECT

This is a line of argument that can work in two directions: either arguing from an effect back to a cause or starting with a cause and arguing that it will produce a particular effect or effects. This type of argument is found in 11 where I argue that the cause of getting wrapped up in rituals leads to the effect of cold formalism. I also use cause and effect in 16 to explain my feelings.

CHIAS. - CHIASMUS

The Greek for "criss-cross," which is a reversal of grammatical structures in successive phrases or clauses such as in the sentence, "It is hard to make money; to spend money it is easy." I did not use this figure of speech in my discourse but I could have used it quite easily at the end of 14 had I said something like, "With their parents, decent kids; but trashy heathen, with their peers."

CLIM. - CLIMAX

The arrangement of units of meaning (words, phrases, clauses or sentences) in an ascending order of importance until a high point of interest is reached. See Romans 5:3-5 for an example. This figure of speech is found in the series of questions in 12 and in 34 in the last sentence.

COMM. - COMMAND

This exclamatory rhetorical device is found in the first line of 42.

CONCLU. - CONCLUSION

This is the last part of a chain of reasoning or the final thought in an argument that is based on evidence stated previously. Often called an inference, you can see examples of this in 14 and 17, where summary sentences at the ends of the paragraphs nail down the exact argument that is being stated and refer back to the evidence given in the paragraph.

CON. ABS. - CONCRETE AND ABSTRACT DICTION

This is the use of very descriptive or colorful particular things to describe abstractions such as the concrete words like Ku Klux Klan and "grand master, honorable matron" in 35 to describe abstractions like "foolish ritualism." Notice also in 40 how the abstraction of Yeshua's Lordship is made real by using concrete words like "social director" and "dietician." Generally speaking, the more concrete and pictorial the word is, the better it communicates than abstract words. In 40 it would have been somewhat boring to say that "Yeshua should have control over our social life and should be our guide in daily living." By using concrete words this is avoided.

COND. - CONDITIONAL

This is a line of argument which argues that hypothetically, if a certain condition is or is not met, then something will or will not follow. In 11 it is a conditional argument to say that if the substance gets lost in the form, then a structural weakness will be created. This type of argument is different from the cause and effect argument because what it is that's being argued is set in a hypothetical framework referring to conditions in the future.

CONN. - CONNOTATION

The implication of the word beyond its strict meaning (denotation). In 36 I could have used a word with fairly neutral connotation for Hollywood theatres, calling them movie theatres, but instead I used negative connotations in "pornography places." Also in 43 instead of saying "worldly *inessentials*" I used stronger connotation and said "worldly *garbage*." It's important to be careful about the use of connotation. For example, the word "politician" denotes something that "statesman" does not. Connotation is the implication of the word, what it suggests emotionally to the hearer.

CONTRAD. - CONTRADICTIONS

This is a line of argument in which two propositions are stated in such a way that the truth of one requires that the other be false. This kind of argument is running beneath the surface in 24 where the implication of my logic is that either Heb. 13:17 applies to everybody or it applies to nobody. Since it cannot be that Heb. 13:17 applies to nobody, it must apply to everybody, *leaders* and followers alike.

CONTRAR. - CONTRARIES

An argument based on contraries has its strength in contrast. In 47 to be a rebel is bad because it is contrasted with being submissive which is good, since this behavior describes Yeshua. The force of the argument that to be a rebel is bad is found in the strength of the contrast.

C.P. - COURTROOM PERSUASION

In contrast with advisory persuasion, this kind of appeal is what the lawyer uses in the courtroom when he pleads the legality of something based on law (in our case, Scripture) or the innocence or guilt of someone based on motives and causes of action. Very often in our speaking we have to level charges against the human race and present evidence for guilt; we have to define the nature of the charge that we are making and show how serious it is. At various times in the speech I have to decide whether or not the charge of nominality is just, so far as my own life is concerned and also in terms of certain types of ministers and believers. The lines of argument that are used are what is just or what is right, and what is unjust or wrong. I use courtroom persuasion to defend in 32. Also in my refutation I use courtroom persuasion to defend myself personally for making the stringent moral demands of sanctification that I make. I am countering certain silent charges of being a legalist or a prude or a dictator or a spoil-sport in the style of a lawyer. Very often I am accusing as a lawyer does, or I am defending the truth of the Word of God. I am speaking of what is unjust or unfair or immoral. Very often we attempt to persuade the "jury" in our audience to accept an interpretation of Scripture as authoritative and to agree about guilt or innocence. Very often my remarks tend in this direction: Who is the rebel? Who is the worldly man? Who is the witch? Who is on the Lord's side and who is against him? Who are the guilty ones? What is my answer to my objectors? What kind of people have to be exposed and discredited and why? What does the law (the Bible) say here? One of the weaknesses of my speech might be in that I do not defend enough. It is easier to accuse than it is to defend. Perhaps the speech is too negative and should be more positive. However, if you will notice, there is a great deal of positive material in 40, 45, and 46.

CURR. EV. - CURRENT EVENT

In our speaking we need to be in touch with the daily newspaper and with the recent historical happenings or the popular sayings of the day. Notice I make a reference to a currently popular black comedian named Richard Pryor in 3. It is good to read *Time* magazine or *Newsweek* so that your arguments have an "up-to-date" ring of relevance.

DEDUCT. - DEDUCTIVE REASONING

This is the type of argument that moves from a principle already known or assumed and moves to a conclusion. In 4 the conclusion that we will not tolerate irresponsible members is drawn or deduced from the principle that privilege requires responsibility. The argument runs:

Privilege requires responsibility.
These types of people are irresponsible.
Therefore, they cannot be members.

Anytime you argue from a principle you are arguing deductively and you are using deductive reasoning.

DENOT. - DENOTATION

Direct specific meaning as distinct from additional suggestion which is connotation. In 21 the definition given of presbyter is denotation, the dictionary meaning.

DEF. - DEFINITION

This is a means of describing something or arguing something by breaking the idea down into its various aspects in order to define it more carefully. This I do in 10, 13, 19, and 30. An argument by definition is used whenever you show that what is true of the genus (class) must also be true of the species (member of the class). For instance,we can prove that John Smith will die because he is a member of the class called man. Since all men are mortal, and since mortality is true of the class, it must be true of the species within the class. One of the arguments by definition in my speech is that since nominalism is bad, anything that falls into that category (or is a species in that genus) is also bad by definition.

DEG. - DEGREE

This is the familiar line of argument called *a fortiori* which affirms that whatever is true of the lesser of something must be true of the greater of something and to an even greater extent. This argument is used in 44 to say that if standards are required of a medical school dealing with only physical life, how much more should standards apply to a spiritual school which pertains to eternal life! Actually the *a fortiori* argument can also apply in the opposite direction because in 43 the would-be members of the congregation are arguing that if the greater leaders and voters can do carnal things how much more should the lesser people (the new members) be allowed to do carnal things.

DESCRIP. - DESCRIPTION

Description is picture-painting words that sharpen the audience's view of the speaker's point. In 16, notice that it would have been less persuasive to say, "Until the day they killed Paul," because the descriptive term adds its own persuasion in saying "they cut his head off." Also in 32 it helps to see what nominalism is (a deafness to the Word of God). And this story with all its descriptive details about a little boy listening to a sermon makes nominalism more vivid and real, like photos of a battlefield's carnage can make a war real.

DIFF. - DIFFERENCE

This is a familiar line of argument in which two things are compared and contrasted in order to make an argumentative point. The speaker who contrasts democracy with communism in order to argue for the American way of life is using this line of argument called difference. An example is in 5 to 8 which compares and contrasts God's house and "my house." Here I was able to show how materialistic worldliness can creep into one's home and turn it into an idol. I wanted more than just a bland "word study" definition of God's house. I wanted to polemically define God's house in a way that would spotlight the tension of the entire discourse, which is between rebellious materialistic idolatry and humble submissiveness.

DIV. - DIVISION

Division is enumerating the parts of something in order to more clearly define it. When a man says there are only five possible solutions, a), b), c), d), and e) but then goes through to show that the only true solution is c) he has in effect done argument by division. You can see argument by division in 10, 14, 15, 18, and 30.

ELLIP. - ELLIPSIS

The deliberate omission of a word or words which are readily implied and understood by means of the context. Very often in speech we don't bother to speak in complete sentences. For instance in 11 "Where we don't break through that incessant ritualism to have a real on-going relationship with God" is not a sentence in the strict grammatical sense. It is a fragment, but the staccato pace of what is being said makes the fragment work. Notice also the elliptical questions at the beginning of 44 which are not complete sentences and yet fit because of the rapidity of the thought which they enhance.

EMOT. - EMOTIONAL APPEAL

When we persuade someone, not only is it permissible to get emotional, but it is really necessary because people decide with their emotions as well as their thinking. An example of an emotional appeal in the discourse is 20 where I am speaking about an adulterous minister. My anger is stirred (it is quite genuine) and it is my intention to stir the anger of the audience because without that anger they will not be moved to decide to submit to the authorities that can be used by God to control such an enraging situation, namely the presbyters. There is more emotional appeal of this type in 21. Remember: people do not get angry by thinking about anger. People do not get joyful thinking about joy. Anger and joy arise from the contemplation of enraging things and acts or wonderful things and acts.

ENTHY. - ENTHYMEME

An enthymeme is an argumentative statement that contains a conclusion and one of the premises, the other premise being implied. If both premises are stated you have a syllogism. To state the argument of my speech syllogistically would be to say:

(First Premise) Nominalism destroys congregations.
(Second Premise) High standards protect against nominalism.
(Conclusion) Therefore, we should maintain high standards

However, to compress the argument into the form of an enthymeme would be to simply make a statement like, "We should maintain high standards because nominalism destroys congregations." One of the premises is missing but for the sake of brevity to get on with the argument and to finish the speech, very often if a premise is fairly well understood it does not have to be explicitly spelled out. There are many enthymemes in this speech. The word "because" is usually a signal of an enthymeme since it is a word used to state a conclusion based on some type of support which also involves premises. The last sentence in 43 is an enthymeme because the implied premise that is not stated is that the saved have a responsibility to warn the lost.

EPAN. - EPANALEPSIS

The repetition at the end of a clause of a word that occurred at the beginning of a clause. An example of epanalepsis is in 5 where I say my house is not God's house, repeating the word "house" at the beginning and end of a clause or sentence. I could have used epanalepsis with a phrase like "carnality invites carnality, permissiveness spawns permissiveness, sin begets sin, and rebels breed rebels."

EPIS. - EPISTROPHE

The repetition of a same word or group of words at the ends of successive clauses as in "the battle is within you, and you've *got to win it,* it's within me and I've *got to win it,*" which is found in 42. Another example: In the world, liquor *is sacred,* gambling *is sacred,* illicit love *is sacred.*" This is the use of epistrophe.

ETH. - ETHICAL APPEAL

The character of the speaker is his ethical appeal, as opposed to the emotional frame of mind of the audience toward him or the logical arguments he presents. In II Corinthians, chapters 11, 12, and 13 Paul deals heavily in ethical appeal to make his persuasion. You can see this resorted to in 47 in the last few sentences of the speech.

ETY. - ETYMOLOGY

The business of tracing the original meaning of words by studying their history as they were borrowed from other languages. In 13, although I did not take the time to give the history of the word "nominal" which comes from a Latin word which means "name," at least I gave the etymological definition "in name only." Here, Webster's Dictionary can be helpful because it will give you the etymology. If you look up the word "presbyter" in the Webster's dictionary it will tell you that it comes from a word meaning "elder."

EUPH. - EUPHEMISM

A figure of speech in which something of an unpleasant, distressing or inelegant nature is described in less offensive terms, such as using the words "passed away" for "died." I use a euphemism for the word "cross" in 45, substituting the word "tree" instead. In order not to offend the taste of people it is necessary often to use euphemisms so that there will be no distraction caused by our language and persuasion can still occur.

EXAMP. - EXAMPLE

Any precedent that illustrates a point (be it positively or negatively). In 6 I use the example of getting a new carpet to make a point about idolatry.

EXCLAM. - EXCLAMATION

An exclamation is an excited emphatic statement usually punctuated by an exclamation mark(!). If used sparingly, it is a key way of drawing attention to the most important ideas in the speech. It's used in 29.

EXEG. - EXEGESIS

Exegesis is the science in theology whereby the correct and Scripturally compatible meaning of a particular passage is drawn out and exposed to the reader. When several alternative interpretations are compared and eliminated down to a Scripturally compatible interpretation which does not contradict the relevant Old Testament and New Testament passages, then exegesis is accomplished. Expository preaching is good because it utilizes a sermon development with rich exegesis of the text, its meaning and application.

EXPLAN. - EXPLANATION

The section of the speech known as the Explanation is the portion that follows the Introduction. This is a preliminary explanation of background details in anticipation of the Argumentation portion. In this speech it extends from 3 to 13 and explains the problem of nominalism in a general way in anticipation of the argument which will deal with the specifics of nominalism. This is to prepare the audience and orient them to be able to digest the argument by informing them in advance with the background material of the argument. In many messages this will be the place for exegesis, which is a critical interpretation of the text.

F-I - FACT-INTERPRETATION

A statement is made and then an interpretation from the statement is presented. This is a familiar pattern of rhetoric and is found in 16 where the fact is stated that I wanted to leave and then the interpretation is made that I was rationalizing. Also an example is found in 20 where the fact is stated that ministers have committed adultery in the past. Then the interpretation is made that this is terrible and must be dealt with.

FAL. CON. - FALSE CONCLUSION

This tactic in rhetoric is to offer a posssible deduction which may be in the audience's mind but then point out that it is false, as in 24.

GEN-SPEC. - GENERAL SPECIFIC

An aid to clarity is never leaving a general statement without specifically illustrating it in order to make it clear as in 14 where it says that "Mom loved the Lord" (general statement), "but she let the kids bring acid rock records into the house" (specific statement).

HIST. - HISTORICAL EVENT

A good way of illustrating any message is to refer to an historical event such as in 28 which is a reference to the Jerusalem council meeting in Acts 15.

HUM. - HUMOR

A surprise perception of a disharmony which is usually absurd but also in a sense true at the same time. The surprise may come from a tense expectation suddenly changing to nothing but it may come from a strange reversal from the norm. Examples are found in 3 and 28 which are incidentally two strategic places for humor, in the beginning and the middle of any discourse where the tension may be getting too high or the attention may be getting too low.

HYPER. - HYPERBOLE

The use of exaggerated terms for the purpose of emphasis or heightened effect such as in 42 with the thought, "Don't have a nervous breakdown." Obviously, the term "nervous breakdown" is an exaggeration but is intended for effect to point out that getting upset even a little about such a minor thing is overreacting. Therefore, I use an overly dramatic admonition. Hyperbole is a figure of speech that is an intentional exaggeration for emphasis or comic effect.

INDUCT. - INDUCTIVE REASONING

Reasoning that brings forward a number of particular facts for the purpose of proving a general statement. Inductive reasoning is demonstrated in 43 where a series of little facts move the argument forward all the way to the final general statement which is "Get the blood off your hands." However, to get to that general statement there are a lot of little individual statements that move us forward to the general point. This is inductive reasoning.

INTRO. - INTRODUCTION

The Introduction of a speech is found in paragraphs 1 and 2 where the attention of the audience is gained and the general topic of the speech is presented in the last sentence of 2. The introduction is rather short because there is a good deal of explanation necessary in order to present the argument. The best introductions are usually short ones with perhaps a little humor (if appropriate) as in the last sentence of 1 and with some indications of what the speech is about and the direction that it's going to go.

IRONY - IRONY

A figure of speech in which the real meaning is concealed or contradicted by the literal meanings, as in: "That was a smart thing to do!" (means very foolish). It is an ironic statement. It rises from an awareness of what is and what ought to be and the disharmony between the two. In other words, it's a use of the word in such a way as to convey the meaning opposite to the real meaning of the word. One example of irony in this discourse is 3 where the last sentence says "stalwart" members of the temple and just the opposite meaning is actually conveyed. Also the phrase "it's all wonderful" found in 35 is an ironic statement which is indicated by the tone in a speaker's voice to mean the opposite.

JEST - JEST (PUNCHLINE)

This is a specific kind of humor where a punchline closes off the story as in 32, the last sentence.

KEN. - KENNING

Kenning is a compound of two or more words that is hyphenated and thrown together in such a way as to be highly descriptive such as "whale-path" for sea. An example is found in 11 where "Talmud-idolatry" becomes an invented name for a judao-pagan religion which claims to be Jewish but in actuality is not. The other example is found in the very long kenning on 20 which forms a highly descriptive adjective.

LAW - LAW

This type of argument utilized any statute, contract, testament, record or document that can be used to substantiate or refute a claim. For the believer this is any Scripture verse from the Bible. An example of the use of law for an argument is "obey your leaders" (24) which is a divine law which no one including pastors can break without suffering the consequences.

LIT. - LITOTES

A deliberate use of understatement not to deceive someone but to enhance the impressiveness of what we say. In Acts 21:39 Paul uses litotes when he says, "I am a Jew, from Tarsus in Cilicia, a citizen of no mean city," which is like saying "I am from New York, a citizen of no hick town." It is an understatement in the sense that Tarsus was an illustrous city in Cilicia. In 28 when I say that Peter and James were not drinking buddies, I am using an understatement. They were hardly that!

LOG. - LOGICAL APPEAL

There are two ways to argue logically against a proposition: We can prove that a proposition that is just the opposite is true, which will demolish the proposition that is being attacked; or we can undermine the argument by which the proposition is supported. This is a logical appeal as opposed to an emotional or ethical appeal.(42)

METAPH. - METAPHOR

An implicit comparison between two unlike entities which does not use the words "as" or "like." There is a metaphor on 20 where presbyters are compared to police and their God-given authority is compared to a club with which to drive unfit ministers from the ministry. Other metaphors are found in 26, 27 and 34.

MAX. - MAXIM

A saying which is a self-evidently true statement and is so widely accepted as true that no proof is needed to make it an acceptable argument. There is an allusion to a maxim in 16 which is the familiar saying that "the grass is always greener on the other side of the fence." Also, in 38 the saying that is very familiar is, "put your money where your mouth is."

OBSERV. - OBSERVANCE PERSUASION

As opposed to Advisory Persuasion or Courtroom Persuasion, this type of persuasion points to the occasion, celebrates the moment, and gives it meaning. Observance persuasion is found in 47 where I speak of the importance of the people coming to the services and being in the seats where they are seated right now. This type of persuasion is used on special occasions and holidays but it's also used during normal times when the meaning of the moment is in the foreground of the argument.

ONOM. - ONOMATOPOEIA

This is the use of words whose sound echoes the sense, as in the sentence, "The guns *boom* in the distance." The use of this figure of speech is found in 7 where the little voice is *clicked* off. Any time the imitation of natural sounds is found in the word formations of the speaker or in the rhythms and textures of his thoughts, he is using this communication technique.

PAR. - PARABLE

Like the fable, the parable is also a simple story. However, unlike the fable, which uses animal characters, the parable uses human characters and shows interest not so much in the story telling as in the analogy drawn between a particular instance of human behavior and human behavior generally. An example is in the analogy drawn between the particular behavior of the Prodigal Son and the behavior of humans generally. In this discourse, the story about the little boy counting the light bulbs and dreaming of Hollywood (32) is a parable, too (although it is also a personal testimony). It is like the parable about the Prodigal Son and also the sower who sowed on bad ground, where the desires for other things choked the word and made the individual unfruitful. Because the story of the little boy and the light bulbs uses a particular human instance to teach a single moral lesson about humanity in general, it is a parable with a teaching point -- that it is folly not to pay attention to the Word of God.

PAR T - PARADOXICAL TERM

This is an apparently self-contradictory term, the underlying meaning of which is revealed only by careful thought. "Less is more" is a paradoxical statement intended to gain attention and provoke fresh thought. Two-word paradoxes are terms like "living death" and "loud silence," or like the term "little tin pope" which is a mixture of opposite or contradictory ideas and is found in 24.

PARODY - PARODY

This is the intentional ridicule of someone which usually involves the imitation of their words. In 28 it is not Paul or Timothy who are being parodied, but it is the ordinary worldly person who is being ridiculed, such as your average bridge player or gambler.

PARAL. - PARALLELISM

This is the use of coordinate ideas arranged in phrases, sentences and paragraphs that balance one element with another of equal importance and similar wording. Scriptural examples of parallelism are in Psalm 78:4, 36. The parallelism in 47 arranges coordinate ideas in contrast: "Don't build with wood or grass or straw; build with presbyters, ordained ministers and voting members." Three ideas are coordinated and contrasted with three other ideas.

PAREN. - PARENTHESIS

A comment that is inserted into another passage with parenthetical markings to bracket it off. Two examples are in 2 and 22.

P.F.F.F. - PAST FACT AND FUTURE FACT

This line of argument is based on the principle that if something has happened before, it can happen again, or if the means has been available, then the end can be accomplished. This line of argument is demonstrated in 31 to show that this type of nominalism has occurred in the past and it can very well occur in the future in the Temple. Also 11 is the same type of argument.

PERIPH. - PERIPHRASIS

The substitution of a descriptive word or phrase for a proper name, or of a proper name for a quality associated with the name, as in the sentence about "Ku Klux Klan ritualism" in 35 or "saying goodbye to Burt Reynolds" in 36 and 45 where "Burt Reynolds" becomes a figure of speech symbolizing the whole of carnal Hollywood. We use this figure of speech every day when we say things like "he's a regular 'Babe Ruth' at baseball."

PERSON. - PERSONIFICATION

Where human qualities or characteristics are attributed to unhuman entities. Anything can be personified from the moon to death to knowledge or even the Devil who is not a human being but is a supernatural spiritual being. Notice the personification in 14 where it says "nominalism *sneaked* into the house." Also 16 where "the enemy was dangling carrots."

PER. EX. - PERSONAL EXPERIENCE

Personal experience is an excellent illustration because besides making good points it also tells the hearer something about the speaker and establishes his ethical appeal. An example is an anecdote that is based on personal experience at the bottom of 6.

POLYPT. - POLYPTOTON

This is the repetition of words derived from the same root, such as John F. Kennedy said in his inaugural, "Not as a call to *battle*, though *embattled* we are." An example of this in the discourse is found 12 where the words *discipline* and *disciples* are used close together.

POLYSYN. - POLYSYNDETON

This is the deliberate use of many conjunctions such as in Genesis 1:24-25. This rhetorical device is used in 31 where the word *and* is repeated several times deliberatly for effect.

P-I - POSSIBLE AND THE IMPOSSIBLE

This line of argument says that if the more difficult of two things is possible, then the easier of two things is also possible. Paul argues this way in Phil. 1:6 when he reasons that if something can be begun it can be finished. An example of this type of argument is found(42)where the text says "keep hanging in here, you'll become a voting member someday." The implied argument is that if it's possible for you to become a believer (which is more difficult) then it's even more possible for you to become a voting member (which is less difficult). And of course the understood assumption here is that all of these things are accomplished by the power of God.

PROP. - PROPOSITION

The proposition of a discourse is the point to be discussed or maintained in the argument and is usually stated in sentence form near the outset. "Privilege requires responsibility" is the proposition that the discourse argues because this is the principle implied in the text, I Cor. 3:10. This same principle is also found in Luke 12:48 which says "To whom much is given much is required." The science of homiletics (homiletics means saying the same thing) is concerned with saying only what the Bible says, no more, no less. It is difficult to expound or argue the depth of meaning of a passage of Scripture unless one can see the specific truth in the passage and argue the acceptance of that truth propositionally. The proposition is the compressed argument of the discourse stated as a principle or fundamental truth. To state a proposition is to predicate (assert) that one thing is true about another thing. In fact, the word "predication" used to actually mean "an act of preaching or proclaiming." A proposition is a statement that preaches that x is true of y. Put mathematically, the proposition has a simple formula: x = y. In the discourse the argument looks like this: x (the requirement of responsibility) = (is true of) y (priviledge). Or, to state it as a sentence with a subject and predicate it reads: Privilege requires responsibility. A message should deal with one proposition only and attempt to say only one thing. This message was attempting to say one thing: that privilege requires responsibility. In other words, the message could have begun by saying: Today I want to talk about privilege. I want to tell you one thing about it, and that is its requirement of responsibility. Notice, to have a proposition you must have a subject (privilege) and a predicate (requires responsibility). The predicate is the part of the sentence that "predicates" (asserts) something about the subject. To have an argument you must have more than a subject, you must also have an assertion to make about the subject. You can't argue something if you don't know what you're arguing. You must find the proposition that you are arguing before you can begin to support it. This is why you need to look at a text and study it carefully to see what one subject it's actually talking about and what argument about that one thing it is making. You should ask yourself the question, "what proposition am I trying to support by the use of this text?" (See paragraph 4.)

PUN - PUN

A play on words that sound alike but have different meanings. A pun is found in 13 where I say "some of this might come a little close to *home*," which is a play on words, since I am using the word *home* in two different senses. A famous pun is when Benjamin Franklin said, "If we don't *hang* together we'll *hang* separately.

PUR. - PURPOSE

Any time you see the words "in order that" or "so that" these words signal a purpose sentence. Ideally, there should be a statement of purpose at the beginning or early in the discourse as it is in 2 and this purpose should be reiterated from time to time as it is in 9 and 39. The purpose of the discourse will be accomplished if the arguments convince the hearers to take the line of action that is advised by the message.

Q-A - QUESTION AND ANSWER

This rhetorical device is to help the audience follow the line of thought. A question is asked and then answered. In the case of a rhetorical question, no answer is expected but is understood because of the obviousness of the answer. An example of question and answer is 9 and 22.

QUO. - QUOTATION

A quotation can be a very effective way of supporting an argument. This is why *Barlett's Familiar Quotations* has been a best seller for so long and is also why *Great Treasury of Western Thought* is included in this syllabus, because of the great wealth of extremely effective quotations that it contains. A quotation used in this discourse is found in 32 where C. S. Lewis is quoted.

REFUT. - REFUTATION

The Refutation is the portion of the speech which comes after the statement of the argument and is placed there in order to defend the argument against its attackers. Any time an argument is made there are objections that are raised in the minds of the hearers and these objections have to be dealt with or the argument will not effectively stand. The Refutation portion of this discourse goes from 39 to 47. During this portion the objectors who may be thinking that the speaker is a prude or kill joy or legalist are being disarmed of their objections. However, the Refutation does not always take place neatly in one particular portion following the Argumentation. For instance, refutation is seen in the speech almost immediately when the speaker throws a grenade, as it were, at his objectors in 3 by satirizing them with the business meeting announcement. This is refutation by wit. There is also refutation by emotional appeal as in 43 where the speaker's anger is stirred against the people who want to bring the "garbage" in. There is refutation by ethical appeal in 40 where the character of Yeshua is held up to refute the objectors. There is also refutation by logical appeal in 44 where the irrationality of lowering standards is shown. A good way of refuting a point which is not used in the message is to put the argument of the opponent into a syllogism which is absurd by the very erroneousness of the premises and conclusion. Once the opinions of men are shown to be contradictory to reason, they are refuted.

RESTA. - RESTATEMENT

To restate something is to say it again in other words. This is used in 21 where the idea of the presbyter being a territorial overseer is restated in that he is also said to be"over certain congregations in the area" which is really saying the same thing but saying it in different words so that it can be understood more readily. This is another method of definition.

R.P. - ROLE PLAYING

This dramatic device is illustrated in 28 where the speaker becomes two people and converses in their characters, playing different roles.

REPET. - REPETITION

In 20 the word "power" is repeated for emphasis. Repetition can be effective in driving home the point being made. However, it can also be tiresome if not used with constraint. For example, the phrase "let me tell you something" is repeated too frequently in this speech and it becomes a little tiresome.

SAR. - SARCASM

Sarcasm is a cutting rebuke such as in the phrase "little tin pope." In 24 sarcasm is directed against the pastor who is so cock sure of himself and independent that he is a rebel and will not listen to those over him in the Lord.

SAT. - SATIRE

A satire is a verbal caricature that shows a deliberately distorted image of a person, institution or society. The technique of the satirist is to exaggerate the disapproved features of what he is attacking. Paragraph 3 contains a satire of the typical church announcement which is heard every Sunday without fail. Like all satires, it mixes the familiar with the absurd. Notice the familiar sentence, "A good time will be had by all" but also the absurdity.

SEQ. - SEQUENCE

This is where an argument hinges on the time that a thing occurred, whether it was previous to something else or after it occurred. In the beginning of 16 you see how sequence is used to state temporal relationships in order to make the argument clear.

SIM. - SIMILARITY

This is a line of argument based on resemblance such as in 36.

SIMILE - SIMILE

This is a comparison with the words "as" or "like" used so that the comparison is more explicit. Paragraph 27 is a simile but instead of stating it directly as the speaker should have, he used an overworked, trite expression "kind of" when he should have stated the simile directly using either "as" or "like." Then he would have said, "It's *like* an insurance policy."

STA. - STATISTICS

Using figures or numbers to make an argument can be very effective because these are facts verifiable in an Almanac. A good place where a statistic could have been used is in 33. The speaker could have said something like "in the last 20 years suicides among youth have gone up 20%. This shows how teenagers are increasingly being sucked into hell, not in any overnight way but in a gradual way."

SUBJ. - SUBJECT

A formal discourse should have a subject and that's why the theme is stated at the beginning as "a sermon on standards for ministers and voting members." This is the subject or theme of the discourse.

SUM. - SUMMING UP

Paragraph 47 contains the Summing Up portion of the discourse. This is where the final opportunity occurs for the speaker to inspire his audience, to leave a favorable impression of himself and what he's been trying to say, to amplify the force of the point that he's been making, to extinguish the force of a point made by the opposition, to arouse the appropriate emotions in the audience, to lead them to an opportunity to make the decision he's been pleading for, and to restate in a summary way the facts and arguments that have been made in the entire discourse.

SYNEC. - SYNECDOCHE

A figure of speech in which a part stands for the whole, such as in "Give us this day our daily *bread*" where the word "bread" stands for all the food that we need for the day, not just bread. Other examples are in 39 where "toes" is a part standing for the whole person offended or in 42 where the word "blood" is a part standing for the whole person irresponsibly lost. The same figure of speech is employed in 43 and 47.

SYNON. - SYNONYNS

Words having nearly the same meaning, as in "free-wheeling, independent" in 25.

TEST. - TESTIMONIAL

A personal experience used to make a point which is generally one in which the person admits failure and also points to the grace of God as in 16.

TITLE - TITLE

A discourse should have a title that states the subject in a very poignant and dramatic way, one that is catchy to the memory and can be referred to easily, such as "Building with Silver and Gold."

HEBREW*

Jeremiah 31:31-34

days Behold

31 כָּל־הָאָדָם הָאֹכֵל הַבֹּסֶר תִּקְהֶינָה שִׁנָּיו׃ הִנֵּה יָמִים

when I
(of) house and (of) house will the
Judah \ Israel make Lord says coming

בָּאִים נְאֻם־יְהוָה וְכָרַתִּי אֶת־בֵּית יִשְׂרָאֵל וְאֶת־בֵּית יְהוּדָה

in their I which like
day fathers made covenant Not .new covenant

32 בְּרִית חֲדָשָׁה׃ לֹא כַבְּרִית אֲשֶׁר כָּרַתִּי אֶת־אֲבוֹתָם בְּיוֹם

to bring
they Egypt from them by I
broke which the land out the hand took them

הֶחֱזִיקִי בְיָדָם לְהוֹצִיאָם מֵאֶרֶץ מִצְרָיִם אֲשֶׁר־הֵמָּה הֵפֵרוּ

the the to a although
covenant this But says husband I
(is) .Lord them was my covenant

33 אֶת־בְּרִיתִי וְאָנֹכִי בָּעַלְתִּי בָם נְאֻם־יְהוָה׃ כִּי זֹאת הַבְּרִית

I
says days will which
those after Israel house make

אֲשֶׁר אֶכְרֹת אֶת־בֵּית יִשְׂרָאֵל אַחֲרֵי הַיָּמִים הָהֵם נְאֻם־

and I I will in their my
will write their and inward Torah I'll the
be it hearts on parts (Word) put Lord

יְהוָה נָתַתִּי אֶת־תּוֹרָתִי בְּקִרְבָּם וְעַל־לִבָּם אֶכְתֳּבֶנָּה וְהָיִיתִי

(each) they And my to will and their to
man teach not people me be they God them
again \ / /

34 לָהֶם לֵאלֹהִים וְהֵמָּה יִהְיוּ־לִי לְעָם׃ וְלֹא יְלַמְּדוּ עוֹד אִישׁ

his
all for (the) Know brother (each) companion
/ Lord / saying man

אֶת־רֵעֵהוּ וְאִישׁ אֶת־אָחִיו לֵאמֹר דְּעוּ אֶת־יְהוָה כִּי כוּלָּם

I the to the from they
will for Lord says greatest the me shall
forgive of them least (of them) know

יֵדְעוּ אוֹתִי לְמִקְּטַנָּם וְעַד־גְּדוֹלָם נְאֻם־יְהוָה כִּי אֶסְלַח

I and
again will not their their
remember sin iniquity

לה לַעֲוֺנָם וּלְחַטָּאתָם לֹא אֶזְכָּר־עוֹד׃

*For Hebrew Pronunciation Key, see Page 158 in *Everything You Need to Grow a Messianic Synagogue.*

SHALOM ALECHEM

messengers	ministering	angels	you with (be)	PEACE*
mal-a-chey	ha-sha-ret	mal-a-chey	a-le-chem	sha-lom
מלאכי	השרת	מלאכי	עליכם	שלום

he (be)	blessed	One Holy the	Kings of	King	King of	(the of) high most
hoo	bah-rooch	ha-ka-dosh	ham'-la-cheem	mal-chey	mee-mel-ech	el-yohn
הוא:	ברוך	הקדוש	המלכים	מלכי	ממלך	עליון

high most	messengers	peace (of)	angels	in peace (be)	May coming your
ey-yon	mal-a-chey	ha-sha-lom	mal-a-chey	l'sha-lom	bo-a-chem
עליון	מלאכי	השלום	מלאכי	לשלום	בואכם

,he (be)	blessed	One Holy the	Kings of	king	king of
hoo	bah-rooch	ha-ka-dohsh	ham'la-cheem	mal-chey	mee-meh-lech
הוא:	ברוך	הקדוש	המלכים	מלכי	ממלך

(the of) high most	messengers	peace (of)	angels	peace with	me Bless
el-yohn	mal-a-chey	ha-sha-lom	mal-a-chey	l'sha-lom	bar-choo-nee
עליון	מלאכי	השלום	מלאכי	לשלום	ברכוני

,he (be)	blessed	One Holy the	kings of	king	king of
hoo	bah-rooch	ha-ka-dohsh	ham'la-cheem	mal-chey	mee-meh-lech
הוא:	ברוך	הקדוש	המלכים	מלכי	ממלך

messengers	peace (of)	messengers	peace in (be)	going your May
mal-a-chey	ha-sha-lom	mal-a-chey	l'sha'lom	tzet-chem
מלאכי	השלום	מלאכי	לשלום	צאתכם

blessed	the One Holy	kings of	king	king of	high most (the of)
ba-rooch	ha-ka-dohsh	ham'la-cheem	mal-chey	mee-meh-lech	el-yon
ברוך	הקדוש	המלכים	מלכי	ממלך	עליון

(be) he
hoo
הוא:

*For Hebrew Pronunciation Key, see Page 158 in *Everything You Need to Grow a Messianic Synagogue.*

LECHAH DODI

welcome us let	Sabbath (the of)	presence	bride	meet to	friend my	Come
n'kah·b'lah:	shab-baht	p'nay	cah'lah	leek-raht	doh-dee	l'chah
נְקַבְּלָה:	שַׁבָּת	פְּנֵי	כַּלָּה.	לִקְרַאת	דוֹדִי	לְכָה

the only	God	caused us to hear	a single	in utterance	remember and observe (the Sabbath day)	
Ha-m-yoo-chad	el	heesh-mee-ah-noo	eh-chad	b'dee-boor	v'zah-chor	sh'mohr
הַמְיֻחָד.	אֵל	הִשְׁמִיעָנוּ	אֶחָד.	בְּדִבּוּר	וְזָכוֹר	שָׁמוֹר

and (his) glory	to (his) renown	(is) one	and (his) name	(is) one	The Lord
oo-l'teef-eh-ret	l'shem	echad	oo'sh'moh	echad	ah-do-nye
וּלְתִפְאֶרֶת	לְשֵׁם	אֶחָד.	וּשְׁמוֹ	אֶחָד	יְיָ

it is	for	(And) let us go	Come	the Sabbath	to meet	and his praise
hee	kee	v'nayl·chah	l'choo	shab-baht	leek-raht	v'leet-hee-lah.
הִיא	כִּי	וְנֵלְכָה.	לְכוּ	שַׁבָּת	לִקְרַאת	וְלִתְהִלָּה:

(in) production	last	it was ordained	from of old	From the beginning	blessing	a wellspring of
mah-ah-seh	sohf	n'soo-chah	mee-keh-dem	may-rohsh	hah-b'rah-chah	m'kohr
מַעֲשֶׂה	סוֹף	נְסוּכָה.	מִקֶּדֶם	מֵרֹאשׁ	הַבְּרָכָה.	מְקוֹר

arise	regal	city	King	(O) sanctuary of our	first	in thought
koo·mee	m'loo-chah	eer	meh-lech	meek-dahsh	t'chee-lah.	b'mah-cah-shah-vah
קוּמִי	מְלוּכָה.	עִיר	מֶלֶךְ	מִקְדַּשׁ	תְּחִלָּה:	בְּמַחֲשָׁבָה

in the valley	hast dwelt	thou	long enough	(thy) overthrow	from	go forth
b'eh-mek	she-vet	lach	rahv	hah-hah-feh-chah	mee-tohch	ts'ee
בְּעֵמֶק	שֶׁבֶת	לָךְ	רַב	הַהֲפֵכָה.	מִתּוֹךְ	צְאִי

	upon thee	have compassion	(verily) he will	of weeping
chem-lah	ah-lye-yeech	yah-chah-mohl	v'hoo	hah-bah-chah
חֶמְלָה:	עָלַיִךְ	יַחֲמוֹל	וְהוּא	הַבָּכָה.

THE BARCHU

The Invocation to Prayer

The Reader:

who is (to be) blessed	/(the) Lord		Bless ye
ha-m'voh-rach	ah-doh-nye	et	bar-choo
הַמְבֹרָךְ׃	יְיָ	אֶת	בָּרְכוּ

The Congregation:

and ever	forever	who is (to be) blessed/	(the) Lord	(is) Blessed
vah-ed	lee-olahm	ham-m'voh-rahch	ah-doh-nye	bah-rooch
וָעֶד׃	לְעֹלָם	הַמְבֹרָךְ	יְיָ	בָּרוּךְ

The Shema, Our Confession

one	(is) Lord	Our God	(the) Lord	Israel	(O) Hear
echahd	ah-doh-nye	elo-hey-noo	ah-doh-nye	yees-rah-el	sh'mah
אֶחָד׃	יְיָ	אֱלֹהֵינוּ	יְיָ	יִשְׂרָאֵל	שְׁמַע

and ever	forever	(is)	Kingdom	(whose) glorious	(his) Name	Blessed (be)
vah-ed	l'ohlahm		mal-choo-toh	kah-vohd	shem	bah-rooch
וָעֶד׃	לְעוֹלָם		מַלְכוּתוֹ	כְּבוֹד	שֵׁם	בָּרוּךְ

(is) Lord	the Messiah	Yeshua	Lord	Lord
ah-doh-nye	ha mashiach	yeshua	ah-doh-nye	ah-doh-nye
אָדֹנָי	הַמָּשִׁיחַ	יֵשׁוּעַ	אָדֹנָי	אֲדֹנָי

our God	(O) Lord	thou (art)	Blessed
elohenu	ah-doh-nye	atah	ba-ruch
אֱלֹהֵינוּ	יְיָ	אַתָּה	בָּרוּךְ

Deuteronomy 6:5

thine heart	with all	thy God	(the) Lord		And thou shalt love
l'vahv-cha	b'chol	eloh-heh-cha	a-doh-nye	et	v'ah-hav-tah
לְבָבְךָ	בְּכָל	אֱלֹהֶיךָ	יְהוָה	אֵת	וְאָהַבְתָּ

thy might	and with all	thy soul	and with all
m'oh-deh-cha.	oo-v'chol	nahf-sh'cha	oo-v'chol
מְאֹדֶךָ׃	וּבְכָל	נַפְשְׁךָ	וּבְכָל־

MEE CHAH-MOH-CHA

glorious	is like unto thee	who	(O) Lord	among the mighty ones	is like unto you who
neh-dahr	chah-moh-chah	mee	ah-doh-nye	bah-eh-leem	mee chah-moh-cha
נֶאְדָּר	כָּמֹכָה	מִי	יְהוָה	בָּאֵלִם	מִי־כָמֹכָה

thy sovereign power	wonder(s)	doing	(in) praises	revered	in holiness
mahl-choo-t'chah	feh-leh.	oh-seh	t'hee'loht	noh-rah	bah-koh-desh
מַלְכוּתְךָ	פֶלֶא׃	עֹשֵׂה	תְהִלֹּת	נוֹרָא	בַּקֹּדֶשׁ

my God	this (is)	Moses	before	(the) sea	as thou didst cleave	Thy children	beheld
eh-lee	zeh	moh-sheh	leef-ney	yahm	boh-key-ah	vah-neh-chah	rah-oo
אֵלִי	זֶה	מֹשֶׁה	לִפְנֵי	יָם	בּוֹקֵעַ	בָנֶיךָ	רָאוּ

and ever	for ever	shall reign	(the) Lord	and said	they exclaimed
vah-ed.	l'oh-lam	yeem-lach	ah-doh-nye	v'ahm-roo.	ah-noo
וָעֶד׃	לְעֹלָם	יִמְלֹךְ	יְיָ	וְאָמְרוּ׃	עָנוּ

from the hand	and redeemed him	Jacob		(the) Lord	hath delivered	for	And it is said
mee-yahd	oo-g'ah-loh	yah-a-kohv	et	ah-doh-nye	fah-dah	kee	v'neh-eh-mahr
מִיַּד	וּגְאָלוֹ	יַעֲקֹב	אֶת־	יְיָ	פָדָה	כִּי־	וְנֶאֱמַר

Israel	who hast redeemed	(O) Lord	art thou	Blessed	than he	of him that was strong(er)
yees-rah-el	ga-ahl	ah-doh-nye	ah-tah	bah-rooch	mee-meh-noo.	chah-zak
יִשְׂרָאֵל׃	גָּאַל	יְיָ	אַתָּה	בָּרוּךְ	מִמֶּנּוּ׃	חָזָק

On Sabbaths:

	to observe	the Sabbath		Israel	the children of	And shall keep
et	lah-ah-soht	hah-shah-baht	et	yees-rah-el	b-nay	v'shahm-roo
אֶת	לַעֲשׂוֹת	הַשַּׁבָּת	אֶת	יִשְׂרָאֵל	בְנֵי	וְשָׁמְרוּ

and (between)	between me	(for) an everlasting	covenant	throughout their generations	the Sabbath
oo-vayn	bay-nee	oh-lahm	b'reet	l'doh-roh-tahm	ha-shah-baht
וּבֵין	בֵּינִי	עוֹלָם׃	בְּרִית	לְדֹרֹתָם	הַשַּׁבָּת

days	(in) Six	that	forever	It is	a sign	Israel	the children of
yah-meem	shey-shet	kee	l'oh-lahm	hee	oht	yees-rah-el	b'nay
יָמִים	שֵׁשֶׁת	כִּי־	לְעֹלָם	הִיא	אוֹת	יִשְׂרָאֵל	בְּנֵי

and on day	the earth	and	the heavens		(the) Lord	made
oo'v-yohm	hah-ah-retz	v'et'	hah-shah-my-yeem	et	ah-doh-nye	ah-sah
וּבַיּוֹם	הָאָרֶץ	וְאֶת־	הַשָּׁמַיִם	אֶת־	יְהוָה	עָשָׂה

and ceased from his work	he rested	the seventh
vah-yee-nah-fahsh.	shab-vaht	hahsh-vee-ee
וַיִּנָּפַשׁ׃	שָׁבַת	הַשְּׁבִיעִי

KIDDUSH

(who) createst	the universe	King (of)	our God	(O) Lord	art thou	Blessed
boh-ray	ha-oh-lahm	meh-lech	elo-hey-noo	ah-doh-nye	ah-tah	bah-rooch
בּוֹרֵא	הָעוֹלָם	מֶלֶךְ	אֱלֹהֵינוּ	יְיָ	אַתָּה	בָּרוּךְ

King (of)	our God	(O) Lord	art thou	Blessed	the vine	the fruit of
meh-lech	elo-hey-noo	ah-doh-nye	ah-tah	bah-rooch	ha-gah-fen.	p'ree
מֶלֶךְ	אֱלֹהֵינוּ	יְיָ	אַתָּה	בָּרוּךְ	הַגָּפֶן׃	פְּרִי

in us	and hast taken pleasure	by the commandments	hast sanctified us	who	the universe
v'rah-tsah	vah-noo	b'meets-voh-tahv	keed-sha-noo	ah-sher	ha-oh-lahm
בָנוּ	וְרָצָה	בְּמִצְוֹתָיו	קִדְּשָׁנוּ	אֲשֶׁר	הָעוֹלָם

hast given us an inheritance	and (in) favor	in love	(the) holy	and Sabbath
heen-chee-lah-noo	oov-rahts-ohn	b'ah-ha-vah	kahd-shoh	v'shah-baht
הִנְחִילָנוּ	וּבְרָצוֹן	בְּאַהֲבָה	קָדְשׁוֹ	וְשַׁבַּת

the first	day	that	(also) being	creation	of the	a memorial
t'chee-lah	vohm	hoo	kee	v'ray-sheet,	l'mah-ah-seh	zee-kah-rohn
תְּחִלָּה	יוֹם	הוּא	כִּי	בְרֵאשִׁית.	לְמַעֲשֵׂה	זִכָּרוֹן

us	For	from Egypt	of the departure	in remembrance	holy	of the convocations
vah-noo	kee	meetz-rah-yeem	lee-tsee-aht	zay-cher	koh-desh	l'mik-ray-ay
בָנוּ	כִּי־	מִצְרָיִם.	לִיצִיאַת	זֵכֶר	קֹדֶשׁ	לְמִקְרָאֵי

and Sabbath	(the) nations	above all	sanctified	and us	thou hast chosen
v'sha-baht	ha-ah-meem	me-kohl	kee-dahsh-tah	v'oh-tah-noo	vah-chahr-tah
וְשַׁבַּת	הָעַמִּים	מִכָּל־	קִדַּשְׁתָּ	וְאוֹתָנוּ	בָחַרְתָּ

art thou	Blessed	hast given us as an inheritance	and favor	in love	(the) holy
ah-tah	bah-rooch	heen-chahl-tah-noo.	oov-rah-tsohn	b'ah-ha-vah	kahd-sh-cha
אַתָּה	בָּרוּךְ	הִנְחַלְתָּנוּ׃	וּבְרָצוֹן	בְּאַהֲבָה	קָדְשְׁךָ

the Sabbath	who hallowest	(O) Lord
ha-sha-baht.	m'kah-desh	ah-doh-nye
הַשַּׁבָּת׃	מְקַדֵּשׁ	יְיָ

THERE IS NONE LIKE OUR GOD

none	like King our	none	Lord our like	None	like (is) God our	None
aye	k'mahl-kay-noo,	ayn	kah-doh-nay-noo	ayn	keh-loh-hay-noo,	ayn
אֵין	כְּמַלְכֵּנוּ.	אֵין	כַּאדוֹנֵינוּ.	אֵין	כֵּאלֹהֵינוּ.	אֵין

who	Lord our like	who	God our like (is)	who	Saviour our like
mee	chah-doh-nay-noo	mee	che-loh-hay-noo,	mee	k'moh-shee-aye-noo.
מִי	כַּאדוֹנֵינוּ.	מִי	כֵּאלֹהֵינוּ.	מִי	כְּמוֹשִׁיעֵנוּ:

God our unto	thanks give We	saviour our like	who	King our like
leh-loh-hay-noo,	noh-deh	ch'moh-she-aye-noo	mee	ch'mahl-kay-noo
לֵאלֹהֵינוּ.	נוֹדֶה	כְּמוֹשִׁיעֵנוּ:	מִי	כְּמַלְכֵּנוּ.

saviour our unto	thanks give We	King our unto	thanks give We	Lord our unto	give we thanks
l'moh-shee-aye-noo	noh-deh	l'mahl-kay-noo	noh-deh	lah-doh-nay-noo	noh-deh
לְמוֹשִׁיעֵנוּ:	נוֹדֶה	לְמַלְכֵּנוּ.	נוֹדֶה	לַאדוֹנֵינוּ.	נוֹדֶה

King our	be Blessed	Lord our	be Blessed	God our	be Blessed
mal-kay-noo,	ba-rooch	ah-doh-nye-noo	ba-rooch	elo-hay-noo,	ba-rooch
מַלְכֵּנוּ.	בָּרוּךְ	אֲדוֹנֵינוּ.	בָּרוּךְ	אֱלֹהֵינוּ.	בָּרוּךְ

(art)	Thou	God our	(art)	Thou	saviour our	be Blessed
hoo	ah-tah	elo-hay-noo	hoo	ah-tah	moh-shee-aye-noo	ba-rooch
הוּא	אַתָּה	אֱלֹהֵינוּ.	הוּא	אַתָּה	מוֹשִׁיעֵנוּ:	בָּרוּךְ

saviour our	(art)	Thou	King our	(art)	Thou	Lord our
moh-shee-aye-noo	hoo	ah-tah	mahl-kay-noo	hoo	ah-tah	ah-doh-nay-noo
מוֹשִׁיעֵנוּ.	הוּא	אַתָּה	מַלְכֵּנוּ.	הוּא	אַתָּה	אֲדוֹנֵינוּ

ADON OLOM

was formed	creative	any	ere yet	reigned	who	(the) universe	(He is) Lord of
neev-rah	y'tseer	kohl	b'teh-rehm	mal-lach	ah-sher	oh-lahm	ah-dohn
נִבְרָא:	כָּל־יְצִיר		בְּטֶרֶם	מָלַךְ.	אֲשֶׁר	עוֹלָם	אֲדוֹן

his name	King	Then	all things	by his desire	were made	at the time when
sh'moh	me'lech	ah-zay	kohl	v'chef-tsoh	nah-ah-sah	l'et
שְׁמוֹ	מֶלֶךְ	אֲזַי	כֹּל.	בְחֶפְצוֹ	נַעֲשָׂה	לְעֵת

shall reign	he alone	all things	shall have had an end	And after	was proclaimed
yeem-lohch	l'vah-doh	ha-kohl	keech-loht	v'ah-chah-ray	neek-rah
יִמְלוֹךְ	לְבַדּוֹ	הַכֹּל.	כִּכְלוֹת	וְאַחֲרֵי	נִקְרָא:

in glory	will be	and who	is	(and) who	was	(and) who	the dreaded one
b'teef-ah-rah.	yee-yeh	v'hoo	hoh-veh.	v'hoo	ha-yah	v'hoo	noh-rah.
בְּתִפְאָרָה:	יִהְיֶה	וְהוּא	הֹוֶה.	וְהוּא	הָיָה	וְהוּא	נוֹרָא:

to consort with him	to him	to compare	second	And there is no	one	And he (is)
l'hach-bee-rah.	loh	l'hahm-shel	shay-nee	v'ayn	eh-chad	v'hoo
לְהַחְבִּירָה:	לוֹ	לְהַמְשִׁיל	שֵׁנִי.	וְאֵין	אֶחָד	וְהוּא

(the) strength	(And) to him belong	end	without	beginning	without
ha-ohz	v'lon	tach-leet.	b'lee	ray-sheet	b'lee
הָעֹז	וְלוֹ	תַכְלִית.	בְּלִי	רֵאשִׁית	בְּלִי

in my travail	and a rock	my Redeemer	(And) liveth	my God	And he is	and dominion
chehv-lee	v'tsoor	goh-ah-lee.	v'chye	ay-lee	v'hoo	v'hahm-mees-rah.
חֶבְלִי	וְצוּר	גֹּאֲלִי.	וְחַי	אֵלִי	וְהוּא	וְהַמִּשְׂרָה.

my cup	the portion of	my	and refuge	my banner	And he is	distress	in time of
koh-see	m'naht	lee.	oo-mah-nohs	nee-see	v'hoo	tsah-rah.	b'ayt
כּוֹסִי	מְנָת	לִי.	וּמָנוֹס	נִסִּי	וְהוּא	צָרָה:	בְּעֵת

and when I wake	I sleep	when	my spirit	I commend	In his hand	(when) I call	on the day
v'ah-ee-rah.	ee-shahn	b'ayt	roo-chee	ahf-keed	b-yah-doh	ehk-rah	b'yohm
וְאָעִירָה:	אִישַׁן	בְּעֵת	רוּחִי.	אַפְקִיד	בְּיָדוֹ	אֶקְרָא:	בְּיוֹם

I will fear	and not	is with me	The Lord	my body (also)	my spirit	And with
ee-rah	v'loh	lee	ah-doh-nye	g'vee-yah-tee.	roo-chee	v'eem
אִירָא:	וְלֹא	לִי	יְיָ	גְּוִיָּתִי.	רוּחִי	וְעִם

THE LORD'S PRAYER

Our Father	which are in heaven	hallowed be	thy name	Come
ah-vee-noo	sheh-bah-shah-mye-eem	yeet-kah-dash	sh'meh-chah	tah-voh
אָבִינוּ	שֶׁבַּשָּׁמַיִם	יִתְקַדֵּשׁ	שְׁמֶךָ :	תָּבֹא

Thy Kingdom	be done	Thy will	as it is	in heaven	
mahl-choo-teh-chah	yeh-ah-seh	r'tzohn'chah	k'moh	vah-shah-mye-eem	ken
מַלְכוּתֶךָ	יֵעָשֶׂה	רְצוֹנְךָ	כְּמוֹ	בַשָּׁמַיִם	כֵּן

in earth		bread	our daily	Give	us	this day	And forgive
bah-ah-retz.	et	lechem	choo-keh-noo	ten	lah-noo	hah-yohm	oo-s'lach
בָּאָרֶץ :	אֶת־	לֶחֶם	חֻקֵּנוּ	תֶּן־	לָנוּ	הַיּוֹם :	וּסְלַח־

us		our debts	as	we forgive		
lah-noo	et	choh-voh-tey-noo	kah-ah-sher	sah-lach-noo	gahm	ah-nach-noo
לָנוּ	אֶת־	חֹבוֹתֵינוּ	כַּאֲשֶׁר	סָלַחְנוּ	גַּם־	אֲנַחְנוּ

our debtors	And not	lead us	into	temptation	but
l'chah-yah-vey-noo.	v'ahl	t'vee-ey-noo	lee-day	nee-sah-yohn	eem kee
לְחַיָּבֵינוּ :	וְאַל־	תְּבִיאֵנוּ	לִידֵי	נִסָּיוֹן	כִּי אִם־

deliver us	from	evil	for	thine (is)	the Kingdom	and the power
chal-tsey-noo	meen	hah-rah	kee	l'chah	hah-mahm-la-chah.	v'hah-g'voo-rah
חַלְּצֵנוּ	מִן־	הָרָע	כִּי	לְךָ	הַמַּמְלָכָה	וְהַגְּבוּרָה

and the glory	forever	Amen
v'hah-teef-eh-ret	l'ol-mey oh-lah-meem	ah-meyn.
וְהַתִּפְאֶרֶת	לְעוֹלְמֵי עוֹלָמִים	אָמֵן :

BENEDICTION

Numbers 6:24-26

bless the	(The) Lord	and keep thee	make, shine	The Lord
y'vah-reh-ch'chah	ah-doh-nye	v'yeesh-m'reh-chah	yah-ehr	ah-don-nye
יְבָרֶכְךָ	יְהוָה	וְיִשְׁמְרֶךָ :	יָאֵר	יְהוָה

his face	upon thee	and be gracious unto thee	lift up	The Lord	his countenance
pah-nahv	eh-leh-chah	vee-choo-neh-chah.	ye-sah	ah-doh-nye	pah-nahv
פָּנָיו	אֵלֶיךָ	וִיחֻנֶּךָּ :	יִשָּׂא	יְהוָה	פָּנָיו

upon thee	and give	thee	peace
eh-leh-chah	v'yah-seym	l'cah	sha-lom.
אֵלֶיךָ	וְיָשֵׂם	לְךָ	שָׁלוֹם :

11

Pioneering a Messianic Jewish Day School

By Phillip Goble

In the eyes of many Jewish parents, the faith that Yeshua is the Messiah is not a real option to them within their cultural perspective. Why? One reason is that the existing church does not provide a Jewish education or the bar or bas mitzvah training they desire for their children. Even though these Jewish parents may not understand much about the Church *or* the Jewish religion, they know their children are going to be bar mitzvah! That in itself is enough to make many reject the Good News.

Of course, in the early church in Jerusalem, the little Jewish boys were allowed to grow up in the messianic faith identifying with their own people in their Jewishness. In Acts 21:21, we hear that the church in Jerusalem was extremely zealous for the Jewish *mitzvot* or Hebrew laws, which have helped to sustain the Jewish people in their identity and cultural heritage. And even the Encyclopedia Judaica's article on the Bar Mitzvah shows there was a functional equivalent ceremony for the Bar Mitzvah in Jerusalem at the time of the early church. Therefore, if we have an understanding of the Good News as the Messiah's Torah or teaching (Messiah himself being the indwelling personal law of the New Covenant), then there is no theological objection to messianic Bar or Bas Mitzvah or Jewish training in the Body of the Lord, provided it is Messiah-centered and Scripturally sound.

If even ordinary churches know the benefits derived from offering religious-based education, how much more needed is this kind of education for a messianic Jewish congregation! If Gentile unbelievers will eventually attend a church because they first felt the need of putting their children in that church's day school, how much more may Jewish unbelievers (with children) respond to a congregation (with a messianic Jewish day school).

Now suppose someone in your group has a Jewish heart and has started a Bible Study that is getting ready to become a messianic congregation. Suppose the weekend services are just getting underway and the core group wants to begin a messianic Jewish day school. How do they begin?

First of all, to get started, someone who has done pioneer work in this field should be contacted, like Mrs. Daniel Juster, Beth Messiah Congregation, 2208 Rockland Avenue, Rockville, Maryland 20851. She could, through correspondence, direct the inquirer to the curriculum materials being developed so far by people affiliated with the Messianic Jewish Alliance. Also, a good book to read is Rabbi Hayim Halevy Donin's *To Raise A Jewish Child*, Basic Books, 1977. This book plus a few field trips to Jewish day schools and Hebrew schools would give your pioneers an idea of what Jewish educators are doing. The school administrators will sometimes give you brochures describing their school philosophy and curriculum. If you live in a city with a large Jewish population (like Los Angeles) you can find out from the school which Jewish bookstore is their textbook distributor. Then you can go there and examine first-hand the kinds of books in use. A good Jewish library in a Temple or Jewish Center might also be helpful.

Now consider the basic logistics involved in starting a school in connection with a congregation. A pastor, who has done or is now doing this, can be a helpful resource person. There are Christian curriculum publishing companies who offer one week training courses to pastors and their staff on the ABC's of starting a religious school. Talk to a few pastors in your area who have started a school by means of this kind of training. What they have learned can help you get started. You may want to take such a training course.

Of course, some of these Christian curriculum publishing companies have textbooks that are unsuitable to a messianic Jewish school. If the terminology would create culture shock, or if the materials could not be selectively purchased (since some textbooks might be completely inappropriate), then the company might not be right for your school.

Two that are recommended by messianic Jewish Day School pioneers are A Beka Book Publications, Pensacola Christian College, 125 St. Johns Street, Pensacola, Florida 32503 (good for History, Science and Social Studies textbooks), and Scott Foresman and Company, 1900 East Lake Avenue, Glenview, Illinois 60025 (good for Math and Reading textbooks).

If Bible-based educational curricula such as the above were combined with Hebrew classes for all ages, a beginning could be made with just a few children, starting with the couples that you now know. As long as you abide by the laws, a school can begin anywhere, with the most modest facilities and school staff. Much prayer and a burdened, competent, educational pioneer are the key ingredients. He or she will have the burden to work with the congregation leadership to get the school started.

On pages 197-215 in Donin's *To Raise A Jewish Child*, there is an excellent bibliography of the Jewish books presently available and even the address of Jewish bookstores in the different states that carry these books. Some of these books will be useable, also, in a messianic Jewish day school. Some may not be useable, or may only be partially useable, because of incorrect teaching about the Messiah.

In doing your research before you officially open your school, find out from successful Jewish and Christian Day School administrators how they attract their students: word-of-mouth, newspaper advertising, bulletin boards, neighborhood canvassing with questionnaires, direct mailing, etc.

Prayerfully seek the Lord's guidance on how you should advertise. Keep in mind that some Jewish groups will be highly threatened by you, viewing your school as a cult, a den of spiritual child molesters. You must use wisdom and discretion in avoiding the harassment and bad publicity these groups may try to bring on you.

However, also remember that the vast majority of the Jewish community is still fairly well outside the influence of the synagogue. Like Gentile parents, many Jewish parents rely on secular schools to educate their Jewish youth. As drugs, violence, and the other social ills of our day continue to invade secular schools, the need for religious-based education will be more keenly felt.

The fact that you have a day school, a summer camp, and a bar or bas mitzvah training program (administered either by your school or under the tutelage of one of the elders in your congregation) will make your faith a more viable option to many Jewish families in your city. The fact that you offer more than secular humanism in a Jewish package, but instead a vibrant life-changing faith that transforms troubled youth into loving new persons, will make what you offer attractive to almost anyone. If your school communicates to children a spiritual sense of Jewish roots, destiny and practical daily living, it will make a strong statement to those who argue that faith in Jesus is always a step toward cultural assimilation and Jewish genocide.

12

A Vital Area for Pastoral Counsel: If You Were To Be Deprogrammed

By Moishe Rosen

A self-styled task force of wolves in sheep's clothing has taken upon itself what it considers to be a mission of mercy. These are the "deprogrammers," a group comprised mostly of concerned parents and religious Jews who seek by nefarious methods to destroy the faith of young Jewish believers in Christ. Many of these deprogrammers actually believe that Jews who believe in Jesus are emotionally unsound and that those who try to dissuade them from their beliefs are doing the work of God. They justify their methods by treating Jewish faith in Christ as a mental and social abberation. There is a vital need for both Gentile and Jewish Christians to be educated and warned about these deprogrammers so that they can deal intelligently and effectively with this insidious threat.

HOW THE DEPROGRAMMERS OPERATE

Separation. The deprogrammers operate on familiar principles. First, the parents of the prospective subject visit the believer and say they would like to be alone with their son or daughter. They invite the believer for a drive or a meal. Once in the car or home, the believer is "kidnapped," and taken to a group of deprogrammers in alien, totally unfamiliar surroundings, often a motel room. The strategy is that the deprogrammers separate the believer from his fellow believers and place him in an unfamiliar situation. In order to do their "work," the deprogrammers must first disorient and intimidate their subject. For this reason they usually don't work with the believer in his parents' home, because the familiarity of those surroundings would serve to remind him of his own identity enough for him to be able to maintain his orientation.

The deprogrammers claim that it is important for them to separate the young believer from his religious community because the Christian leaders or elders have some unusual power over the person. This may be the case in a cult situation, but of course it doesn't hold true in a normal church relationship. In any case, separation from all strong believers is imperative for the deprogrammers' plan, since supportive fellowship of any kind would thwart their purposes.

The deprogrammers agree that one of the first steps in the deprogramming process is to separate the believer from his Bible. Although the deprogrammers sometimes pose as true believers, this approach immediately uncovers their true identity and purpose. Imposed spiritual starvation is never to be regarded as a holy imperative, for the Scripture teaches that we are to consider the Word of God as essential food for nourishment, (I Tim. 3:15, 16).

The Attack Approach. This tactic is not new. It has been used effectively in military spheres for centuries to acquire information from an unwilling prisoner, or to restructure loyalties. In modern language we call it "brain washing." Human beings are creatures with limitations, and in order to achieve the desired results, the deprogrammers have only to attack until they reach the limits of the individual's endurance. The deprogrammers proudly claim that their methods are one hundred percent effective. Nevertheless, as in the foregoing incident, captured Christians have escaped, sometimes with their faith temporarily shaken, but not destroyed.

It's easy for the deprogrammers to trip up even a Christian with this attack approach. In the deprogramming process there are usually six to ten deprogrammers surrounding the believer, sometimes many more. These people eat and sleep normally, while the believer is often deprived of food, granted a bare minimum of sleep, and subjected to a great deal of harassment.

As believers, we have the holy obligation to confess our faith. Therefore, the deprogrammers' questions seem at first like welcome opportunities to share the faith. They ask,

"What do you believe,?" "How did you come to believe this?" "Could you explain to us why you believe?" What Christian could resist such an opportunity? But the Bible admonishes us to be wise as serpents and not to address ourselves to insincere questions.

When a Christian gives his testimony, it is to proclaim the grace and mercy of God in light of his own particular unworthiness regarding salvation. Often the believer will describe a certain problem from which the Lord delivered him. If a person has had a problem of indulgence in dope, degraded sex, or a certain kind of pride, the deprogrammers might reintroduce this to the believer. Pride is the easiest stumbling block, as the Bible warns us. Pride tells us that we "deserve" something. If the deprogrammers can get the subject hooked into a pride trip, then they can get him hooked on almost any old habit (Proverbs 16:18). The Christian in such a situation, must remember that he is bought with a price and doesn't deserve any kind of self indulgence.

Guilt. Another prime tactic the deprogrammers use is the appeal to a young believer's love for his parents, combined with his susceptibility to guilt feelings. Most people have at one time or another done things, or displayed attitudes towards their parents for which they are genuinely sorry. Since all Christian teaching points to the necessity for love and restitution, the young believer is eager to become the child he feels his parents expect him to be. This good motive is used by the deprogrammers as a lever to increase the believer's guilt feelings. In this early state, the parents or the deprogrammers appeal to the believer that for the sake of his family, he ought to sever his relationship with the particular fellowship of believers from which he has been kidnapped. The deprogrammers don't at first ask the believer to renounce Christ, but that is only steps away. Few can resist this technique, and once the believer has accepted the deprogrammers and parents as his friends, who only have his "best interests at heart," it's just a matter of time until he succumbs and reaches their intended conclusion. The deprogrammers have all the time in the world. They will work on a person for days, however long it takes.

Renunciation. Toward the end of the deprogramming, when the subject is broken in spirit, the deprogrammers goad him into performing some act of renunciation. This act may be to slander the names of the people he knew, especially the elders or the minister of the fellowship or church. In some cases, it might be something more unspeakable, such as cursing the name of Jesus, or spitting on the Bible. Once the person has done something of that magnitude, the deprogrammers remind him of how difficult it would be to return to the fellowship he attended, and often they convince him that he has committed an "unpardonable sin."

HOW CAN WE ANTICIPATE DEPROGRAMMING?

We must expect that many parents will be very receptive to the idea of cooperating with deprogrammers to "free" their victimized children from the "Jesus trip." They will provide all necessary funds and go to great lengths to accomplish the desired end, but there is much that God would have us do to prepare for such a possibility.

The Word of God. Every believer requires the consumption and digestion of the Word of God for spiritual sustenance. Bible memory work is imperative to strengthen a person against the threat of being deprogrammed. The deprogrammers may take away your Bible, but they can't take away your memory. Furthermore, knowledge of the Bible must exist on an independent basis. That is, it must stem from private thought and study, not group teaching. Too much of our Bible "knowledge" is made up of predigested conclusions based on what our particular group of believers assumes. A believer should always be able to back up his faith with Scripture. Know why you believe what you believe.

Forgiveness. Remember that there is no act that can be committed that will take a believer out of salvation and away from God if he truly repents and wants to have the Lord. Where there is repentance, there is always forgiveness. It is the responsibility of the elders in Christ to teach new believers the depth and extent of Christ's forgiveness. One of the tactics used by the deprogrammers is to convince the "broken" victim that his renunciation or slander of his fellowship or testimony is too great a sin to be forgiven by his old friends. They convince him that it will be no use ever to try to reinstate himself into that fellowship. We must remember that the blood of Christ can cleanse us from ALL unrighteousness if we confess our sins to the Father. Likewise, as brothers and sisters in Christ, we, too, should be quick to show forgiveness to one who has stumbled. Remember, no one is saved because of what he deserves. God is the one who pieces us into the body of Christ, and it is His grace that will keep us there.

Emotions. Don't allow love for any person to be used as a lever against your faith. The parents of the deprogramming victims often try to appeal to their emotions by saying, "If you really love us, then come away where we can sit together and talk." The believer will usually comply, because he wants to do all he can to show his love and respect for his parents' wishes. New Christians should be instructed that there is a point at which they should not allow their love to be used in this way.

Also, there is a time to witness, and a time not to witness. The time not to witness is in a situation contrived by someone who doesn't want to hear, but rather wants to dissuade the believer from his faith. Conditioned to be harmless as doves, we, as Christians, sometimes forget to be also as wise as serpents. We must be prepared to keep our emotions from endangering us or our brothers and sisters in Christ. A good idea when being approached by a parent or other family member in this way is to take along another believer. There's safety in numbers.

Humility. Christian faith is not a rational process by which a believer comes to a logical conclusion that Jesus is Lord. Faith is a gift from God whereby we believe that which the natural man is incapable of believing: spiritual truth. There is much to learn about our faith, and God has given us all eternity to grow in understanding and wisdom. Therefore, a new believer should realize that just because he may not have an answer to a question, that is no reason to think that there is no answer. To think that at any point you must be able to come up with perfect answers to a person's questions is to fall into the trap of pride. Never let yourself believe that you know everything that is in the Bible and everything that God has inferred in His Word. Above all, don't confuse paradoxes with contradictions when examining Scripture. A believer should be humble enough to allow a great margin for the things he doesn't understand, and faith-filled enough to believe that God is making him into the kind of person who can and will be trusted with more and more spiritual insight.

HOW TO DEAL WITH THE ENEMY

The deprogrammers, no matter how convinced they may be that they are doing God a service, are the enemies of your soul. If encountered by such people, here are some recommendations on handling the situation.

Cooperation. NEVER talk to someone and try to persuade him while you are being held against your will. Only a free man can talk and think straight. You have to be able to eat when you want, sleep when you want, and have the right of privacy and the choice to leave or stay. Just the fact that you're being held against your will is enough to interfere with your being able to think clearly and to comprehend.

Different groups of deprogrammers allow the victim varying degress of freedom, but in some cases it has been reported that the parents themselves actually slept across the threshold or doorway of a room in order to prevent the possibility of escape. Often the deprogrammers count on the fact that most people, especially Christians, prefer to avoid making a scene. The victims, being in unfamiliar territory and often without money in their pockets, are apt to decide that cooperation is the best way to meet the situation. DO NOT BE COOPERATIVE! Tell anyone who is holding you that you are being held against your will, and you refuse to talk to them.

Deprogrammer Ted Patrick was once quoted in *Time* Magazine as saying, "If I can get them communicating, I can always win. I say, 'Prove you are a Christian.' This shows up the person's own frailties." Don't accept any kindness from the deprogrammers, and don't communicate with them. Accept the fact that anyone who would interfere with your walk with God in this way is your enemy. Soldiers in wartime are taught not to communicate with the enemy. If captured, they are to state only their name, rank, and serial number. You, too, can refuse to talk. Some of this deprogramming is demonic-Remember to resist the devil and he will flee.
Prayer. Talk to Jesus within yourself, but don't let your captors hear you. Remember the promises of God in Scripture and recite verses to yourself. Dwell on past experiences of answered prayer. Don't let the deprogrammers get into your mind. Don't reveal to them what you're thinking, except to express resistance. To keep your mind busy, recite poetry to yourself, or count the cracks in the floor or ceiling. DO NOT OPEN UP.

Fasting. Another effective technique that has been used to defeat the deprogrammers is to go on an extended fast, which the captors interpret as a hunger strike. Such a fast, accompanied by prayer, is actually strengthening under these circumstances, and it puts the moral responsibility for the consequences on the captors. If the captive can find the strength from God to maintain absolute silence, physical passivity to violence, and complete refusal to ingest either food or water, the chances of his being released soon are much better. In that situation, you should remember to continue your refusal to eat and drink and remain absolutely passively uncooperative until you are away from the deprogrammers and back to complete safety. Otherwise, the deprogrammers might trick you into eating or drinking or communicating with them by saying they have decided to let you go. This happened to someone who was being held, where his captors said they were releasing him. They stopped the car in a gas station and someone brought cokes to the car. The victim drank one, whereupon the deprogrammers, no longer worried about his becoming dehydrated, refused to release him and continued their harassment.

Dealing with Physical Violence. The main tool that the deprogrammers use is psychological duress, but sometimes they try to induce this by physical violence or the threat of physical violence. Then they resort to kicking, slapping, and shoving the victim in order to intimidate him. In one bizarre case, a girl was repeatedly raped and tortured and told that her religion made her subhuman. Serious physical attack of this kind is rare. Nevertheless, should the victim encounter any degree of physical violence, it's best just to go limp. Don't make the mistake of thinking of yourself as a martyr for the faith, because such pride works against you.

The best way to endure physical violence is to remember that it is not directed against you as a person, but against Christ who is in you. Separate the physical pain from the psychological pain. Don't allow yourself to be shocked if you are slapped, shoved, or slammed up against a wall. One way to handle the pain is to compare in your heart what you are enduring to the agony Christ suffered at Calvary. In the light of His sufferings, almost any pain seems small and insignificant by comparison.

It's very important that you don't shove back, scream, or respond in any manner. If you were to fight back, your captors would consider that justification for further acts of violence. God built the human body in such a way that if the physical pain becomes too great to bear, a person loses consciousness. Remember that He will not tempt you above that which you are able to bear, but will, with the testing, make a way of escape for you. (I Cor. 10:13). If pain is happening to you, He has already given you the strength to bear it and to endure.

Humiliation. Part of the intimidation process is humiliation. The deprogrammers might hold their victim in such confines that he cannot tend to his personal toilet or relieve himself. This is extremely embarrasing to most people. One person broke during deprogramming when he wasn't allowed the use of a bathroom. When he could no longer contain himself and defecated, the deprogrammers made him sit in his own filth. This humiliated and embarrassed him to the point of tears. If you ever find yourself in such an embarrassing or humiliating situation, remember that a believer who has been cleansed by Christ cannot be defiled by any bodily function over which he has no control. Only the thoughts of his heart can defile him.

Accusations of Insanity. While being held, you might encounter a statement like this: "We think you're insane. If you'll just talk to us and show us that you're a reasonable person, we won't have you committed to a mental institution." Denying insanity won't work, because insane people never admit to being insane. Remember, anyone can be driven insane by pressure tactics and the withholding of bodily necessities like food and sleep. Do not try to manipulate the deprogrammers. They are not bound by Christian ethics. They have only one job to do, and that is to get you to renounce your faith at all costs. Never fake insanity as a means of escape, because they might have you committed to a mental institution. While being held, never take any medication from anyone purporting to be a doctor.

Escape. One article about deprogrammers reports that a number of abductees have managed to escape through windows. One girl said that she felt they were going to kill her anyway, and that it was worth the risk of jumping. Don't do anything foolhardy, but do try to escape. If you succeed, go to the police and tell them that you have been held against your will. Volunteer to take a battery of tests that comprise a legal sanity hearing on which to base your case. If you can't find police, go to a nearby church and report what has happened to you. Try to call your pastor or Christian friends collect, and seek their help.

It's not wrong to go to the police. We have been conditioned not to complain against parents. But when parents declare that they will stop at nothing to get their sons and daughters to renounce their faith, then those sons and daughters must, at all costs, protect themselves, their personal freedeom, and particularly the future freedom of others.

Capsule Advice to Deprogramming Victims. If captured by deprogrammers, behave like a prisoner of war. You must fight the deprogrammers all the way, as though they were going to kill you. Remember to resist but remain passive. When you are confronted with what seems like a monolithic force, you can be brought to the point of believing anything. But remember, as a Christian, stronger is He that is in you than he that is in the world.

The law is now being brought into question concerning some of the deplorable tactics of the deprogrammers. Every person has the right to freedom of religion and freedom of choice. Furthermore, as creatures of God, we should demand and expect the same kind of choice from the world that we have received from the Lord. Jesus said, "Behold, I stand at the door and knock." God does not abduct His children!

In conclusion, there is no "cure" for a real case of Christianity. The deprogrammers will never be one hundred percent effective, because the experience of knowing Christ keeps on in a person even when he has been brought low. Keep in mind the disciple Peter who denied the Lord three times, saying, "I never knew him." Peter came back to become the strongest of the apostles. The Lord can always forgive and reinstate His children and accomplish through each one what He has purposed to do. Remember the promises of God in Christ!

Never give anyone up to the deprogrammers. A few might actually renounce the Lord under extreme pressure; yet there is the probability that if they do, they will still repent and come back. And when someone returns to Christ after such an ordeal, treat him with a double measure of welcome and rejoicing, like the "prodigal son."

Appendix
By-Laws

ARTICLE I - NAME OF ORGANIZATION

The name of this organization shall be: BETH MESSIAH CONGREGATION, INCORPORATED; hereafter referred to as BETH MESSIAH CONGREGATION.

ARTICLE II - OBJECTIVES:

SECTION I - SPIRITUAL:

A. To foster the spiritual growth of those Jewish people who have already asked Messiah Yeshua into their hearts.

B. To win other Jewish people to Messiah Yeshua.

SECTION II - SOCIAL:

To provide occasions for fellowship among Messianic believers.

SECTION III - CULTURAL:

A. To identify with our Jewish people everywhere.

B. To assist in worthwhile Jewish causes by practical participation.

ARTICLE III - MEMBERSHIPS:

SECTION I - REGULAR MEMBERSHIP:

Messianic believers, their spouses, and their child-rent may apply for regular membership.

SECTION II - APPLICATION: For reception into membership, applicants must:

A. Be at least 18 years of age.

B. Have confessed and repented of their sins and asked Messiah Yeshua into their hearts and lives.

C. Have followed Messiah Yeshua into the mikveh (Baptism).

D. Have completely filled out and signed the membership application form.

E. Give evidence of agreement with the Congregation's doctrinal statement in their interview with the Membership Committee.

F. Have the approval of the Board of Elders. The Elders will carefully weigh the view of the Membership Committee.

SECTION III - REMOVAL:

The Board of Elders may remove any person at any time from the membership rolls for unworthy conduct, lack of attendance, or discontinuance of faith in the Messiah and in the Scriptures. Such removal shall be in accord with biblical principles of testimony and the judicial authority of the body of believers (Matthew 18).

SECTION IV - ANNUAL BUSINESS MEETINGS:

A. There shall be at least one annual business meeting of the entire membership.

B. The annual business meeting shall be conducted in the month of May.

SECTION V - VOTING:

Members may vote on the removal of elders or Executive Director/Rabbi, may as a group suggest candidates for eldership, vote on disposition of property and amendments to by-laws.

ARTICLE IV - BOARDS OF ELDERS AND DEACONS

SECTION I - COMPOSITION:

A. Beth Messiah's Board of Elders shall be comprised of individuals as prescribed in the Bible which are members in good standing.

B. Beth Messiah's Board of Deacons shall be comprised of individuals as prescribed in the Bible which are members in good standing.

SECTION II - SELECTION:

A. The Board of Elders as a whole, or a designated part of the Board of Elders, shall serve as a Nominations Committee.

B. The Elders shall at least four weeks before the annual meeting present those whom they perceive as called to serve in the positions of Elder and Shamash. This process of nomination includes elders and shamashem whose terms have expired and who are eligible for reaffirmation. The Congregation shall have the opportunity to affirm or not affirm the nominees. Two-thirds affirmation from those who cast ballots at the meeting will be necessary before the assumption of the position.

C. If affirmation is not forthcoming, the Elders may lower the set number of members on either board or may, through the Nominations Committee, present names at a future time to fulfill the position(s). Vacancies due to resignation or removal may also be filled by the same process. All names presented for affirmation shall be announced four weeks before any special affirmation meeting.

D. The original selection of an elder or shamash (deacon) is for a three-year term or for the duration of the term of any elder or shamash who vacates his or her position.

SECTION III - DUTIES:

A. The Board of Elders shall manage and direct the affairs of Beth Messiah, and within the limits of constitutional powers set forth herein, are the highest authority of Beth Messiah. They shall oversee all the various areas of congregational life.

B. The Shotrim Board (deacons) shall oversee the Scriptural responsibilities assigned to them as well as other tasks assigned to them by the Board of Elders. The Shotrim Board shall be under the authority of the Board of Elders and shall regularly report to the Board of Elders.

C. The Board of Elders shall have the power to appoint department heads and chairmen of standing and special committees.

SECTION IV - MEETINGS:

The boards of Beth Messiah shall meet as needed but will seek to usually meet on a monthly basis.

SECTION V - QUORUM:

If less than a majority of board members of either board are present, action taken shall be submitted to the other members of the Board of Elders by mail for their written approval.

SECTION VI - REMOVAL:

Elders may be removed at any time by a two-thirds majority of members present at a duly called meeting.

SECTION VII - MODERATORS:

The Spiritual Leader shall be the moderator of the Board of Elders and an ex-officio member of the Shotrim Board and all committees. Committee chairpersons shall moderate the meetings of their commitees. The Shotrim Board shall be moderated by either an elder appointed for this purpose or by a chairperson of this board who is appointed by the elders and who is a duly active member of the Shotrim Board. In making the selection of committee chairpersons and the Chairperson of the Shotrim Board, the elders shall seek to ascertain the sense of the various committees and the Shotrim Board as to whom they believe would make good leaders in these areas. All moderators and chairpersons shall be responsible to regularly report on their areas of oversight to the Board of Elders. Hence the elders shall ultimately oversee all projects and areas of congregational life and shall have the authority to approve, disapprove, and direct subject to the directives of Scripture and the limitations of this constitution.

SECTION VIII

No person who is ordained or who has served as a congregational Spiritual leader shall function in the capacity of a lay elder unless he relinquishes this ordination and assumes office as a regular lay elder among the rest of the lay elders.

ARTICLE V - THE EXECUTIVE DIRECTOR:

SECTION I - NOMINATION:

An Executive Director/Rabbi shall be determined by two-thirds of the Board of Elders and ratified by two-thirds of members present at a duly-called business meeting.

SECTION II - COMPENSATION:

The Executive Director shall be compensated in such an amount and with such benefits as determined by the Board of Elders and approved by a two-thirds majority of members present at a duly-called business meeting.

SECTION III - DUTIES:

A. The Executive Director/Rabbi shall execute the directives of the Board of Elders and acts as its agent when it is not in session.

B. The Executive Director/Rabbi shall have the prime responsibility for the successful operation of Beth Messiah. To this end, he shall aid and exhort its members to do their part in every way possible.

C. He is an ex-officio member of every committee; with voice. As Spiritual Leader, his sense of leading shall be carefully and seriously considered. As moderator, however, he shall only vote in the meetings he moderates (elders and general congregational meeting) to break a tie.

SECTION IV - AUTHORITY:

A. The Executive Director/Rabbi shall have the authority to make such purchases as he deems necessary for the functioning of Beth Messiah within the financial limits set by the Board of Elders.

B. The Executive Director/Rabbi shall have the authority to engage, dismiss and to set the salaries of staff members of Beth Messiah with the approval of the Board of Elders.

SECTION V - REMOVAL:

The Executive Director/Rabbi of Beth Messiah may be removed upon the recommendation of the Board of Elders and the two-thirds approval of members present at a duly-called business meeting.

ARTICLE VI - FINANCES:

SECTION I - BANK ACCOUNT AND RECORDS:

Beth Messiah shall keep a bank account and maintain records of all of its finances.

SECTION II - DEPOSIT, CHECKS AND LOANS:

A. Deposits may be made by the treasurer or the Executive Director/Rabbi.

B. Checks may be drawn by any authorized member of the Board of Elders.

C. Loans may be made for Beth Messiah in the amounts approved by the Board of Elders.

SECTION III - FISCAL YEAR:

The fiscal year of Beth Messiah shall be from January 1 to December 31.

SECTION IV - BUDGET:

An annual projected budget shall be prepared by the elders and approved by the congregation each May.

ARTICLE VII - BUSINESS MEETINGS:

SECTION I - RULES OF ORDER:

Roberts Rules of Order shall govern the parliamentary procedure at all business meetings.

SECTION II - QUORUM:

A quorum shall consist of those members present at a duly-called meeting.

SECTION III - A DULY-CALLED MEETING:

A. A duly-called meeting of the Board of Elders is one in which the time and place of the meeting has been submitted in written form to each member of the Board of Elders at least three days prior to the meeting.

B. Emergency meetings of the Board of Elders may be called and action confirmed at the next duly-called meeting.

C. A duly-called meeting of the entire membership of Beth Messiah is one in which the time, place and purpose of the meeting is announced at least seven days prior to the meeting.

D. Business meetings or Board meetings may be called by either the Executive Director/Rabbi or a majority of the Board.

SECTION IV - RECORDS:

The Clerk or Secretary of the Board of Elders shall keep minutes of all elders' board meetings as well as congregational meetings. The minutes of each previous meeting shall be read to begin each session. The Shotrim shall also keep regular minutes of their meetings. These minutes shall be ultimately stored in the Congregational file.

Other Committees shall keep minutes sufficient for their orderly functioning.

ARTICLE VIII - AMENDMENTS:

SECTION I - SUBMITTAL:

By-laws Amendments must be submitted in written form to the Board of Elders by any regular member of Beth Messiah.

SECTION II - CONSIDERATION:

Amendments to the by-laws must be approved by a majority of the Board of Elders.

SECTION III - APPROVAL:

A. Proposed amendments to these by-laws approved by the Board of Elders are to be sent to each member of Beth Messiah in written form at least seven days prior to a duly-called business meeting at which the amendments will be voted upon.

B. The membership of Beth Messiah can then adopt the amendment(s) by two-thirds of the members present at the said duly-called meeting.

ARTICLE IX - DISSOLUTION:

No part of the net earnings of the corporation shall inure to the benefit of or be distributable to its individual members, directors, officers or other private persons, except that the corporation shall be authorized and empowered to pay reasonable compensation for services rendered and to make payments and distributions in furtherance of the purposes set forth in Article II thereof. No substantial part of the activities of the corporation shall be the carrying on of propaganda, or otherwise attempting, to influence legislations, and the corporation shall not participate in, or intervene in (including the publishing or distribution of statements) any political campaign on behalf of any candidate for public office. Notwithstanding any provision of these articles, the corporation shall not carry on any other activities not permitted to be carried on by a corporation exempt from Federal Income Tax under Section 501(c) of the Internal Revenue Code of 1954 (or the corresponding provision of any future United States Internal Revenue Law). Upon the dissolution of the corporation, the Board of Directors shall, after paying or making provision for the payment of all liabilities of the corporation, dispose of all the assets in such manner, or to such organizations organized and operated exclusively for charitable, educational, religious or scientific purposes as shall at the time qualify as an exempt-organization or organizations under Section 501(c)(3) of the Internal Revenue Code of 1954 (or the corresponding provision of any future United States Internal Revenue Law), as the Board of Directors shall determine.

Notes

Chapter 1

[1]Hugh J. Schonfield, *The History of Jewish Christianity*, p. 122.

[2]Martin Luther, *Luther's Works*, Vol. 45, p. 200.

[3]*Ibid*, Vol. 47, p. 268f.

[4]Isaac DaCosta, *Israel and the Gentiles*, p. 519.

[5]As quoted by *Jewish Series No. 10*, Presbyterian Evangelism Department, p. 107.

[6]*Ibid*, p. 109.

[7]Albert Huisjen, *The Home Front of Jewish Missions*, p. 192.

Chapter 2

[1]This is by implication since the baptismal formulae of Matt. 28:19 and Acts 2:38 refer to the God of Israel.

[2]See Matt. 23:15 where Jesus condemns only the results of the Pharisees' proselytizing and not their zeal. See also Bamberger, *Preselytism in the Talmudic Period*, p. 267f.

[3]See extensive documentation from rabbinic literature in Bamberger, *Proselytism in the Talmudic Period*, p. 175f.

[4]Of course, Gal. 6:15 makes it clear that for Gentiles, being born again is what is important, not being Jewish. However, when Paul speaks of the new birth, he speaks of becoming a spiritual or true Jew -- see Rom. 2:28, 29 and Phil. 3:3. Care must be taken by a Gentile Christian not to usurp the term "Jew" so completely (or arrogantly) that he minimizes the promises made to the Jewish remnant that will one day have expanded so that all Israel is saved (Romans 11:26). Therefore, a Gentile Christian may want to identify himself as one with a "Jewish heart." This is much more satisfactory to many messianic Jews.

[5]Joseph Hertz, *Authorized Daily Prayer Book*, p. 251.

[6]See Brown, Driver, and Briggs, *A Hebrew and English Lexicon of the Old Testament*, p. 402.

[7]Hertz, *Authorized Daily Prayer Book*, p. 149.

[8]Oesterley, *The Jewish Background of the Christian Liturgy*, p. 90. See James 2:2 where the church is called a synagogue in the Greek New Testament.

[9]See the five contacts with Jerusalem that Paul has in the book of Acts. 1) Acts 9:26-30. 2) Acts 11:29-30. 3) Acts 15. 4) Acts 18:22. 5) Acts 21:18-25.

[10]"Antinomian" is a term that does not normally refer to "ceremonial law" nor even to the Torah, but contrasts instead with legalism and means lawless. However, here it is used in the sense of a reaction against "Torah" Judaism in favor of a "Torah-free" Christianity, i.e., a religion free from the life-style created by the ceremonial law, rather than the more usual sense of "libertine."

[11]Schmithals, *James and Paul*, p. 37.

[12]Haenchen, *The Acts of the Apostles*, p. 267.

[13]Contra Brandon, *The Fall of Jerusalem and the Christian Church*, p. 127.

[14]See Brandon, *The Fall of Jerusalem*, pp. 27 and 152.

[15]Compare Jas. 2:14 and Gal. 5:16.

[16]Compare Jas. 3:17-18 and Gal. 5:22-25.

[17]Compare Ro. 2:13 and Jas. 2:24.

[18]Compare Jas. 1:22-23; 2:18-25 and Gal. 5:13-15.

[19]See Schmithals, *James and Paul*, p. 93.

[20]See Romans 3:1f; 7:12; I Cor. 9:20; Acts 18:18; 20:16; 21:26.

[21]Brandon, *The Fall of Jerusalem*, p. 135.

[22]*Ibid*, p. 135.

[23]See Schmithals, *James and Paul*, p. 20.

[24]*Ibid*, p. 35.

[25]*Ibid*, p. 97.

[26]*Ibid*, pp. 28-30.

[27]Zech. 12:10; Matt. 23:38-39; 24:32-33; Luke 21:29-31; Ro. 11:15.

[28]See Gal. 2:9. Also note Acts 8:14 and 9:32 where Cornelius is seen by Peter to be something of an exception in that his ministry even as late as Acts 15:6-11 is mainly to Jews. Peter's previous contact with the church at Antioch shows by his blunder that he was a specialist out of his own mission field. Note the cultural specialization possibly implied in Acts 11:19, where some of the Hellenists go to "the Jews only and to no others."

[29]See Luke 2:41-52 which alludes to Yeshua's bar mitzvah, according to G. B. Caird, *The Gospel of Saint Luke*, p. 66. Note also the *Encyclopaedia Judaica*, Vol. 4, p. 244, which says that a tradition recorded in Talmudic literature (Sof. 18:7, ed. M. Higger 1937) alludes to the fact that during the period of the Second Temple it was customary for the sages to bless a child who had succeeded in completing his first fast day at 12 or 13. This would be the equivalent of a bar mitzvah ceremony at that time and would justify Luke 2:41-52 being interpreted in that light.

[30]Brandon, *The Fall of Jerusalem*, p. 184.

[31]See *Encyclopaedia Judaica*, Vol. 4, p. 244 for historical background documentation.

[32]See Acts 2:46, 47; 5:13-14; 6:7; 9:31; 21:20.

Chapter 3

[1]Judah Benzion Segal, *The Hebrew Passover: From the Earliest Times to A.D. 70*, p. 257.

[2]E. O. James, *Origin of Sacrifice: A Study in Comparative Religion*, p. 192.

[3]Roland de Vaux, *Ancient Israel: Religious Institutions*, Vol. 2, p. 490.

[4]*Ibid*, p. 484.

[5]George Buchanan Gray, *Sacrifice in the Old Testament: Its Theory and Practise*, p. 385.

[6]e.g. Joachin Jeremias, *The Eucharistic Words of Jesus*, p. 146.

[7]See also Angus John Brockhurst Higgins, *The Lord's Supper in the New Testament*, p. 50.

[8]Gray, *Sacrifice: Theory and Practise*, p. 357.

[9]*Ibid*, p. 376.

[10]Vaux, *Institutions*, p. 427.

[11]Geerhardus Vos, *Biblical Theology: Old and New Testaments*, p. 135.

[12]Segal, *Passover*, p. 183.

[13]*Ibid*, p. 183.

[14]Exod. 13:3; see Childs' commentary, *The Book of the Exodus*, p. 204.

[15]Pss. 113, 114, 115, 118, 135, 136, 146-150.

[16]"In the Old Testament the terms 'to be unclean' and 'to defile' have always a moral no less than a levitical connotation." William David Davies, *Paul and Rabbinic Judaism*, New York, 1948, p. 255.

[17]See Mishnah *Pesahim* 8.8, Herbert Danby, translator. *The Mishnah*, p. 148.

[18]Segal, *Passover*, p. 171.

[19]Leon Morris, *The Apostolic Preaching of the Cross*, p. 77.

[20]Dennis J. McCarthy, *Old Testament Covenant: A Survey of Current Opinions*, p. 4.

[21]See Gen. 17 and 22. See also the lifesaving significance of the blood of circumcision in Exod. 4:25, 26.

[22]Henry Clay Trumbull, *The Blood Covenant, A Primitive Rite and Its Bearings on Scripture*, p. 280.

[23]Segal, *Passover*, p. 177.

[24]*Ibid*, p. 266.

[25]Gray, *Sacrifice: Theory and Practise*, p. 362.

[26]Trumbull, *Blood Covenant*, p. 231; *The Threshold Covenant, or the Beginning of Religious Rites*, p. 203f.

[27]See Trumbull, *Threshold Covenant*, pp. 216-217.

[28]*Ibid*, p. 209.

[29]*Ibid*, p. 216.

[30]See Segal, *Passover*, p. 106.

[31]See Trumbull, *Threshold Covenant*, p. 69.

[32] *Ibid*, p. 203.

[33] *Ibid*, p. 206.

[34] Segal, *Passover*, p. 165.

[35] See Gen. 14:18, 26:28-30, 31:44; Exod. 24:8-11.

[36] L. Kohler, "Problems in the Study of the Language of the Old Testament," *FSS*, 1, 1956, 4-7 as quoted in McCarthy, *Old Testament Covenant*, p. 3.

[37] McCarthy, *Old Testament Covenant*, p. 30.

[38] Trumbull, *Threshold Covenant*, p. 212.

[39] *Ibid*, p. 212.

[40] *Ibid*, p. 214.

[41] Mowinckel, *The Psalms in Israel's Worship,* Nashville, 1962, Oxford, 1963, 2 Vol.

[42] Segal, *Passover*, p. 184.

[43] George F. Moore, *Judaism in the First Centuries of the Christian Era*, Vol. II, p. 41 and note 7.

[44] Danby, *Mishnah Pesahim*, 10.4-5, p. 150-151.

Chapter 4

[1] There is no need to rehearse here the various arguments for and against the Synoptic dating of the Last Supper. For a good summary, see Jocz, *The Covenant*, p. 185f. Also Higgins, *The Lord's Supper in the New Testament*, p. 17.

[2] For a nearly exhaustive listing of the various theories of the Last Supper and the scholars that espouse them, see Jocz, *The Covenant*, p. 186.

[3] Ralph P. Martin, "Passover," *New Bible Dictionary*, p. 750.

[4] George Buchanan Gray, *Sacrifice in the Old Testament: Its Theory and Practise*, p. 383.

[5] See William David Davies, *Paul and Rabbinic Judaism*, p. 250 and note especially I Cor. 5:7; 10:1-4; 15:23.

[6]*Ibid*, p. 253.

[7]E. O. James, *Origin of Sacrifice: A study in Comparative Religion*, p. 209.

[8]See Leon Morris, *The Apostolic Preaching of the Cross*, p. 78.

[9]Elmert J. F. Arndt, *The Font and the Table*, p. 71.

[10]Morris, *Apostolic Preaching*, p. 105.

[11]Arthur C. Cochrane, *Eating and Drinking with Jesus*, p.28.

[12]Henry Clay Trumbull, *The Threshold Covenant, or the Beginning of Religious Rites*, p. 274.

[13]See Isa. 42:6 and Mal. 3:1 where the covenant is associated with an individual who mediates it to Israel.

[14]The mikveh is the purification bath whereby a proselyte turns in repentance to God and becomes incorporated into Judaism. The bris is the act of circumcision whereby one becomes a Jew, and with a spiritualized meaning, becomes a spiritual Jew. See Col. 2:11-13 where baptism is described as the rite of spiritual circumcision, the ritual associated with the new birth through faith. A spiritual heathen would be the equivalent of one "uncircumcised in heart" (Acts 7:51), i.e., one who has not been born again, regardless of whether he was Jewish or Gentile in a physical sense. The whole message of Scripture is that the true spiritual Jew is one who is in a covenantal relationship with God, which, according to Heb. 8:13, can only be the followers of Yeshua.

[15]Delbert R. Hillers, *Covenant: The History of a Biblical Idea*, p. 187.

[16]Joachim Jeremias, *The Eucharistic Words of Jesus*, p. 159.

[17]Mishnah, *Perakoth*, 288.

[18]Jeremias, *Eurcharistic Words*, p. 246.

[19]J. J. Petuchowski, *Journal of Biblical Literature*, 76 (1957), p. 294-295.

[20]A. R. Millard, "Covenant and Communion in First Corinthians," *Apostolic History and the Gospel*, ed. W. W. Gasque and R. P. Martin, p. 247.

[21] Millard, "Covenant and Communion," p. 243.

[22] Jeremias, *Eating*, p. 251.

[23] Millard, "Covenant and Communion," p. 245.

Chapter 5

[1] For those who would hesitate on grounds that the Seder was traditionally a home ceremony, see Deut. 16:2, 7; II Kgs. 23:21-23 where the Passover was in fact transferred to the central Sanctuary in Jerusalem.

[2] Jean-Jacques Von Allmen, *The Lord's Supper*, p. 42.

[3] Karl Barth, *Church Dogmatics*, IV, 3, p. 878.

[4] Dom Gregory Dix, *The Shape of the Liturgy*, p. 81.

[5] Arthur C. Cochrane, *Eating and Drinking with Jesus*, p. 88.

[6] Elmer J. F. Arndt, *The Font and the Table*, p. 21.

[7] Alan Marshall Stibbs, *Sacrament Sacrifice and Eucharist: The Meaning, Function and Use of the Lord's Supper*, p. 46.

[8] Allmen, *The Lord's Supper*, p. 37.

[9] *Haggadah of Passover*, translator Naurice Samuel.

[10] Arndt, *Font and Table*, p. 18.

[11] H. L. Strack and P. Billerbeck, *Kommentar Zum Neuen Testament aus Talmud Und Midrash* (Munich: C. H. Becksche Verlagsbuchhandlung, 1922-) Vol. II, p. 246f as quoted in Cochrane, *Eating and Drinking with Jesus*, p. 158.

[12] Dix, *Shape of the Liturgy*, p. 49.

[13] *Ibid*, p. 48.

[14] See the liturgy in the author's book, *Everything You Need to Grow A Messianic Synagogue*, pp. 59-69.

[15] Stibbs, *Sacrament Sacrifice*, p. 53.

Chapter 6

[1]See the liturgy in the author's book, *Everything You Need to Grow a Messianic Synagogue*, pp. 95-139.

[2] Joseph Hertz, *The Authorized Daily Prayer Book*, p. 345. Also see Exod. 25:31f for a Biblical precedent for a kindled light in Jewish worship.

[3]See I Cor. 14:26; Eph. 5:19; Col. 3:16.

[4]See Oesterley, *The Jewish Background of the Christian Liturgy*, Gloucester, Mass., P. Smith, 1965, p. 81, where he shows that the Ten Commandments were discontinued from the synagogue liturgy for anti-Christian reasons since in the Jerusalem Talmud *Berakhoth* 1.8 it says "of right they should read the ten words every day. And on account of what do they not read them? On account of the cavilling of the heretics (minim), so that they might not say, these only were given to Moses on Sinai."

[5]See Oesterley, *The Jewish Background of the Christian Liturgy*, p. 139, where he connects this benediction with an early Christian liturgical prayer.

[6]See Hertz, *Prayer Book*, p. 468.

[7]See Gustaf Dalman, *Jesus - Yeshua*, S.P.C.K., New York, 1929, p. 41.

[8]See Oesterley, *The Jewish Background of the Christian Liturgy*, p. 40.

Bibliography

Allmen, Jean-Jacques Von, *The Lord's Supper*, Richmond: John Knox Press, 1966.

Arndt, Elmer J.F., *The Font and the Table*, Richmond: John Knox Press, 1967.

Aron, Robert, *The Jewish Jesus* translated by Agnes H. Forsyth and Anne-Marie de Commaille and in collaboration with Horace T. Allen, Jr., Maryknoll, New York: Orbis Books, 1971.

Ausubel, Nathan, *The Book of Jewish Knowledge*, Crown Publishers, New York, 1964.

Bamberger, Bernard Jacob, *Proselytism in the Talmudic Period*, New York: KTAV Publishing House, 1968.

Bloch, Abraham, *The Biblical and Historical Background of the Jewish Holy Days*, New York: KTAV Publishing House, 1978.

Blumberg, Harry and Lewitter, Mordecai,*Modern Hebrew*, Hebrew Publishing Co., 1963.

Brandon, S. G. F., *The Fall of Jerusalem and the Christian Church*, London: S.P.C.K., 1968.

Brown, Edward, Driver, S.R. and Briggs, Charles A., *A Hebrew and English Lexicon of the Old Testament*, Oxford: Clarendon Press, 1907.

Buksbagen, Victor, *The Gospel in the Feasts of Israel*, Philadelphia: The Spearhead Press.

Caird, G. B., *The Gospel of Saint Luke*, Great Britain: Penguin, 1963.

Campbell, Roderick, *Israel and the New Covenant*, Philadelphia: Presbyterian and Reformed Publishing Co., 1954.

Campbell, Alexander, *The Covenant Story of the Bible*, Philadelphia: United Church Press, 1963.

Charnock, Stephen, *Christ our Passover*, Evansville, Indiana: Sovereign Grace Book Club, 1959.

Chill, Abraham, *The Mitzvot, the Commandment and Their Rationale*, Keter Publishing House, Jerusalem, 1974.

Cochrane, Arthur C., *Eating and Drinking with Jesus*, Philadelphia: Westminister Press, 1974.

Cohen, A., *Everyman's Talmud*, E. P. Dutton, New York, 1949.

Coopersmith, Harry, *The Songs We Sing*, New York: The United Synagogue Commission on Jewish Education, 1950.

Corbett, Edward, *Classical Rhetoric for the Modern Student*, Oxford University Press, 1971.

Cullmann, Oscar, *Early Christian Worship* translated by A. Stewart Todd and James B. Torrance, London: SCM, 1953.

DaCosta, Isaac, *Israel and the Gentiles*, London: Nisbet, 1850.

Dalman, Gustaf, *Jesus-Yeshua*, Paul P. Levertoff, translator, New York: S.P.C.K., The MacMillan Co., 1929.

Danby, Herbert, translator, *The Mishnah*, London: The Clarendon Press, 1933.

Danielou, Jean, *The Theology of Jewish Christianity*, translated and edited by John A. Baker, London: Darton, Lougman and Todd, 1964.

Davies, William David, *Paul and Rabbinic Judaism*, New York: Harper, 1948.

Davis, W.D., *Paul and Rabbinic Judaism*, London, 1949.

Dix, Dom Gregory, *The Shape of the Liturgy*, 2nd Ed., London: Dacre Press, 1945.

Donin, Hayim Halevy, *To Be a Jew*, New York: Basic Books, 1972.

Donin, Hayim Halevy, On developing Messianic Jewish parochial schools see pp. 164-185 *To Raise a Jewish Child*. See Appendix A in the bibliography for "Resources for the Jewish Education of Children."

Douglas, J.D., *The New Bible Dictionary*, Grand Rapids: Eerdmans, 1962.

Dugmore, Clifford William, *The Influence of the Synagogue upon the Divine Office*, Westminister, S.W.: Oxford University Press, 4 Milford, The Faith Press LTD, 7 Tufton St., 1944.

Engstrom and Dayton, *The Art of Management for Christian Leaders*, Word Books, 1976.

ed Gasque, Woodrow Ward and Martin, Ralph P., *Apostolic History and the Gospel*, Grand Rapids: Eerdmans, 1970.

Goble, Phillip, *Everything You Need to Grow a Messianic Synagogue*, Pasadena: William Carey Library, 1974.

Graetz, Heinrich, *History of the Jews*, Philadelphia: The Jewish Publication Society of America, 1891-98.

Gray, George Buchanan, *Sacrifice in the Old Testament: Its Theory and Practise*, Oxford: The Clarendon Press, 1925.

Guilding, Aileen, *The Fourth Gospel and Jewish Worship: A Study of the Relation of St. John's Gospel to the Ancient Jewish Lectionary System*, Oxford: Clarendon Press, 1960.

Haenchen, Ernest, *The Acts of the Apostles*, Philadelphia: Westminister Press, 1971.

Heller, Abraham Mayer, *The Vocabulary of Jewish Life*, Hebrew Publishing Company, 1942.

Herford, R.T., *Judaism in the New Testament Period*, London, 1928.

Herford, R.T., *The Ethics of the Talmud: Sayings of the Fathers*, Schocken Books, 1962.

Hertz, Joseph H., *The Authorized Daily Prayer Book*, New York: Bloch Publishing Co., 1948.

Higgins, Angus John Brockhurst, *The Lord's Supper in the New Testament*, London: SCM, 1952.

Hillers, Delbert R., *Covenant: The History of a Biblical Idea*, Baltimore: John Hopkins Press, 1969.

Holy Scriptures (The Tenach),Hebrew Publishing Company, New York.

Hoon, Paul Waitman, *The Integrity of Worship: Ecumenical and Pastoral Studies in Liturgical Theology*, Nashville: Abingdon Press, 1971.

Hort, Fenton John Anthony, *Judaistic Christianity*, New York: Macmillan and Co., 1904.

Huisjens, Albert, *The Home Front of Jewish Missions*, Grand Rapids: Baker Book House, 1962.

Idelsohn, A.Z., *Jewish Liturgy and Its Development*, New York: Schocken, 1960.

James, E. O., *Origin of Sacrifice: A Study in Comparative Religion*, Port Washington, New York: Kennikat Press, 1971, Oxford, 1933.

____________. *Seasonal Feasts and Festivals*, New York, Barnes and Noble, 1961.

Jeremias, Joachim, *The Eucharistic Words of Jesus*, Oxford: Blackwell, 1955.

Jocz, Jakob, *The Covenant*, Grand Rapids: Eerdmans, 1968.

____________. *The Jewish People and Jesus Christ*, London: S.P.C.K., 1949.

Knox, Wilfred L., *St. Paul and the Church of Jerusalem*, London: The Cambridge University Press, 1925.

____________. *St. Paul and the Church of the Gentiles*, London: The Cambridge University Press, 1939.

Levi and Kaplan, *Guide for the Jewish Homemaker*, New York: Schocken.

Levitt, Zola, *Confessions of a Contemporary Jew*, Tyndale Publishing House, 1975 (pp. 106-111 gives the description of a messianic bar mitzvah service).

Luther, Martin, "On the Jews and their Lies" (1943), translated by Martin H. Bertram, edited by Franklin Sherman, *Luther's Works*, Vol. 47, Fortress Press, Philadelphia and Concordia Publishing House, St. Louis, 1962-1974.

____________. "That Jesus Christ Was Born a Jew" (1923), translated by Walter I. Brandt, ed. *Luther's Works*, Vol. 45.

McCarthy, Dennis J., *Old Testament Covenant: A Survey of Current Opinions*, Virginia: 1972.

Menkus, Belden, ed. *Meet the American Jew*, Broadman Press, 1963.

Mielziner, Moses, *Introduction to the Talmud with a New Bibliography by Alexander Guttman*, Block Publishing, 1968.

Montefiore, Claude, *Rabbinic Literature and Gospel Teaching*, Library of Biblical Studies, New York: KTAV Publishing House, 1970.

Moore, George F., *Judaism in the First Centuries of the Christian Era*, Vol. II, New York: 1958.

Morris, Leon, *The Apostolic Preaching of the Cross*, Grand Rapids: 1955.

Murray, Andrew, *The Two Covenants and the Second Blessing*, London: 1899.

Osterley, William Oscar Emil, *Jewish Background to the Christian Liturgy*, Gloucester, Mass: P. Smith, 1965.

Paterson, Moira, ed., *The Bar Mitzvah Book*, New York: Praeger Publishers, 1975.

Posner, Kaploun, Cohen, eds., *Jewish Liturgy: Prayer and Synagogue Service Through the Ages*, Jerusalem: Keter Publishing House, 1975.

Rendall, Gerald H., *The Epistle of St. James and Judaic Christianity,* London: Cambridge University Press, 1927.

Rosenbaum, Samuel, *To Be a Jew,* Knopf, 1969.

Routtenberg, Lilly S. and Seldin, Ruth, *The Jewish Wedding Book,* New York: Schocken Books, $3.95.

Schauss, Hayyim, *Guide to Jewish Holy Days: History and Observance,* New York: Schocken Books, 1938.

Schlatter, Adolf, *The Church in the New Testament Period,* translated by Paul R. Levertoff, London: SPCK, 1955.

Schmithals, Walter, *Paul and James,* Chatham, England: SCM Press, Mackay LTD, 1965.

Schoeps, Hans-Joachin, *Jewish Christianity,* Philadelphia: Fortress Press, 1969.

____________. *Paul,* Westminister Press, 1961.

Schonfield, Hugh J., *The History of Jewish Christianity,* London: Duckworth, 1936.

Segal, Judah Benzion, *The Hebrew Passover: From the Earliest Times to A.D. 70,* London: Oxford University Press, 1963.

Srawley, James Herbert, *The Early History of the Liturgy* -- [Eng.] -- Cambridge University Press, 1947.

Stibbs, Alan Marshall, *Sacrament Sacrifice and Eucharist: The Meaning, Function and Use of the Lord's Supper,* London: The Tyndale Press, 1961.

Streeter, Burnett Hillman, *The Primitive Church,* London: Macmillan and Co., 1929.

Talbot, Louis, *Christ in the Tabernacle,* Moody Press, 1978.

Tanenbaum, Wilson and Rubin, eds. *Evangelicals and Jews in Conversation,* Baker Book House, 1978. (Marvin Wilson who teaches at Gordon College, Wernham, Massachusetts has prepared a Study Guide for this book which is published by Gordon College Press.)

Trumbull, H. Clay, *The Threshold Covenant,* New York: C. Scribner's Sons, 1896.

____________. *The Covenant of Salt,* New York: C. Scribner's Sons, 1899.

____________. *The Threshold Covenant, or the Beginning of Religious Rites,* New York: C. Scribner's Sons, 1896.

____________. *The Blood Covenant, a Primitive Rite and Its Bearings on Scripture,* Grand Rapids: Zondervan, 1958.

Vaux, Roland de, *Ancient Israel: Religious Institutions,* Vol. 2, New York: 1965.

Vos, Geerhardus, *Biblical Theology Old and New Testaments,* Grand Rapids: W. B. Eerdmans Pub. Co., 1948.

Werner, Eric, *The Sacred Bridge,* New York: Schocken Paperback, 1970.

Williams, Arthur Lunky, *The Hebrew-Christian Messiah,* London: S.P.C.K., 1916.

Winter, Roberta, *Once More Around Jericho,* Pasadena: William Carey Library.

Helpful Resources Worth Knowing About

Evangelism Explosion, P. O. Box 23820, Ft. Lauderdale, Florida 33307, (305) 781-7710. (This is an international ministry specializing in seminars to train congregational laymen in house visitation evangelism. Their methodology, if culturally adapted, could make a messianic synagogue double in size overnight.)

House of David, Box 777, Lakewood, New York 14750. (This is a messianic Jewish literature and religious gift store, as well as a mail order clearinghouse for most of the messianic books and music, etc. The catalogue is a very important reference work which every yeshiva library would need to be aware of. Send to the above address for a copy of the catalogue. The Hebrew books they offer are excellent, especially those of David Bivin.)

Church Growth Book Club, William Carey Library, P. O. Box 128C, Pasadena, California 91104. (All the books in the William Carey Library catalogue dealing with Theological Education by Extension and the American Church Growth Book Club are important to a Yeshiva. Also the books in popularizing missions and the theology of missions show the essentially missionary nature of the people of God under both the Old and New Covenants, a concept that must not be forgotten in a messianic synagogue, lest it become a Jewish ghetto unburdened for a lost world.)

U.S. Center for World Mission, 1605 East Elizabeth Street, Pasadena, California 91104. (This is a cooperative frontier missions nerve center dedicated to helping existing agencies and churches launch a new era of outreach to the world's 16,750 Hidden Peoples. A Hidden People is an ethnic group (like the Jews) that are unreached by conventional evangelism because they do not have an indigenous church in their culture and geographical area. The U.S. Center is located near William Carey University, a secular campus where students can prepare for service to the Great Commission. The Institute of International Studies exposes students to world missions here as well.)

Open Door Community Church, 1151 North Western Avenue, Hollywood, California 90029. (This is a community of house churches rapidly multiplying in Los Angeles. Dr. P L. Hymers, the founder and superintendent has written a doctoral dissertation entitled, *Guidelines for House Churches: a study on organizing and developing house churches*. It could be called, "Everything You Need to Form a Mini-Denomination," because it describes in painstaking detail how to quickly mobilize men and women through your own Bible School and into pastorates over their own growing flocks. Organizational genius is what can be gleaned from these pages, whether or not one agrees with all in the book.)

Missions Advanced Research Communication, World Vision, 919 West Huntington Drive, Monrovia, California 91016. (They have published a directory edited by Ed Dayton called Mission Handbook which lists all the North American Missions agencies and missions professors in colleges and seminaries.)

Dr. Phil Goble, Yeshiva Israel Institute and Center for the Arts, PO Box 2056, New York, NY 10017, (212) 581-7375. Write for more information on leadership training and ministries through the arts.